S0-BXV-342

Marcia Bench

MARCIA BENCH

AN INSIDER'S GUIDE TO

CAREER COACHING

THE STEP-BY-STEP ROADMAP TO COACHING JOB AND CAREER SATISFACTION

ADVICE FROM AMERICA'S PREMIER CAREER COACH

An Insider's Guide to Career Coaching
Published by High Flight Press 2002

Copyright © 2002 by Marcia Bench

All rights reserved.

Reproduction or translation of any part of work beyond that permitted by the 1976 United States Copyright Act without the express written permission of the copyright owner is unlawful. Requests for permission or further information should be addressed to Permissions Department, High Flight Press, 1799 Kiowa #107-526, Lake Havasu City, AZ 86403.

This publication is designed to provide accurate and authoritative information in regard to the subject matter covered. It is sold with the understanding that the publisher is not engaged in rendering professional services. If legal, accounting, medical, psychological, or any other expert assistance is required, the services of a competent professional person should be sought. Client names have been changed to protect identities.

Library of Congress Cataloging-in-Publication Data:

Bench, Marcia
    An Insider's Guide to Career Coaching: The Step-by-Step Roadmap to Coaching
Job and Career Satisfaction / Marcia Bench
    Includes index
    ISBN 0-9724955-0-9
    1. Coaching 2. Job search   3. Career coaching

Printed in the United States of America

AN INSIDER'S GUIDE TO CAREER COACHING

TABLE OF CONTENTS

PART FIVE: THE CAREER COACH'S TOOLBOX

ACKNOWLEDGEMENTS

This book – including the content drawn from live class sessions – could not have been written without the support and assistance of many people over the past two years. The author wishes to thank the following for their input, editing assistance, ideas, client stories, and other contributions to the book:

Joyce Baker	www.coachingyourbusiness.com
Denise Bane	www.orriscenter.com
Scott Blanchard	www.coaching.com
Wendy Enelow	www.cminstitute.com
Timi Gleason	www.executivegoals.com, www.hrce.com
Tracy Heller	www.tracyheller.com
Geri Jamison	www.administrativevirtual.com
Tom Jones, CCC	www.careerplanninguniversity.com
Meg Montford, CCC	www.abilitiesenhanced.com
Janine Moon, CCC	www.cpcoaching.com
Ann Ronan, CCC	www.authenticlifeinstitute.com
Donna Andronicos	
Jennifer Bergeron	
Kathy Keeton	
Laurie Toyama	

I must also acknowledge all of the students in the Career Coach Institute program – past, present and future! – and to my personal career coaching clients, for the richness you have brought to my life and that of your classmates and clients just for being willing to follow your own callings and assist others in following theirs.

Finally, to my husband, Jay, and the many people who have supported me in my recent battle with breast cancer and in my dedicated quest to get the material in this book into a form in which I can share it with a larger audience than those who have heard it to date, thank you.

My heartfelt desire is that each of us can identify and pursue the work that has such meaning and passion for us that as we wake up in the morning, we can't wait to get started doing those things that express our Authentic Vocation™!

Marcia Bench

INTRODUCTION

If you're thinking about becoming a career coach – whether working for yourself or coaching within your organization – then this book is written for you.

It is written with several purposes in mind:

1. **To articulate definitions and standards for career coaching.** While the field of career guidance has a 100-plus year history, the field of coaching is less than 15 years old. And combining the two into career coaching has only been done in the past 5-10 years at most. As the director of the premier career coach training organization, Career Coach Institute, I will share with you the definitions, standards, and models we teach our students, with the hope that it will become the recognized standard in the career coaching community.

2. **To debunk the myths and misunderstandings about career coaching.** In talking to both coaches and client representatives worldwide, it is clear that very different concepts of the qualifications for career coaching exist. For example, in Australia and much of Europe, it is commonly thought that a career coach should have a psychology degree and/or background in order to coach. In the U.S., this is not the understanding. We will unravel this and other myths about career coaching to create greater clarity for our clients and ourselves.

3. **To help more people enjoy their work.** Over the past 15-20 years, one statistic has not changed: 80-90 percent of people *still* do not enjoy their work. This book will contribute to changing that fact in two ways: first, by people entering the field of career coaching and experiencing the satisfaction that comes from this work, and second, as more career coaches work with clients to help them discover their Authentic Vocation™, then what the client does for a living will be congruent with who they are, increasing their satisfaction as well.

The book is patterned after the curriculum we teach at Career Coach Institute (www.careercoachinstitute.com), outlining the key principles career coaches need to know to work effectively with clients. Part One introduces you, the reader, to the field of career coaching and its history, and clarifies how career coaching differs from related fields. The ethics of coaching are also addressed.

In Part Two, all 8 elements of our Authentic Vocation™ model of career exploration are explained in detail, together with coaching tips and resources to use with clients.

Part Three provides you with the best current thinking on all aspects of the job search mechanics, from which strategies to use for various client needs to resume design, interviewing techniques, and negotiation of the compensation package.

Then, in Part Four, we shift gears and explain the QuantumShift!™ model of coaching to draw forth the elements of our clients' Authentic Vocation™ and help them move quickly to the work that is most satisfying for them. QuantumShift!™ also enables clients to overcome obstacles that may be standing in the way of their ideal work, whether they have to do with the circumstances of their life or their belief system or identity. All 70 of the coaching skills required of coaches certified by the International Coach Federation are touched upon in this Part, culminating with a chapter discussing coach self care and the importance of being client-centered.

Finally, in Part Five we provide you with over 20 forms and tools for your Career Coach's Toolbox. You are free to use any of these with your individual clients if they help you implement the concepts and principles outlined in the book. If you wish to use them in a classroom setting, we ask that you contact us directly at coach@careercoachinstitute.com to describe the type of use so that we can determine whether any use fee should be assessed.

To conclude, we provide an appendix of frequently asked questions about career coaching as well as a list of the ICF coaching competencies for your reference.

We hope that if you find value in the concepts in this book, you will use them to facilitate transformation and new discoveries in your clients. And if you would like to experience the power of exploring them in the context of a learning community, you may wish to consider an upcoming career coach training program with Career Coach Institute (some detail provided at the end of the book, additional information on our web site at www.careercoachinstitute.com).

We share this material in book form to demonstrate our core commitment to operate from an abundance mentality. If you use any of the content of this book in written materials – whether on the Internet, in a magazine or journal, or in the classroom – we simply ask that you respect our copyright and give credit where credit is due.

Happy coaching!
—Marcia Bench

LIST OF FIGURES

PART ONE

THE PRACTICE OF CAREER COACHING

THE FIELD OF CAREER COACHING: WHAT IT IS AND IS NOT

"The secret of happiness is not in doing what one likes, but in liking what one does."

—James M. Barrie

"Working with people is difficult, but not impossible."

—Peter Drucker

Career coaching is one of the most exciting and fast growing professions to enter today. Emerging from the roots of career development established by Frank Parsons in the early 1900's, coaching is the newest methodology to assist people in achieving job and career satisfaction. Whether making job or career changes, retiring, or searching for greater fulfillment at work, people and organizations increasingly see a need for career coaching.

Consider these facts about the need for and growth of career coaching:

- Most people change careers (not jobs, but careers) 5-9 times in their lifetime
- Home-based and virtual businesses are increasing so quickly that the U.S. Department of Labor predicts that by 2010, the number 1 employer will be "self"
- *Business Start-up* magazine recently rated coaching the number 1 home-based business to start, and *Money* magazine named it the fastest growing profession behind management consulting

- The events of 9/11/01 have caused everyone to question their priorities and, in many cases, commit to a life with greater meaning

And correspondingly, the corporate environment is rapidly changing:

- "The corporation as we now know it will not exist in 25 years," according to business guru Tom Peters
- Hundreds of thousands of employees have been laid off by corporations of all sizes in recent years due to consolidation and downsizing in virtually every industry, the hardest hit being the information technology industry
- Sixty-seven percent of the skills needed for success today are emotional competencies or "soft" skills, according to *Emotional Intelligence* author Daniel Goleman
- Ethics and values have taken center stage as Enron, Worldcom, and Arthur Andersen, among others, have had systemic alleged breaches of ethics revealed, resulting in stricter standards for reporting in all major corporations

How do people make sense of this changing climate? Often, they seek a career coach. One of my clients, Debbie, had been employed by a world leader in the wireless telecommunication industry for 8 years, beginning at the onset of the IT boom. She worked her way up from a sales representative position to senior account manager, having direct contact with new and existing corporate clients for the company's products. Then, in a reorganization of her department, she was relegated to sales administration – a "back office" position, which significantly decreased Debbie's job satisfaction. What she enjoyed most was having direct contact with the clients and "making the deals." Debbie's employer had made a generous stock options program for its employees, and her options had been steadily increasing in number and projected value. This created a dilemma for Debbie.

When the reorganization occurred, Debbie began exploring, during personal hours, other positions, both within her employer and in other companies. A young software company expressed interest in hiring her and ultimately offered her a position as their Vice President at an increased salary over her previous position. One factor that made the position even more appealing was that they wanted her to work from home, allowing her to spend more time with her two young children. However, her stock options were expected to total $250,000 within 2 years.

It was at this point that Debbie came to me for career coaching. If she left the company, she could lose virtually all of her options. She sought my assistance to help her make this difficult decision and facilitate her transition or ongoing job search, depending on which option she chose. Through our coaching, she was able to more objectively see the conflicting values involved in the situation, the implications of the various possibilities, and after some reflection, she decided to take the new position. She has thoroughly enjoyed her newfound independence and family time, though we did discuss how to help her fully take advantage of the opportunities presented. Debbie feels challenged by her new duties. And as it has turned out, the stock options formerly valued at a quarter of a million dollars are now nearly worthless and, had she stayed at the firm, she would have lost their value either way, a tough situation to predict. She is exceedingly glad she followed her passion. The emotional toll from staying in the unfulfilling job would only have been compounded by the loss of her stock option "nest egg."

Debbie is just one example of how career coaching can benefit individuals faced with transition. One of the responses of organizations to these shifts is to bring in coaches to help employees to be more productive. They may explore shifts in responsibilities among employees or team members, developing alternative career paths, cross-training or mentoring programs, or otherwise applying the coaching methodology. Here are some of the results:

- Six out of every 10 companies now offer coaching or similar services to their managers and executives
- The blockbusting best-seller *First Break All the Rules* outlined Gallup organization research that showed that in companies where the employees are "engaged," or fully involved in and matched well with their work, the company will experience a rise in sales, customer loyalty, and profits
- Companies who offered training alone experienced a 22 percent increase in productivity, but when combined with coaching it rose to 86 percent

- Coaching provided to Fortune 100 companies provided a return on investment of 5.7 times the cost of the coaching in a Manchester, Inc. study

The Coaching Industry

As an industry, coaching is only about 12 years old. Thomas Leonard, founder of Coach University (the first coach training organization) in 1992, the International Coach Federation in 1994, and Coachville in 2001, is credited with first applying the term and concept of coaching outside the athletic context. From its origins in the late 1980's, the International Coach Federation (ICF), the primary trade association for coaching, was incorporated in 1995 and currently has over 4000 members. Its membership, conference attendance, and programs have grown significantly. In addition to serving as a membership organization for coaches, it also offers a coach referral service by which clients can find coaches meeting their stated criteria, it sets the ethical standards for the industry (see chapter 2), and it accredits coach training organizations.

Another new organization serving coaches which was founded in 2001 is Coachville, which as of this writing has over 20,000 members and is free. Coachville also licenses coaches using its own certification body, the International Association of Certified Coaches.

Currently, there are over 75 coach training organizations, over 60 of which have begun offering their services since 2000. Career Coach Institute, of which this author is founder and director, was the first coach training organization to focus on the niche of career coaching. Coaching has only recently (in the past 5 years) been applied to career guidance.

Since coaches are not required to register with any association or body in order to begin practice, it is difficult to determine exactly how many coaches are currently in practice. However, best estimates show that there are between 10,000 and 30,000 coaches in practice part-time and full-time around the world. That number has been growing by at least 20 to 25 percent per year for the past 5 years.

We expect the growth in the coaching profession to continue indefinitely. As the workplace evolves and the corporation yields to new ways of doing business, career coaching will play a key role. And as individuals seek more "high touch" to compensate for the "high tech," as John Naisbitt has described it in his books *Megatrends* and *High Tech, High Touch,* career coaching can be one of the channels for a personal touch, to help workers cope with an unsettled workplace.

Specialties in Coaching

Although coaching is a relative young profession, most successful coaches find they need to specialize. Specializing allows the coach to claim a niche in the marketplace and to establish a discrete set of issues on which to focus and develop competence. Among the specialties coaches may choose are:

- Career coach
- Corporate coach
- Personal coach
- Human resource coach
- Sales coach
- Marketing coach
- Networking coach
- Relationship coach
- Parenting coach
- Team coach
- Transition coach
- Nutrition coach
- Fitness coach
- Wellness coach
- Creativity coach
- Book coach
- Financial coach
- Success coach
- Speakers' coach
- Accountants' coach
- Lawyers' coach
- Therapists' coach
- Attraction coach
- Addiction coach
- Communication coach
- Image coach
- Computer coach
- Writers' coach
- Organization coach
- Web coach
- Spiritual coach
- Executive coach
- Entrepreneurial coach
- Life coach
- Life purpose coach
- Marketing coach
- Retirement coach

Even within the field of career coaching, many subspecialties are beginning to emerge, including:
- Executive career coaching
- Career coaching for the retiring employee
- Industry-specific career coaching (e.g., information technology, banking, sales people, attorneys in transition, etc.)
- Coaching the transition from corporate position to entrepreneur
- Spiritual career coaching
- Internal career coaching (i.e. coaching within an organization

to develop and implement a career development initiative company-wide, of which coaching is one component)
- Career coaching for women
- Interview coaching

Definitions of Coaching

So what is this thing called coaching anyway? And how does it differ from counseling, mentoring, and other related specialties? Simply stated, coaching is a series of interactions between coach and client, including questioning, observations, and many other techniques, in which both parties explore the issue(s) the client wishes to resolve, clarify, or understand, and together develop actionable outcomes for the client to implement or work on between sessions.

While there are many definitions of coaching, the one that is most universally accepted is that of the International Coach Federation:

The ICF Philosophy of Coaching

"The International Coach Federation adheres to a form of coaching that honors the client as the expert in his/her life and work, believes that every client is creative, resourceful, and whole. Standing on this foundation, the coach's responsibility is to:
- Discover, clarify, and align with what the client wants to achieve
- Encourage client self-discovery
- Elicit client-generated solutions and strategies
- Hold the client responsible and accountable."

The ICF Definition of Coaching

"Professional Coaching is an ongoing professional relationship that helps people produce extraordinary results in their lives, careers, business or organizations. Through the process of coaching, clients deepen their learning, improve their performance, and enhance their quality of life.

In each meeting, the client chooses the focus of conversation, while the coach listens and contributes observations and questions. This interaction creates clarity and moves the client into action. Coaching accelerates the client's progress by providing greater focus and awareness of choice. Coaching concentrates on where clients are now and what they are willing to do to get where they want to be in the future, recognizing that results are a matter of the client's intentions, choices and actions supported by the coach's efforts and application of the coaching process."

International Coach Federation
(www.coachfederation.org)

At Career Coach Institute, we carry many of the same elements into career coaching, but further elaborate on the application of coaching to job and work-related issues. With this in mind, career coaching can be defined as follows:

"Career coaching is an interactive process of exploring work-related issues – leading to effective action – in which the coach acts as both a *catalyst* and *facilitator* of individual and, in turn, organizational development and transformation.

"Career coaches connect people with their passion, purpose, values and other critical aspects of their ideal work. They equip their clients with career management skills that can be used in future transitions in addition to enhancing one's current work. They also facilitate the client's process of developing and implementing a job search or business start-up plan to activate the client's Authentic Vocation.™ The desired outcomes of career coaching include enhanced self-awareness, clarity about the individual's life purpose and goals, increased ability to be effective in today's changing workplace, and overall betterment of one's quality of life."

—Marcia Bench, MCCC

There are several critical elements here:

- **"Interactive"** – Unlike some of the related roles such as consulting and managing, coaching is characterized by its interactivity. Client and coach have what are referred to as "strategic conversations" in which the coach asks probing questions of the client about what's most important to them and how they wish to be assisted in moving forward.
- **"Work-related issues"** – This distinguishes career coaching from other types of coaching such as life coaching, business

coaching, executive coaching, spiritual coaching, etc., in that career coaching specializes in work-related issues. These may include both determining one's overall career direction as well as job search techniques such as resume-writing, interviewing practice, negotiation assistance, and the like. Internal coaches as well as external coaches may also assist with enhancing work satisfaction, career development planning, and similar issues.

- **Catalyst** – The dictionary defines "catalyst" as "one that precipitates (brings on or begins) a process or event." A coach, therefore, precipitates the process of learning at three levels: behavior, beliefs, and identity. In chemistry, as in coaching, the catalyst usually does not break down during the chemical process, but rather stimulates, by its very presence, a change in the nature of the other compounds present.

- **Facilitator** – To turn again to the dictionary, to "facilitate" means "to make easier." All of us have what in coaching are referred to as "blind spots" resulting from disappointments, childhood messages, role models or other experiences that are unconscious. These "filters" make it difficult for us to see life as it is. An effective coach penetrates these blind spots, explores the client's strengths, and thereby furthers the process of transformation as the client moves through those hindrances and fully embraces his/her true self.

- **Individual and, in turn, organizational development and transformation** — An organization is comprised of individuals. As each person transforms by enhancing his/her work enjoyment, the organization moves, too.

- **Ideal work** – Most career coaches are not content to help people find just another job. Rather, they seek to help the client find work that is truly fulfilling, that allows them to make the contribution they believe they have come to earth to make (assuming this is the client's goal, of course!) This emphasis on "ideal" work, rather than "suitable" or "acceptable" work, sets career coaches apart. Employment agencies, many career counselors, and the purveyors of skills-based assessments often overlook life purpose and deeper motivators in suggesting next career moves to a client. Since most workers will change careers 5 to 10 times during their lives, many of which occur during midlife when priorities are shifting, the focus on ideal work is an important enhancement of the life journey for career coach and client to explore together.

- **Equip clients with career management skills** – The Bible compares giving a man a fish so he can eat for a day with teaching a man to fish so he can eat for a lifetime. Similarly, coaching aims to teach the client to self-coach, and to learn skills he can use again when similar situations arise, instead of just telling him which kind of work to pursue. That is the key reason why the best coaches are known for asking the right questions, not giving the right answers.
- **Authentic Vocation™** – Part Two will elaborate on this 8-phase model as a preferred approach to career coaching.

Distinguishing Career Coaching from Other Roles

In each of the following sections, we will contrast and compare coaching with similar functions. A chart at the end of this section summarizes the similarities and differences.

Coaching vs. career counseling

Though the lines are often blurred between career coaching and career counseling, some distinctions can be made. Coaching is generally more results-oriented, less structured, and guided by the client's agenda in comparison to counseling. Another distinction is that counseling (and therapy) often seeks to fix pathology, whereas coaching focuses on developing possibilities, leveraging the clients' strengths, and helping them achieve their goals.

Career coaches may work with the client throughout the search; career counselors generally stop when the client knows what his/her next job will be. Coaching closes the gap between the client's current situation and their desired state. Career counselors may get more in-depth training in the use of psychological assessments, and will typically use a battery of such assessments at the outset of the counseling relationships. While career coaches may be trained in and/or use some assessment tools, they only do so as the client's presented needs require.

Coaching vs. consulting

The simplest way to distinguish coaching from consulting is this: coaching focuses on asking the right questions; consulting focuses on solving problems through providing the right answers. Coaching and consulting can overlap, but they are not synonymous. Consultants are experts in a specific topic area and are paid to provide advice, do analyses, write reports and make recommendations within that subject area. The consultant typically has business experience and/or education in the client's business or in the discipline about which they are consulting (marketing, operations efficiency, etc.).

Coaches, on the other hand, need not have had experience in the client's business at all. The primary experience they need is practice doing coaching using an articulated model that leads to clients obtaining their desired results.

Coaching vs. therapy

Both coaching and therapy are discrete skillsets and professions. Therapy focuses on exploring the origins of current emotional and/or psychological problems, often drawing on the past and trying to better understand it to resolve current issues. Coaching, in contrast, begins in the present and focuses on moving the client forward to get more of what they want in the future. It is action-oriented and results-focused. Coaching is not a substitute for therapy, and in fact can be used together with therapy when the client's situation warrants it.

Coaching vs. mentoring

Mentoring is a related skill to coaching which nevertheless can be distinguished in several ways.

> "Mentoring is a method of teaching and learning that can occur among all types of individuals across all kinds of knowledge bases and settings. In the workplace, mentoring normally consists of teaching, giving feedback, coaching on the job, counseling through change, and structuring ongoing contact over a designated time period."
>
> "Mentoring for Performance Improvement,"
> Great Circle Learning (www.gclearning.com)

As Figure 1 illustrates, mentoring is somewhat more directive than coaching in that a goal of most mentoring programs or relationships is to pass on information or knowledge from the mentor to the mentee. However, because the ultimate goal is to help the mentee act independently, the mentor may use coaching techniques and questions to help the mentee think for him/herself about the skills or situations which are the subject of the mentoring relationship.

Figure 1: Comparing Coaching with Other Roles				
Factor	Career Coach	Career Counselor	Consultant	Manager as Coach
Focus	Questions	Q&A	Answers	Q&A
Agenda	Client's	Shared	Consultant's	Company's
Conflict of Interest	No	No	No	Yes
Orientation	Process, what's possible, results	Process, next logical step	Results, solving problems	Results
Education	Coach training	Master's degree preferred	Varies	Varies
Voluntary?	Yes	Usually	Sometimes	No
Time perspective	Present, future	Past, present	Present, future	Present, near future
Use of Assessments	Yes, as appropriate	Yes, standardized	Sometimes	360 most common
Time to results	Quickly!	Slower than coaching	Sometimes never!	Varies
Ownership of results	Client	Counselor	Consultant	Manager and employee

Coaching vs. managing with a coaching approach

Thomas Crane, in his book *The Heart of Coaching*, defines transformational coaching for managers as:

"a comprehensive communication process in which the coach provides performance feedback to the coachee [employee]. Topics include broad, work-related dimensions of performance (personal, interpersonal, or technical) that affect the coachee's ability and willingness to contribute to meaningful personal and organizational goals."

It is increasingly accepted that coaching has a place in the manager's toolkit. However, one critical difference between an independent coach and a manager as coach within an organization is that the manager (or a coach who is within the human resources umbrella) has a built-in conflict of interest in coaching the employee. Since the manager/coach is often also responsible for performance review of the employee, making decisions about salary increases and promotions, and disciplining the employee, it is difficult (perhaps impossible) for the employee to be completely candid with the manager. He or she will preserve his/her job security over personal disclosures in most cases!

Another important factor in making these distinctions is where the primary focus lies, whether with the professional (of whatever discipline) or the client. The following graphic demonstrates this continuum:

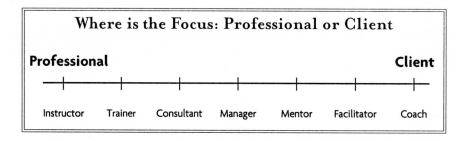

Where is the Focus: Professional or Client

Professional   **Client**

Instructor   Trainer   Consultant   Manager   Mentor   Facilitator   Coach

Is Career Coaching Right for You?

So how do you know whether career coaching is a field you should consider? The most successful career transitions are carefully thought out and the risks of the decision tested. The students in the Career Coach Institute program come from a wide variety of backgrounds. Some representative examples of people who have completed the CCI program and became Certified Career Coaches™ include:

- Meg had started her own resume writing service after a 13-year career in private and nonprofit employment industry positions. She found herself giving away substantial amounts of advice and time to clients who wanted her to write their resumes, but didn't know what jobs they were targeting. She wanted to be generous, but since she couldn't build a business with un-billable

hours she looked for a productive way to help clients
- Jeff was a therapist who had worked both within corporations and with individuals on career issues (as well as other issues from a therapeutic standpoint), and had even completed another coach training program prior to ours. However, that program didn't specialize in career, and he wanted to hone his expertise to get faster, more lasting results with clients. In addition, he wanted to do work that had a more positive focus than much of his therapy, which dealt with pathological conditions in his clients.
- Peg had transitioned from corporate communications to a position in organizational development within a pharmaceutical firm. A highly achievement-oriented woman in her late 50's, Peg wanted to both expand her skills for the coaching she did within the company she worked for and learn a specialty that she could use independently in retirement.
- Gina had been an independent recruiter for over 10 years and had been very successful in that field, particularly when the economy in the U.S. was strong. When the recession began, her business fell off and she began to seek other ways to leverage her substantial experience in business and the careers field. Like Meg, she found herself giving a lot of advice and time away to candidates (even though her actual client was the company seeking to hire them). She wanted to find a way to get paid for coaching job seekers and recruiting candidates.

Dozens of other examples could be given to illustrate the diversity of backgrounds of people entering the field of career coaching. Whether you have no experience or an advanced degree and 25 years of professional experience, career coaching may be right for you *if* you possess the traits needed for success.

The self-assessment in Figure 2 will help you decide whether independent career coaching is right for you:

Figure 2: Is Independent Career Coaching Right For You?

Question	Yes	No
Is it important to you to accomplish something meaningful with your life?		
Are you passionate about helping others?		
Do you usually set and achieve your goals?		
Do you enjoy working independently?		
Can you think strategically?		
Are you self-directed?		
Do you like to be in control of your working environment?		
Do you take full responsibility for your successes *and* failures?		
Are you in excellent physical, mental and emotional health?		
Do you have the drive and energy to create a successful business?		
Do you have a basic knowledge of career transition or career development or job search? (If not, CCI's Authentic Vocation™ Course can help!)		
Do you long for work that makes you so engrossed in it that time passes unnoticed?		
Do you consider "failures" as opportunities to learn and grow?		
Can you hold to your ideas and goals even when others disagree with or discourage you?		
Are you willing to take moderate risks to achieve your goals?		
Can you afford to lose the money you invest in your business?		
When the need arises, are you willing to do a task that may not interest you?		
Can you establish the appropriate amount of interaction with people to balance working largely on the phone and internet?		
Do you usually stick with a project until it is completed?		
Can you ignore the distractions inherent in working at home?		

17-20 "yes"   Career coaching is for you!

14-17 "yes"   You may be suited to career coaching

10-14 "yes"   Work within a team or organization may be a better fit than self-employment

5-10 "yes"   Carefully examine your choice to be sure career coaching is what you want to do!

0-5 "yes"   Independent career coaching is probably *not* your best career choice

What the Client Wants

We have surveyed dozens of individuals over the past two years to find out what they would look for as important traits, from the client's perspective, in a career coach. Here are a few:

- Current knowledge regarding industries and the job market
- Someone who can motivate me, provide support and confidence
- Some credential/credibility
- Customize approach to learning style, age group, etc.; good soft skills
- Able to reduce search time
- Skilled in helping the client discover his/her talents and gifts
- Good listener
- Experience in job/life experience
- Open, uses intuition
- Nondirective, facilitative
- Workable job search strategies
- Responsive
- Confident

To complete the picture, certain business skills such as bookkeeping, strategic planning, marketing, public relations, budgeting, and the like will be required. However, these can be learned if you have the basic traits for success.

Key Coaching Concepts:

1. Career coaching is a growth field because of the number of career and job changes the typical worker makes today during their life, the revolution in how corporations are doing business worldwide, and the increasing public awareness of their need for and the value of coaching.
2. The field of coaching is just 12 years old, and its application to career as a specialty only 5-10 years old.
3. A working definition of career coaching is: "Career coaching is an interactive process of exploring work-related issues – leading to effective action – in which the coach acts as both a *catalyst* and *facilitator* of individual and, in turn, organizational development and transformation."
4. Career coaching can be distinguished from other related fields such as mentoring, therapy, consulting, career counseling, and manager as coach based on the focus of the work, who sets the agenda, the nature of the process itself, the education required, time perspective, use of assessments, and who owns the results.
5. To be a career coach requires certain personality traits, traits clients want, and business skills.

2. ETHICAL CONSIDERATIONS IN COACHING

"Ethics stays in the prefaces of the average business science book."

— Peter Drucker

"A man is ethical only when life, as such, is sacred to him, that of plants and animals as well as that of his fellow man, and when he devotes himself helpfully to all life that is in need of help."

—Albert Schweitzer

Most of the so-called "helping professions" such as counseling, ministry, and social work are governed by a set of ethical standards. Coaching is no exception. And with the allegations of serious ethical breaches in corporate America by such icons as Arthur Andersen, Enron, Martha Stewart, and Worldcom, ethics and integrity have taken a more central focus than at any time in recent history.

For a coach, adhering to a set of ethical standards adds credibility to what can be an otherwise intangible service for the client or prospect to understand. This is particularly true if you share with clients the standards to which you hold yourself, and by which you expect them to abide during the coaching relationship, as part of the intake process.

The ICF Standards of Ethical Conduct

The model set of ethical standards in coaching is that articulated by the International Coach Federation. Compliance is required of ICF members; it is optional – though recommended! – for non-ICF member coaches.

Those standards (current as of July, 2002) follow:

ICF Ethical Standards

1. I will conduct myself in a manner that reflects well on coaching as a profession and I will refrain from doing anything that harms the public's understanding or acceptance of coaching as a profession.

2. I will accurately identify my level of coaching competence and I will not overstate my qualifications, expertise or experience as a coach.

3. I will ensure that my coaching client understands the nature of coaching and the terms of the coaching agreement between us.

4. I will not intentionally mislead or make false claims about what my client will receive from the coaching process or from me as their coach.

5. I will respect the confidentiality of my client's information, except as otherwise authorized by my client, or as required by law.

6. I will obtain informed permission from each of my clients before releasing their names as clients or references or any other client identifying information.

7. I will be alert to noticing when my client is no longer benefiting from our coaching relationship and would be better served by another coach or by another resource and, at that time, I will encourage my client to make that change.

8. I will seek to avoid conflicts between my interests and the interests of my clients.

9. Whenever any actual conflict of interest or the potential for a conflict of interest arises, I will openly disclose it and fully discuss with my client how to deal with it in whatever way best serves my client.

10. I will disclose to my client all anticipated compensation from third parties that I may receive for referrals or advice concerning that client.

11. I will honor agreements I make in my coaching relationships, and construct clear agreements that may include confidentiality, progress reports, and other particulars [and] will obtain the express consent of the person being coached before releasing information to another person compensating me.

12. I will not give my clients or any prospective clients information or advice I know to be misleading or beyond my competence.

13. I will respect and honor the efforts and contributions of others.

14. I will respect the creative and written work of others in developing my own materials.

15. I will use ICF member contact information (email addresses, telephone numbers, etc.) only in the manner and to the extent authorized by the ICF.

Case Studies

Let's see how these ethical standards apply in two actual coaching situations:

1. You are coaching two different clients who happen to know each other because Nancy, client #1, has a contract at the company where Joe, client #2, works. On your call this week, Joe happens to share some company-insider information with you about Nancy that could cause her to lose the contract if she doesn't act to stop it. Nancy doesn't seem to be aware of this information, but she has shared with you that she is concerned about how the contract has been going. Neither Joe nor Nancy knows that you coach the other person.

   What standard(s) is/are at issue here? What should you do? (Note to the reader: try to analyze this yourself before you look at the answers below.)

   The ethical standards at issue here are 5, 6, and 9. Absent client authorization, you must respect confidentiality of the client's "information," which includes their identity and the fact that you are coaching them. If you are to disclose to either Joe or Nancy the fact that you are working with the other, you must get the other's permission to do so. Standard number 6 prohibits giving anyone client information known to be confidential. Based on this standard, the company-insider information mentioned above may not be disclosed to Nancy. There is also a potential conflict of interest here between your relationship with Joe and your relationship with Nancy. Standard number 9 dictates that what Joe shares in a session is confidential, but it is material to the welfare of another of your clients, who has shared concerns with you about it. Best course of action: do not disclose the information, and consider withdrawing from one of the coaching relationships on the basis of conflict of interest.

2. In his first conversation with a new client, Jill, Mark made the following statements in response to Jill's question as to what she could expect from the coaching session. "If you coach with me," Mark said, "I guarantee that you will find a job you absolutely love, making more money than you have ever made. In fact, just last week I helped Mary Jones get a job with Quantel Computers making $85,000. With my 25 years of experience in all aspects of career coaching, you can't go wrong with me."

    How many of the ethical standards were violated here? Which ones? (Note to the reader: try to analyze this yourself before you look at the answers below.)

    Mark violated Standards 1, 2, 4, 5, 6, and 12. He misrepresented what he could deliver as a career coach. Guaranteeing that a client will find a job is outside the scope of ethical representations. Capping this off by pointing to his years of experience (implying that he could help anyone with any issue) violated standards 1, 2, 4 and 12. And by stating whom he worked with previously (Mary Jones) and who she went to work for and at what salary, he inappropriately disclosed client information in violation of standards 5 and 6.

Critical Thinking Pathway

"How will I know if I've crossed the line from doing the right thing to participating in an unethical activity?" "What will I do if I feel I have crossed that line or that my client has?"

To answer these and other difficult questions that can arise regarding the ethical standards, the "critical thinking pathway" can help. The critical thinking pathway can be summarized as an eight-step process:

1. State the central moral dilemma as clearly and briefly as you can. Remember there are two sides to a dilemma.
2. Describe the two sides as completely and clearly as you can.
3. Gather facts pertinent to each side of the dilemma. Move toward discovery of a resolution.
4. Identify your bias(es) in the matter. This can assist in determining whether or not you are truly objective about the situation, and where you are not so that you may be more open in your thinking about it.
5. Bring in new or alternative views of the dilemma. This may be a sort of brainstorming process which considers every idea - from the silly to the sublime, to the logical to the dramatic.
6. Begin to weigh the various alternatives identified
7. Bring in experts, if needed.
8. Preview the consequences of this or that decision about the matter.

At this point you may have a resolution and you may also very well have a dilemma of your own: "Should I go public with this matter?" That is not necessarily an easy question depending upon the situation and going public requires that you consider all stakeholders in this matter, including yourself and your family. Preview those consequences. Once you have made a choice then make your decision.

When working with a client, the coach can introduce the technique of working through a dilemma using the critical thinking pathway. It is the client's task to work through the issues. Most of us are brought up in this culture to know "the right thing to do" and simply go about our lives making ethical decisions without undue stress. When a major ethics dilemma is before us, that is when we welcome a way to resolve it.

(The author acknowledges Christine M. Martin, *MA, MBA, MCC, Member, ICF Ethics & Standards Committee,* who submitted this idea. Reprint by permission of the International Coach Federation.)

Key Coaching Concepts:

1. Coaches are encouraged, but not required (unless ICF members) to comply with the Ethical Standards promulgated by the ICF.
2. Stating clearly to a client the ethical standards to which you (and they) must comply adds credibility to your coaching practice.
3. The Critical Thinking Pathway is a process by which to navigate the difficult ethical dilemmas that can arise in coaching.

PART TWO

THE AUTHENTIC VOCATION™ MODEL OF CAREER DESIGN

OVERVIEW OF AUTHENTIC VOCATION

"This book is about a search, too, for daily meaning as well as daily bread, for recognition as well as cash, for astonishment rather than torpor; in short, for a sort of life rather than a Monday through Friday sort of dying."
—Studs Terkel, *Working*

"[W]hen you work you fulfil a part of earth's furthest dream, assigned to you when that dream was born, And in keeping yourself with labour you are in truth loving life, And to love life through labour is to be intimate with life's inmost secret."
—Kahlil Gibran, *The Prophet*

From the time we enter school, we are asked, "what are you going to be when you grow up?" The question is not "what will you *do*?" but "what will you *be*?" The question itself suggests that we integrate a part of ourselves in what we do. Certainly, this notion can be taken too far if we overly identify ourselves with our occupation, for we are each far more than what we do for a living. But the typical person spends over 100,000 hours working during his/her lifetime. And fully 90 percent of people do not enjoy their work. The Authentic Vocation™ model asks, why not enjoy the time you work and feel like you're contributing your unique gifts in the process?

It has become common to dread going to work on Monday (or any other day!), and to bring less than our full self to work (since our other gifts may not be valued or appreciated if we share them). We begin chanting "TGIF" (Thank God It's Friday) as we walk into work for "casual day" at the end of the work week. Then we cram all of the shopping, errands, household tasks and a quick movie or concert into the busy weekend and begin the process again. Somewhere in this routine, many people find that their true Self has been left behind. They wonder where they gave up their dreams, their values, and their excitement about doing something meaningful with their life.

One of my clients, Sally, hired me during a career and life crossroads. She was living apart from her estranged husband, but still owned a share in their hotel in a tourist location. Every two to four weeks, Sally went back to the hotel and the town where she and Don had lived together to do the books for the business and deal with any business issues that needed resolution. Sally had an MBA emphasizing finance, and had worked for over 15 years in a CFO capacity in the hotel, later dabbling in a position as a stock broker but feeling like that didn't really fit her. Her creativity had been stifled for years, mainly because the role she had in the family business didn't require it as much as her "hard" business skills.

Simultaneously with the work we did in exploring the 8 factors of her Authentic Vocation™, Sally was also working with a therapist and reading books on assertiveness. As she learned to stand up for herself (which she did little of during her marriage) and claim what she wanted, her career exploration also blossomed. What Sally was seeking was work that would blend the various parts of herself into work that was fun and meaningful. That, in short, is what Authentic Vocation™ is all about. (We'll return to Sally's story later in this chapter.)

What Authentic Vocation™ Is

The fulfillment through work that Kahlil Gibran describes at the beginning of this chapter is a far cry from the experience of the typical worker today. Instead of viewing it as "life's inmost secret," most people find themselves complaining about that @#!$ boss and planning how they can get more time off. In fact, 67 percent of workers would take a cut in pay to have one additional day off, according to recent research. We find an entirely different attitude among people who see their work as the expression of their Authentic Vocation.™ They may find it hard to break away from their work because they're having so much fun, and view the challenging people in their life as catalysts for their learning and growth. Sound impossible? It's not!

One way to explain Authentic Vocation™ is to define the terms, elements and principles involved, but observing and listening to people who are working in what they consider their Authentic Vocation™ is the true explanation. We will do both. "Authentic," as used here, means "real," "genuine," or "aligned with one's essential self;" "vocation" means "a calling," "a profession to which one is particularly suited," or "a life's work." In other words, work that meets this standard emanates from one's authentic self and allows a person to be who they truly are while doing what they most love, feel passionate about, and find meaning.

There are 8 elements of Authentic Vocation,™ each of which will be explored in detail in upcoming chapters:

1. Life Purpose - what is the core theme or message of your life?
2. Values - what matters most to you?
3. Motivators and Interests - what motivates you to do something well?
4. Skills, Knowledge and Abilities - what natural talents do you have? And what other marketable skills have you developed that you enjoy using? What education have you obtained?
5. Work and Other Experience - what kinds of work experience have you had? What about volunteer or a vocational experience?
6. Desired Job/Career Target(s) - what kinds of jobs or careers do you want to pursue next?
7. Work Environment - what is the best fit for you in the place where you work, considering 7 different factors?
8. Business Reality - are the options you have selected financially viable? Do you have a realistic view of the job search process and probabilities?

Three principles form the foundation of Authentic Vocation™:

1. Every person has a central life purpose that, if fulfilled through one's work as it develops and changes over time, generates optimum work fulfillment.

2. It is possible to find or create work for each individual that expresses his/her purpose, utilizes his/her skills, meets a need in the world, and is financially viable to pursue.

3. To achieve this ideal, the individual's purpose, values, motivators, interests, skills and desired work environment must be determined and then filtered through business reality.

While this may sound like a tall order, I suggest that this experience is available to everyone, and that no matter what your client's situation, he/she can move closer to their Authentic Vocation.™ Whether janitors or CEO's, new graduates or professionals near retirement, individuals or teams, there is something special for them to do. If they haven't found it yet, the factors in Authentic Vocation,™ coupled with skilled coaching and creative intuition, can open the doors to fulfillment. Sometimes it's a combination of personal exploration and shifting one's attitude around a common purpose, what we call life purpose for the individual. Consider this example from Charles Garfield in his book, *Peak Performers*:

> "A senior vice-president of an aerospace company in Southern California piqued my curiosity one afternoon as we talked about a series of workshops I had just conducted for his managers and technical people. Developing a sense or mission makes sense at the middle and higher levels of a company, he said. But he suggested that there must be levels at which peak performance is just impossible because people have so little control of their circumstances."
>
> "'For instance,' he said, 'there's a group here that puzzles me. They maintain the pipes in our thermodynamics plant, checking temperatures and pressures. The situation makes me nervous. On the one hand, the work is mechanical and repetitive; essentially it's plumbing, and it seems impossible to me that anybody would find it even interesting, much less an occasion for peak performance. But here is the surprise: this group's attendance record is terrific; they have the lowest turnover in the entire company; their motivation is obviously high; their productivity and performance are excellent. How come?'"

"I went to visit the department. Sam Harrison, the foreman, gave me a tour. At one point I asked why all his people wore green surgical smocks. 'Oh, you noticed,' Harrison said. 'I got them from my son. He's a cardiovascular surgeon, and he got them so I could give them to the gang.' 'Ah,' I said, 'you wear them for comfort.'

"'No, no!' Harrison said. 'It's because we are surgeons. Just like my son. He takes care of pipes in the body - you're worried about a heart attack, my son works on your arteries. We take care of pipes in this plant. It isn't going to have any breakdowns as long as we're working on its arteries. We take care of these pipes the way a doctor takes care of your heart.'"

"Sure enough, the stencils on their locker doors said Dr., and Sam used the title - with a grin - as he introduced his colleagues. Their statement of their mission - 'take care of these pipes the way a doctor takes care of your heart' - matched its importance. The way they spoke to one another, the mixed humor and pride with which they used surgery as their metaphor, helped them to share the special value that their work had for them."

Authentic Vocation™ coaching brings that special sense of purpose to each of our client's work and adds the missing dimensions of meaning and fulfillment.

It's More Than Doing What You Love

In the early 1980's, the implied work contract began to change. We moved away from lifetime employment and the Puritan Work Ethic (i.e., work hard and you will be rewarded with consistent employment and a pension and gold watch at retirement) to an era of free agents and the Fulfillment Work Ethic (i.e., choose the work that offers greatest fulfillment, changing employers when needed, and you will contribute more to the workplace and society). At that time, books abounded encouraging people to "do what you love, the money will follow" and "follow your bliss." But too many times, people identified what they loved and the money didn't follow. This is almost worse than never pursuing Authentic Vocation™ at all, because the job seeker becomes disillusioned, cautious, and doubts whether they will ever be able to merge their passion with their pocketbook.

The Authentic Vocation™ model addresses this concern. Merely finding one's passion is not enough. The acid test for Authentic Vocation™ is the following 4 criteria:

Authentic Vocation™:

1. **Is in integrity with the worker's core purpose, values, motivators and passions.**   The chosen job and career are consistent with what is most important to the client, both in terms of what has most meaning for them and what they feel most passionate about.

2. **Facilitates the use of one's gifts and talents, often referred to as knowledge, skills and abilities (KSA's).** In addition, the work allows the client to use his/her natural abilities (or "strengths," to use Marcus Buckingham's term in *Now Discover Your Strengths*) and minimizes the use of "compensatory skills," those developed to fill a job description but which do not flow naturally for the person.

3. **Fulfills a need in the world of work/business.** No matter how much one wants to do something like make buggy whips or another job that is outdated, is too far ahead of its time, or addresses a dying market, he will not be able to find an employer who will hire him for the position. (In fact, it wouldn't even be suitable for an entrepreneurial venture.) Whatever the work is must fulfill an actual need in the business world, even if it extends or modifies what is currently being done.

4. **Meets the worker's financial needs.** Finally, the actual and/or projected wage or salary for the job must meet an individual's needs. For some people, it must also meet many of their wants! But all the passion in the world will not pay next month's mortgage payment or buy groceries and school clothes for the family. When we discuss business reality in chapter 11, we'll talk about what to do if the client's chosen job does not appear to be financially viable - there is hope! But the financial component cannot be avoided if the job is to truly be called one's Authentic Vocation.™

Choosing Authentic Vocation™ can also be thought of as giving up the idea that being less than we are capable of being serves us - or others. It's time to "grow up" and step into our greatness. As Maryann Williamson so aptly put it in *A Return to Love* (Harper Collins 1992):

> "Our deepest fear is not that we are inadequate. Our deepest fear is that we are powerful beyond measure. It is our light, not our darkness that most frightens us. We ask ourselves, Who am I to be brilliant, gorgeous, talented, fabulous? Actually, who are you not to be? You are a child of God. Your playing small does not serve the world. There is nothing enlightened about shrinking so that other people won't feel insecure around you.... And as we let our own light shine, we unconsciously give other people permission to do the same. As we are liberated from our own fear, our presence automatically liberates others."

Authentic Vocation™ suggests that the deep sense of fulfillment that many people seek in mid-career will not occur unless we find work that unites who we are with what we do. Other authors have described this experience in various ways. The renowned psychologist Abraham Maslow observed "peak experiences" among self-actualized people, characterized by seemingly effortless achievement, time passing unnoticed, and often-outstanding outcomes resulting. More recently, Mihaly Csikszentmihalyi in his book *Flow: The Psychology of Optimal Experience* (Harper Collins 1991) and his subsequent books on the "flow" experience describes a similar phenomenon:

> "'Flow' is the way people describe their state of mind when consciousness is harmoniously ordered, and they want to pursue whatever they are doing for its own sake. In reviewing some of the activities that consistently produce flow - such as sports, games, art, and hobbies - it becomes easier to understand what makes people happy."

We can also find a parallel between pursuing Authentic Vocation™ and the "engagement factor" which, in *First Break All the Rules*, the Gallup organization found as the critical connection between job satisfaction and bottom-line performance. When 12 key indicators of engagement were present within a company, inevitably sales, profits, and customer loyalty were greater than when they were not, and employee turnover was significantly less. (More about this in chapter 6.)

So when we help our clients discover and implement their Authentic Vocation,™ we are not only helping them feel more fulfilled; we are also contributing to the productivity and performance of the companies for which they work.

Fitting the Authentic Vocation™ Process to Client Needs

Most current models of career development, including many software programs that claim to help people discover their ideal job, begin by looking at what the client is good at and what he/she has done before - their skills, education, and work experience. While these elements have a place in crafting a next job or career for some clients, for many other clients it does not provide the insights for which they are looking.

What makes the Authentic Vocation™ model so workable is that it is scalable: it allows the coach to meet the client where they are. For the new graduate or the client seeking a new job within their existing industry or occupational area, it may be quite appropriate to begin in the middle of the model with skills, experience, and desired job/career area. If they also decide they want to factor in enhanced satisfaction, the first three elements (life purpose, values and motivators) can be explored as well. This approach may also be advisable for someone who has been laid off without notice and needs to find a new job immediately, but is interested in creating their Authentic Vocation™ once the financial pressure is lessened. For other clients without such pressures but who are seeking enhanced meaning in their work, beginning at factor 1 of the model will be the preferred approach.

Many of the clients who will seek career coaching to pursue their Authentic Vocation™ are, like Sally, at a crossroads where they don't know what to do next. They may have been in one occupation or industry for 20 or more years, or they may have become bored or dissatisfied with what used to challenge them. And often, they have exhausted the resources and techniques that worked for them last time they were in transition - or maybe this is the first time they've considered a change and they weren't taught "Change Management 101" or "Career Choice 101" in school. For these clients, the Authentic Vocation™ approach is ideal. It goes beyond the data that a skills assessment or interest inventory would generate (which for these clients usually doesn't reveal anything they didn't already know about themselves).

What It's Like to Work from Authentic Vocation™

There truly is nothing like finding and beginning to implement one's Authentic Vocation.™ Most clients report that their energy skyrockets, their satisfaction increases, and they have the deeply fulfilling sense that what they do matters - they're making a difference in their segment of the world.

Here are a few representative statements from people who are pursuing their Authentic Vocation™:

"It moves me. It gets me up in the morning excited to go to work. And it fulfills my need to connect deeply with people's lives - to add real value."

— Richard Lieder
The Power of Purpose

"By saying yes to our calls, we align ourselves with the natural forces instead of pitting ourselves against them."

- Gregg LeVoy
Callings

"When you are fulfilling your life's purpose, you are completely absorbed in your activities. You do not notice the passage of time; the activity completely occupies you."

—Marcia Bench
When 9 to 5 Isn't Enough

And from one of our graduates and Certified Career Coaches™:

"I've discovered something I never had before - a life direction that is purposeful, energizing, and absolutely right."

—Janine Moon, M.A., CCC

To return to Sally's story, we worked together for about 8 months. Sally had a different idea nearly each week of our coaching, and I reassured her that at this stage thinking of many different possibilities was normal; that eventually she would settle on one option that stuck with her. And by about the seventh month, that happened. It occurred to Sally that if she combined the training in finance she had with her family-owned business experience and also offered communications skills training, she could form a niche-consulting firm serving family-owned businesses. She is currently launching that practice, feeling a great sense of satisfaction and that she can share the benefit of her experience and learnings with other family-owned businesses.

Figure 3 illustrates the Authentic Vocation™ model of career development.

Figure 3: Authentic Vocation

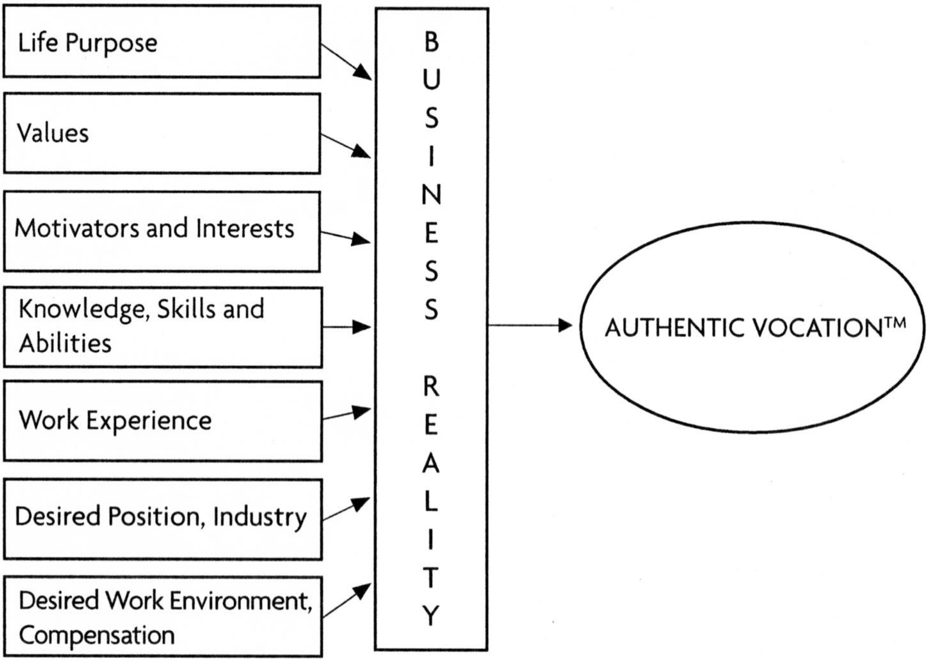

Perhaps poet Robert Frost captured it best in his poem, "Two Tramps in Mudtime":

> My object in living is to unite
> My avocation and my vocation
> As my two eyes make one in sight
> Only where love and need are one
> And the work is play for mortal stakes,
> Is the deed ever really done
> For Heaven and the future's sakes.
>
> —Robert Frost

Key Coaching Concepts:

1. Authentic Vocation™ combines what is genuinely "you" with a vocation, or "calling," resulting in work that is passionate and meaningful.

2. There are 8 factors in Authentic Vocation™ :
   a. Life Purpose
   b. Values
   c. Motivators and Interests
   d. Skills, Knowledge and Abilities
   e. Work and Other Experience
   f. Desired Job/Career Target(s)
   g. Work Environment
   h. Business Reality

3. The test for Authentic Vocation™ consists of 4 elements:
   a. Is in integrity with the worker's core purpose, values, motivators and passions
   b. Facilitates the use of one's gifts and talents, often referred to as knowledge, skills and abilities (KSA's)
   c. Fulfills a need in the world of work/business
   d. Meets the worker's financial needs

4. Pursuing Authentic Vocation™ requires shedding one's "smallness" and saying yes to an inner "calling" that won't let us go

5. The Authentic Vocation™ model is scalable so that it can be tailored to any client's needs, whether first-time job seeker, seasoned worker close to retirement, or midlife career changer.

FACTOR 1 –
LIFE PURPOSE

"Life's purpose can be simply defined as a calling, a mission, or an overall theme for your life that transcends your daily activities. It is the quality you have come to earth to develop, the type of service you are here to render, the segment of the planet you have come to enhance or improve or heal. It is much broader than one job or career; it pervades your entire life."

—Marcia Bench
When 9 to 5 Isn't Enough

"Purpose is the conscious choice of what, where, and how to make a positive contribution to our world. It is the theme, quality, or passion we choose to center our lives around."

—Richard Lieder,
The Power of Purpose

Perhaps the signature trait of the Authentic Vocation™ model is that it begins with life purpose. I have been advocating the importance of life purpose in career decisions since the mid 1980's, but it wasn't until the advent of coaching as a profession that life purpose took the central role it deserves. Now, life purpose is something nearly every coach claims to explore!

The first principle of Authentic Vocation™ is that "Every person has a central life purpose that, if fulfilled through one's work as it develops and changes over time, generates optimum work fulfillment."

Notice first that it doesn't say some special people have a life purpose and others don't (more on this in a moment), but that every person has a central life purpose. It may take a while to discover it (the author spent 18 years exploring the issue before she could clearly articulate it!), but it is there.

Secondly, notice the outcome: optimum work fulfillment. Your clients may express their lack of fulfillment in many different ways, such as:

> "I'm doing well at my job - I'm even considered an outstanding performer - but I feel like something is missing. I'm just not happy."

> "I've been doing the same kind of work for 20 years now and feel bored with it, but I don't know what else I could do."

> "I just kind of 'fell into' the jobs I have had, being in the right place at the right time. I've never consciously designed or chosen my work."

By discovering and beginning to fulfill their life purpose, they will finally feel the fulfillment that has eluded them to date.

Definitions of Life Purpose

What is encompassed by the term "life purpose"? First, in a broad sense, we all have a shared overall purpose, in that we are here to discover as much of our true self as we can and to express our true self through our lives to the greatest possible extent. We do this through all of the experiences we have, the people we relate to, the jobs we choose, and the teachers whose message rings true with us.

But each of us also has a specific purpose. It is a calling, a mission, or an overall theme for our life, which transcends our daily activities. It is the quality we have come to earth to develop, the type of service we are here to render, the segment of the planet we have come to enhance or improve. It is much broader than one job or career; it pervades our entire life.

In fact, most of us will have at least five different careers in our lives. Our purpose is not found in a career area or a job description.

Rather, we use our career (as well as the other aspects of our life) to accomplish our broadly stated purpose. For example, one man's life purpose was to promote peace. He did so by working as a mediator and by consciously pursuing peaceful relationships. Another woman discovered her life purpose was to nurture the earth. She learned all she could about conservation, worked for the park bureau, and soon was in demand as a teacher for other nature guides and conservationists.

If a client does not feel they have experienced the level of success they know they are capable of, or have felt as if something was "missing" from their life, you may want to share with them a very important principle: A person will tend to experience success and fulfillment in their life to the extent that he/she is clear about his/her life purpose.

Qualities of Life Purpose

Life purpose is fun, joyful, and playful. When we are carrying out our life purpose, we find that the time goes by unnoticed. Hours pass in pure bliss. Joseph Campbell and the eastern mystics use the phrase, "Follow your bliss." The dictionary defines bliss as "complete happiness."

Since our life purpose serves as a central theme for our life, it also serves as a filter or criterion on which to decide whether or not to accept a job, whether or not to volunteer for a particular cause, and which kinds of relationships (professional and personal) will best contribute to fulfilling our purpose. There is a sense of "coming home" when one discovers his/her purpose. Not only is the individual client's life incomplete without it; there is something missing in the world if each of us does not contribute the gift(s) we have.

Why It's Important

When life purpose is discovered and expressed, it provides a reason for being, a quality one brings to everyday life, and the motivation for one's activities.

"This is the true joy in life, the being used for a purpose recognized by yourself as a mighty one; the being thoroughly worn out before you are thrown on the scrap heap; the being a force of Nature instead of a feverish selfish little clod of ailments and grievances complaining that the world will not devote itself to making you happy."

—George Bernard Shaw

"The gifts of each of us and the value of serving others provide our mission in life."

—Richard Bolles
What Color is Your Parachute?

In the affluent society of the Western world, it may seem that life purpose would be unimportant. However, research tells us otherwise:

"When 60 college students who had attempted suicide were recently surveyed, and 85% of them said the reason was that 'life seemed meaningless.' Ninety-three percent of them lacked a sense of purpose in their lives despite socially active lives, academic achievements, and supportive families.

"This happens in the midst of affluent societies and in the midst of welfare states! For too long we have been dreaming a dream from which we are now waking up: the dream that if you just improve the socio-economic status of people, everything will be OK, people will become happy. The truth is that as the struggle for survival has subsided, the question has emerged: survival for what? Ever more people today have the means to live, but no meaning to live for."

—Viktor Frankl
Man's Search for Meaning

Clues to Life Purpose

Following are ten clues designed to help in the life purpose discovery process (see Figure 4). They ask the client to look at her life and work from several different perspectives, as though examining a precious stone (or diamond in the rough) from many angles. Then, with a coach's guidance, she uncovers the themes that emerge and, ultimately, a statement of her life purpose. (NOTE: these are included in Authentic Vocation™ Worksheet Number 1 in Part Five, the Career Coach's Toolbox, for your use with individual clients.)

FIGURE 4: 10 CLUES TO DISCOVERING YOUR LIFE'S PURPOSE	
1	WHAT DO YOU LOVE TO DO, WHETHER IN YOUR SPARE TIME OR AT WORK?
2	WHAT PARTS OF YOUR PRESENT JOB OR LIFE ACTIVITIES DO YOU THOROUGHLY ENJOY?
3	WHAT DO YOU NATURALLY DO WELL?
4	WHAT ARE YOUR TEN GREATEST SUCCESSES TO DATE (IN YOUR EYES)?
5	IS THERE A CAUSE ABOUT WHICH YOU FEEL PASSIONATE?
6	WHAT ARE THE TEN MOST IMPORTANT LESSONS YOU HAVE LEARNED IN YOUR LIFE?
7	ARE THERE SOME ISSUES OR PERCEIVED PROBLEMS THAT HAVE OCCURRED OVER AND OVER AGAIN?
8	WHAT DO YOU DAYDREAM ABOUT DOING?
9	IMAGINE YOU ARE WRITING YOUR EPITAPH. WHAT THINGS DO YOU WANT TO BE REMEMBERED FOR AT THE END OF YOUR LIFE?
10	WHAT WOULD YOU DO IF YOU KNEW YOU COULD NOT FAIL?

Taking the answers to the 10 clues, the next step is to notice any themes in the answers, e.g., do many of them relate to being with people in a particular way, or to solving problems or working with your hands?

Other processes that may assist the client in discovering their purpose include:

Listen to your intuition. It is often from our intuition that the hints and key aspects of our purpose emerge. If the client is not accustomed to listening to his/her intuition, the tips and processes in *Practical Intuition* by Laura Day may be helpful (see Resource List in Part Five). The intuition is a window into the most authentic parts of ourselves, as well as to our higher purpose in life. Whether it is experienced as an audible voice, a physical sensation, or just an urge to call someone, buy a particular book, or attend an event we might not otherwise attend, when we follow it the meaning behind the sensation eventually becomes clear.

Decide that you matter, and that you can have clarity about your purpose.

> "A sense of purpose is rarely handed to us. We get it by deciding to have it. We get it by deciding that, yes, I matter. A sense of purpose comes from within, and only we know if we have it."
>
> —Richard Lieder
> *The Power of Purpose*

No matter how much you, the coach, believe the client can have clarity about his life purpose, he will not uncover it until he too believes it is possible for him. Perhaps he is facing one of the obstacles we will discuss in the next section. Or maybe his self-esteem is so low that he needs coaching to raise it before he can meaningfully participate in an exploration of his life purpose.

Discover solitude and meditation. It is only through getting quiet that we can hear the answers to the questions life is asking us at critical junctures such as career crossroads. Otherwise, the busyness of our daily lives crowds out the still, small voice that can provide the answers. One exercise that is simple but powerful is to ask the client to dedicate 15 minutes each morning to just sitting quietly, looking at something beautiful (e.g., scenery out their window) and concentrate on just being there. This is not the time to consciously vision, to solve problems, or to dwell on what isn't working. Rather, it's a time to develop a sense of comfort with oneself, the self that is behind the "doer," that "more of us" that exists apart from our professional or family roles. A specific meditation that facilitates discovery of your purpose is the Symbol Meditation in Part Five.

Obstacles to Discovering Life Purpose

If discovering our purpose were easy, everyone would have already done it. Even answering the ten questions we list above as clues to life purpose will not result in instant awareness for every client. So on the one hand, it is important to be patient with the process and allow it to unfold. On the other hand, clients are often anxious to gain clarity so that their Ideal Job Template (see Part Five) can be completed. One thing that I have discovered is that where it used to take weeks to guide clients to their life purpose, by adding the QuantumShift!™ coaching techniques you will learn in Part Four to the process, the client can usually articulate his purpose statement within a couple of coaching sessions.

There are at least four common obstacles which may arise when clients are having difficulty clarifying their purpose:

1. **It's so obvious that we take it for granted and assume that everyone has the same interest/skill/passion.** Certainly, we all have natural strengths and gifts. And we often tend to overlook the very things that people have always told us we're good at doing, or that have always been our "role" or "duty" when our family or close friends plan an activity. This obstacle requires the objective feedback of a third party (e.g., a career coach) to help the client see their specialness. It is simple, not complex.

2. **My purpose must be completely unique and different from the purposes of anyone else.** Many of the activities and goals represented by a purpose statement are far too large for one person to accomplish, outside of their own individual circle of influence. So for more than one person to be committed to that purpose or a similar one will simply accelerate the transformation process in the world - or the segment in which the client wishes to work.

3. **I don't have time to explore my purpose - I just need to make a living.** This is a common trap, with everyone so busy these days. The pressures of an unexpected layoff may require that the life purpose exploration be deferred temporarily. The coach can help the client evaluate whether the financial issues are so pressing as to require immediate attention. If so, the coach may want to help the client obtain a "transitional" position that will pay their bills - but not require 110% of their time - so that they can then explore their life purpose. Most people will not be fulfilled and satisfied in their work until it becomes an expression of their life purpose (see diagram on page 48).

4. **Only famous writers, artists, musicians and religious leaders [or insert category of your choice] have a life purpose, and I'm not one of those special people.** The truth is, everyone has a purpose, as we expressed in the first principle of Authentic

Vocation,™ and discovering it will increase work and/or life satisfaction. However, some people don't feel the longing to explore it until later in life; others begin early.

Examples Of Purpose Statements

The life purpose statement itself, if it is to be useful as the central theme of one's life, should be articulated in a specific format. It has two parts: the essence, which is relatively unchanged over one's life, and the expression, which changes as life circumstances change.

Following are some samples of the essence portion of several life purpose statements:

- To promote corporate integrity through....
- To increase the harmony and love in the world through...
- To be a positive influence on women and children through...
- To help working mothers achieve the balance they desire through...
- To help people communicate with themselves and others as honestly and courageously as possible through...
- To promote win-win conflict resolution and increase world peace through...
- To find my own path and help others find their path through...
- To provide environments where self-healing can occur through...
- To help people discover their purpose and express their calling while they're still alive through...

While as we mature we may refine the way the "essence" (the part of the statement which precedes the word "through") is stated, the fundamental idea is a theme that we can trace from cradle to grave. It expresses through childhood relationships, college education, early careers, starting our family, releasing our children to move out on their own, retirement, and beyond. These latter circumstances are the changing "expression" which evolves as our life unfolds.

A sample life purpose statement would read:

"My life purpose is to increase the harmony and love in the world through working as a child and family therapist using a harmonious communication approach, pursuing peace in all of my personal and professional relationships, volunteering with Peace on the Planet Foundation, and teaching my children to seek harmony instead of discord."

From the life purpose statement, we may then formulate a business mission statement if we are beginning our own enterprise, or a work mission statement if we are working for a company. These mission statements need to be congruent with the overall life purpose statement.

Implementing Life Purpose

Even as the client begins to explore the other elements of his Authentic Vocation,™ he can begin to live a more purpose-centered life by implementing his life purpose, as he understands it. Here are several easy ways to do this.

1. **Do the activities related to your life purpose first thing in the morning.** This will allow you to do what is important to you before other distractions have a chance to tempt you off course.
2. **Whenever you have a decision to make, ask which of your options will take you closer to your life purpose.** Usually, one of your options will be more joyful than the other(s). This will be the one that leads to the fulfillment of your life purpose. Each small step builds on the last, and soon you are living the life of your dreams!
3. **Be willing to change.** To fulfill your life purpose, you must be willing to change anything that does not take you there. If you are harboring resistance, fear, or old programming, merely stating to the Universe a willingness to chance it will propel you in the direction you want to go. You may not know the precise steps to take, but your willingness will lead you to take the right action for you.
4. **Think of your life purpose as an organizing principle for your life.** (see **Figure 5**) If we imagine that our life purpose is the "hub" of a wheel, we can continue our efforts to implement it by moving out through the other rings of the wheel. Next, we examine our roles: which of them serve our purpose and which do not? Can we, either gradually or immediately, eliminate the roles that no longer serve our newfound purpose? Then we consider our long-term goals and life vision, both. What do we want to have accomplished in 3 years? 5 years? Over our lifetime? Setting long-term goals that facilitate the

expression of our purpose ensures that we will feel fulfilled, not just satisfied that we accomplished another goal, because our purpose is being realized.

For the goals that we wish to accomplish within the next year or so, we then set short-term subgoals articulating the "goals within the goals" that we want to achieve, then the specific actions we will take to do so. And finally, we use principles of time and stress management to daily execute the steps toward our goals. Thus our life purpose becomes an "organizing principle" for the rest of our lives and the basis for a career and life plan. Let's use Sally, our client from chapter 3, as an example of how this process can work.

Example:

Life purpose statement: To help people communicate better and leave a legacy through consulting with family-owned businesses, conscious relationships with my partner and children, volunteering at nonprofit organizations, and building my self-esteem through assertiveness training, physical fitness, and investing toward my retirement.

Role evaluation: current roles include CFO for hotel business, budding entrepreneur (family business consultant), friend, investor, docent at local museum, spiritual seeker, yoga practitioner, lover; desire to phase out of CFO role and expand entrepreneur role with other roles remaining a total of 25% of total

Long-term goal: To become an internationally known speaker in the field of family business

Short-term subgoals:
- Improve speaking skills
- Become visible within local and, eventually, national hotel and family business associations
- Learn how to price and promote speaking services

Action plans:
- Join Toastmasters to improve speaking skills
- Present proposal to speak at regional hotel association conference
- Join National Speakers Association and network with other established professional speakers re: pricing and promotion

Time/stress management: Drawing from assortment of scheduling, organization, relaxation, and other skills, manage time and stress appropriately to execute plan and achieve goals

Figure 5: Life Purpose as Organizing Principle

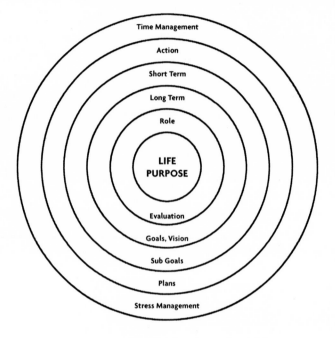

Reprinted from *Thriving in Transition* by Marcia Bench

Key Coaching Concepts:

1. Life's purpose can be simply defined as a calling, a mission, or an overall theme for our life that transcends our daily activities.

2. The first principle of Authentic Vocation™ is that "Every person has a central life purpose that, if fulfilled through one's work as it develops and changes over time, generates optimum work fulfillment."

3. There are 10 questions, or "clues," which can help a client discover their life purpose, articulated in Authentic Vocation™ Worksheet 1.

4. Common obstacles to discovering one's purpose are: it being too obvious, lack of deservingness, lack of time, and the perception that only "special" people have a purpose.

5. A life purpose statement has two parts: essence, which is relatively unchanged throughout one's life, and expression, which reflects the current circumstances through which the purpose is expressed and will change over time.

6. Life purpose can be implemented through consistent focus and through seeing it as an "organizing principle" for the goals and plans one has for each part of his/her life - including but not limited to his/her work.

FACTOR 2 – VALUES

"If I say a [person] is pulled by values, what is implicitly referred to is the fact that there is always freedom involved: the freedom of [that person] to make their choice between accepting or rejecting an offer, i.e., to fulfill a meaningful potentiality or else to forfeit it."

—Viktor E. Frankl,
Man's Search For Meaning

If anyone was ever in a position to speak to the importance of being pulled by values, it is Viktor Frankl. Imprisoned in a Nazi concentration camp for years, he was one of the few people who survived that horrific experience and wrote of his experiences in *Man's Search for Meaning.* He can be a beacon of hope for the millions of workers who experience values conflicts every day in their work. Perhaps it materializes when the narrowness of a job description doesn't allow one's values of creativity and initiative to express. Or it may be the micro-management of an overly controlling boss, squelching the employee's value of autonomy or independence. Even worse, a finance executive may be asked to approve deliberate misstatements of revenues, expenses or profits to shareholders. As widespread practices like these come to light through heightened scrutiny and government investigations, we can hope that fewer such incidents will occur in the future. But the value businesses place on money often far outweighs the value they place on employee morale, congruence between company mission and daily operations, measures to prevent constant "firefighting" or dealing with the crisis of the day, and open communication with staff. Conflicts between individual values and the company values (not the stated values, but rather the actual values as they are practiced each day) can create significant stress in the individual worker.

What are values? Values are simply the things about work that, to us, are intrinsically valuable or desirable. They form the basis for our choices about what we will and will not do. Therefore, they are important to our career decisions and to our Authentic Vocation.™ Each of us has developed a unique system of values that determines how we feel about our work and the contribution it makes to the society. If we choose to pursue a career or an organization with requirements or culture that are at odds with our values, we will not be happy with the choice. Most people who pursue work that is congruent with their values feel satisfied and successful in their careers. Relating our values to our work decisions and choices helps us determine our reasons for wanting to work, the characteristics of occupations that are appealing to us, and our career goals.

Types of Values

There are several ways of categorizing values:

INTRINSIC	EXTRINSIC
The internal values in the work activities themselves, or how the work benefits society (e.g., socially responsible, automates communication)	The external conditions of a job or occupation (e.g., physical setting, salary, or career growth opportunities)
CULTURAL	OPERATIONAL
Pertaining to the purpose, character, and overall direction of one's career development (e.g., responsibility, autonomy)	Those which operationalize the cultural values in day-to-day work (e.g., flexibility, employee orientation)

Three Major Value Systems

Psychologist David McClelland has found that each person places varying levels of importance on each of three primary values: achievement, affiliation and power. They are defined below.

Achievement - Meeting or exceeding a standard of excellence and/ or improving one's own performance. People with a strong value on achievement will often perform better over time, even in the absence of specific demands to do better, because they enjoy mastering challenging tasks.

Affiliation - Establishing, maintaining and avoiding disruption of close, friendly relationships with people. People with strong value on affiliation will, on their own initiative, seek out people to spend time with because they enjoy their company.

Power - Having an influence or making an impact on others. People who value power desire to have an impact. They focus on their reputation and position and feeling or being perceived as strong, effective and influential.

Identifying a Client's Work-Related Values

There are two primary approaches to values clarification in the career context. One is to ask the client to list, without prompting or suggestion, what their most important values are. The other is to provide a list of common work values and have the client rank them in order of importance to them. Authentic Vocation™ Worksheet 2 (see Part Five, Career Coach's Toolbox) combines both of these approaches. First, it asks the client why they work, and what they want to derive from their work. Then, it gives them a list of work values to rank from 1 to 3 in importance, and finally to narrow the list down to their top 5 values. Once the client has identified their top 5 values, use your coaching skills to probe how the client would like to see that value expressed in their next position or employer, what makes that value important to them, etc.

For further values clarification, there are at least three other tools that can be used:

- **Personal Values Questionnaire.** Available from the Hay Group (www.haygroup.com), this questionnaire provides scores for the relative importance of the three values identified by David McClelland: power, achievement, and authority.
- University of Waterloo, Cooperative Education and Career Services, Ontario, Canada offers this values assesment (see Figure 6):

Figure 6
Step 1.3 Understanding Your Values
Copyright Career Services, University of Waterloo, www.cdm.uwaterloo.ca;
Reprinted with Permission

- This exercise will help you to clarify your values
- This process will take 15 – 30 minutes

As with the previous section, you will notice that the checklist is divided into six sections with similar values clusters. You will learn more about these clusters in the section on "Interests". Read your pride stories and scan the checklist. Put a check to show each value that applies to you. Add to the list other values that describe you.

Values Clarification	Story #							Total
Section "R"	1	2	3	4	5	6	7	#
Be able to move around in my work								
Do hands-on work								
Meet clear standards								
See the results of my work								
Work outdoors								
Section "R" Totals								

Section "I"	1	2	3	4	5	6	7	#
Be able to structure my own work								
Be recognized for my knowledge								
Contribute new learning to a field								
Demonstrate high degrees of skill								
Engage in complex questions & demanding tasks								
Section "I" Totals								

Section "A"	1	2	3	4	5	6	7	#
Be able to write or present ideas								
Be free to express my uniqueness								
Be involved in studying or creating beauty								
Create new ideas, programs or structures								
Have personal control over my life & lifestyle								
Section "A" Totals								

Section "S"	1	2	3	4	5	6	7	#
Be involved in helping others directly								
Contribute to the betterment of the world								
Feel that my work is making a difference								
Have opportunities for self-development								
Work with others toward common goals								
Section "S" Totals								

Section "E"	1	2	3	4	5	6	7	#
Be able to get ahead rapidly								
Be in a position to change opinions								
Have a high standard of living								
Have the power to influence others' activities								
Impress others, have respect & status								
Section "E" Totals								

Section "C"	1	2	3	4	5	6	7	#
Carry out responsibilities and meet requirements								
Complete work where attention to detail is required								
Do work where employment is secure								
Do work where tasks are clear								
Have regular hours and predictable work								
Section "C" Totals								

Additional Values	1	2	3	4	5	6	7	#
Additional Values Totals								

Congratulations on clarifying your values! Circle or highlight the top 5 values that are most important for you. This information will be helpful when you get to the section on "Interests".

- **Values Card Sort.** Available through www.careertrainer.com, these tools are particularly good for kinesthetic or young clients who desire to narrow their values but still have some raw data from which to start.

A Hidden Benefit in Values Clarification

At this stage in our coaching process, we are helping the client to clarify their values as part of developing their Ideal Job Template (see Part Five for example). But as one of my colleagues discovered, values can also play an important role in some interviews. My colleague's client, whom we'll call Vicki, was terrified of interviews, and often gave untrue answers just to say something in response to the questions asked. Shortly after she completed Authentic Vocation™ Worksheet 2 on values, she had an interview for an outside sales position with a major telecommunications firm. The interviewer asked her what her top four values were, and she immediately realized that she had an honest answer to the question because of her Authentic Vocation™ work! She stated that one of her top values was "freedom," and when asked why by the Sales Manager, she said, "because I was raised in South Africa where some people are not free - I'm glad I am!"

The Sales Manager congratulated her for being so prepared, and said most sales candidates don't have an answer for this question about values. He also said that because she did have an answer, it was an indicator of success and that she was the kind of person he wanted on his team. She was hired!

Key Coaching Concepts:

1. Values are simply the things about work that, to you, are intrinsically valuable or desirable. They form the basis for our choices about what we will and will not do.
2. Values can be categorized as intrinsic vs. extrinsic or cultural vs. operational.
3. David McClelland identified three primary values on which each individual places varying amounts of weight: power, affiliation and achievement.
4. There are four primary tools to use in identifying a client's values: Authentic Vocation™ Worksheet 2, the Personal Values Questionnaire assessment, the online values questionnaire, and the Values Card Sort.

6

Factor 3 – Motivators and Interests

"Lord, grant that I may always desire more than I can accomplish."

—Michelangelo

"We know nothing about motivation. All we can do is write books about it."

—Peter Drucker

Think back for a moment to the subject you least liked in school. If you're like most of us, you did only enough homework to get a passing grade in the class, were bored during class sessions, and couldn't wait for it to be over, right? Many workers in businesses today have a similar attitude toward many aspects of their jobs. This is the opposite of the kind of motivation we want our clients to experience when they are aligned with their Authentic Vocation™.

Recently, the Gallup organization did a fascinating research project, summarized in *First Break All the Rules*, to determine what highly successful companies were doing that resulted in their employees being so highly motivated. The exact questions they were exploring were "How can you measure human capital?" and "What does a strong, vibrant workplace look like?" They discovered that when certain key factors were present, "engagement" had occurred and productivity increased. These results remained consistent across 2500 business units in 24 companies representing 12 industries. For more information, see *First Break All the Rules* or the Gallup organization web site.

In Factor 3 of Authentic Vocation,™ we explore what motivates and interests the client.

What Motivation Is

To be motivated is to feel inspired, excited, and look forward to doing something. It also means "to provide with a motive," which in turn is defined as "a reason or desire, acting as a spur to action." Each of us is motivated by different factors, and we will not perform at our best unless those factors are present in our work. This includes both the type of work and the environment in which we perform the work (the latter of which we will explore further in chapter 10).

Many of our clients will know the types of duties they want to perform, but they may be unconscious of what really motivates them. Motives are often unconscious, and as such become a driving force that "must" be fulfilled. It may be a need, a want, or a concern; it may be a desired state, and usually includes a desire to reach a certain kind of goal.

For example, when Ashley volunteered for a new project to initiate a joint venture with another complementary firm on a proposal, her motives could have been:

- To obtain recognition
- To step up her responsibilities to position herself for promotion
- To explore positions with the other company
- To facilitate cooperation among the companies

So while the behavior may look the same externally, the internal (and sometimes unconscious) drivers may be quite different.

Several decades ago, psychologist Frederick Herzberg researched employee motivation and how rewards impact it. He found that increasing salary or providing an annual Christmas turkey may appear to improve motivation temporarily, but in the long run, these are merely "hygiene factors" that are required as part of a job. For an employee to truly become more motivated, the employer must adjust the "motivating factors" and do such things as cross training, increasing the challenge of the job, or otherwise making a substantive change, not just a monetary one. This principle remains true today!

Differentiating Motives and Values

It is important to clarify the difference between motives or motivators, and values. McClelland points out that values often influence our choices about where to invest our energies, while motives reflect how much pleasure we get out of certain activities. Values are conscious, whereas motives are unconscious (and motivators are designed to tap into the unconscious motives). Figure 7 explains some of the key differences:

Figure 7: Values vs. Motives

Values	Motives
• Choose areas of importance	• Natural drives
• Conscious Level	• Unconscious
• Help an individual make decisions	• Predict types of behavior a person will gravitate toward over time
• Adaptive-developed from experience throughout one's life	• Basic-influenced by early emotional experiences and perhaps is genetic
• Less difficult to change	• More difficult to change

PVQ Profile & Interpretive Notes-TRG/HayMcBer (reprinted with permission)

In some coaching engagements, you will be seeking to discover the client's motivators in order to determine the best career fit for them; in others you may be seeking to change a motive in order to instigate a behavior change. Both situations are addressed in the tools and techniques you are learning here.

Figure 8 illustrates the respective factors that are at play as we explore our client's issues. Life Purpose, Motive, Traits, Self-Image, and Social Role/Values are below the surface of the water on the iceberg, meaning they're more or less unconscious. Skills and Knowledge are what the rest of the world sees as the 10 percent of the iceberg that is visible.

Figure 8: The Iceberg Metaphor

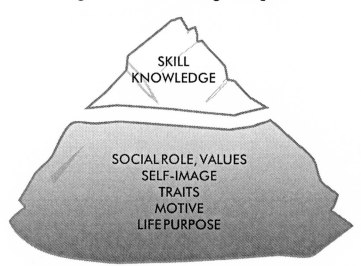

Changing & Increasing Motivation: 5 Basic Steps

Whether the client is seeking to access more of their known motivation regarding their work situation, or to change the motivation behind a troublesome behavior, the following 5 steps will result in a change in both motivation and behavior:

1. **Do self-assessment:** First the client must become aware of how naturally, or habitually, she perceives and thinks about the people and situations she encounters. That is, she must thoroughly understand her present motivation and its consequences. Once she understands it, she can then seek to leverage it in she work. For example, Sue was feeling frustrated with her work as a customer service representative for a software company. Her self-assessment included noticing, throughout the day, which aspects of her job upset her the most. She realized it was the lack of control over the situations she would encounter with customers, their emotional state, and even whether she could successfully resolve their problems.

2. **Define desired state:** Next she needs to fully describe the ideal situation that would allow us to feel motivated, and toward which she wants to move. Sue has several choices here

(though she may not realize it!). She can explore changing jobs, either within her company (e.g., to another department) or to another company. And if she doesn't know what other jobs would suit her, she could work with a career coach to discover it. A second choice would be to change her attitude and approach to her existing job. Instead of insisting on controlling each day's activities and exchanges, she could learn to find motivation in being challenged and delighted by each day's varied experiences. This may change the way she has viewed herself in the past, and in fact may affect other experiences in her life too.

3. **Set goals:** The next step is to set goals, solve problems, plan and act in ways consistent with her new thoughts about people and situations. If Sue chose the first option of seeking a new job, for example, her goals would include identifying her job targets, updating her resume, reactivating her network of contacts, and planning and implementing a job search.

4. **Repeat new motivation:** To fully integrate a new habit, idea, or motivation at the subconscious level, it must be consciously repeated for at least 21 days consecutively. If it is a deep, longstanding belief, it may take longer! In the case of seeking a new job, a powerful repetition technique is to write out a description of the desired work situation each night before going to bed. That allows the subconscious to work on the idea throughout the night and enhances the results obtained from job search activities. Emotions coupled with this reinforcement improve the results still further, as Figure 9 illustrates.

5. **Obtain interpersonal and situational supports:** Finally, she can put herself in situations and be with people who will give her feedback, stimulation, and generally support our new way of thinking and behaving. These situational supports include a coach, a Master Mind group that meets weekly to celebrate victories and provide support during disappointments, or a support group organized around a common situation (e.g., people in job transition, new business owners, etc.). If she isn't working with a coach (or maybe even if she is!), Sue might participate in a job seekers' networking group to support her

job change efforts. These activities work together to create a positive feedback loop, which can continually reinforce the motivation you are trying to change or increase.

Figure 9: Formula for Change

Desired state ➡ repeated thought + strong emotion = desired change

Relationship of Motives and Interests

Often (but not always), when we have a high level of interest in something, we are also highly motivated to do it. Therefore, as we evaluate this factor of Authentic Vocation,™ we can do an interest inventory to identify functional areas within an organization that may be more motivating to the client than others. A caveat here, however: just because someone has a high level of interest in something does not mean that they have any skill (transferable or otherwise) or experience in it. So all of the Authentic Vocation™ elements must be considered together as we work with the client.

One assessment of interests is the Career Transition Report available at www.cpp.com. It evaluates the individual's interest level in ten functional work areas of an organization:

* Administration   * Information Systems
* Customer Service   * Manufacturing/Production
* Finance/Accounting   * Marketing
* General Management   * Research and Development
* Human Resources   * Sales

Each functional work area has a set of tasks associated with it so clients can see which areas and tasks they showed interest in. The Career Transition Report also includes an action plan that advises clients how to effectively apply their results from the report and activities they can do to ease their transition and identify satisfying career options.

Another way to categorize interests is to use the Self-Directed Search (http://www.self-directed-search.com/index.html), developed by career theorist and Case Western Reserve professor John Holland. This model assumes that since vocational interests are one aspect of personality, description of a person's vocational interests is also a description of their personality. Personality traits are identified by indicating preferences for school subjects, recreational activities, work, and hobbies.

The 6 types evaluated by the Self-Directed Search include:

1. **Realistic** - prefer activities involving systematic manipulation of machinery, tools or animals; lack social skills
2. **Investigative** - analytical, curious, methodical, and precise; lack leadership skills
3. **Artistic** - expressive, nonconforming, original, introspective; lack clerical skills
4. **Social** - enjoy working with and helping others; avoid ordered, systematic activities and lack mechanical/scientific ability
5. **Enterprising** - enjoy manipulating others to attain organizational goals or economic gain, avoid symbolic/ systematic activities; lack scientific ability
6. **Conventional** - enjoy manipulating data in systematic way, filing records, and reproducing materials; avoid artistic activities

The results of an interest inventory can affirm your client's current career focus or suggest new areas for exploration.

Key Coaching Concepts:

1. To be motivated is to feel inspired, excited, and look forward to doing something. It also means "to provide with a motive," which in turn is defined as "a reason or desire, acting as a spur to action."

2. Values are different from motives in several aspects including the fact that values are conscious and motives are unconscious; values are adaptive and motives are basic; and values are easier than motives to change.

3. If we wish to change or increase client motivation, we need to facilitate 5 key steps:
   a. Do self-assessment
   b. Define desired state
   c. Set goals
   d. Repeat new motivation with emotion
   e. Obtain interpersonal and situational supports

4. Often (but not always) we are motivated by those activities in which we have a high level of interest. Therefore, administering an interest inventory at this stage can help define motivators.

FACTOR 4 –
KNOWLEDGE, SKILLS
AND ABILITIES

"Knowledge is the only instrument of production that is not subject to diminishing returns."

—J.M. Clark

"The man we call a specialist today was formerly called a man with a one-track mind."

—Endre Balogh

As we have pointed out previously, many current career development models begin with what in Authentic Vocation™ is factor 4: skills. The philosophy, apparently, is that if one does more of what one is good at, satisfaction will surely follow. The problem is, most mid-career coaching clients have already followed that track to the end, and come up wanting when they reach the point where fulfillment is more important than competency.

The dictionary defines "skill" as "proficiency or ability; expertise; an art, trade or technique." Skills are differentiated from experience (the factor we examine in the next chapter) in that skills are specific competencies that can be innate, learned or attained through use, whereas experience refers to job titles and types of work one has actually done. Similarly, knowledge a client possesses may come from formal education, on-the-job training, continuing education, or other means.

Skills fall into three categories: a) technical, "hard," or job-specific skills, which usually require special training or education, like the ability to program a computer or create a spreadsheet; b) non-technical, "soft," or adaptive skills, like loyalty and punctuality, which pertain to one's work style; and c) transferable skills, like leadership and decision making, which are applicable in many different work settings.

The role of one's skills in Authentic Vocation™ will vary somewhat with the reason the client is seeking a job change. If he simply wishes to progress in responsibility or broaden his expertise in an industry or job in which he has experience, skills will be of high importance. The client's marketability will depend on his ability to demonstrate his skills to a prospective employer (even if within the same company!).

If, on the other hand, the client is a mid-life career changer (or would like to be!) who is dissatisfied or unfulfilled with his occupation, technical and non-technical skills *per se* are of less importance, but transferable skills are critical. In determining the type of work that will provide the client with fulfillment, substantial weight would be placed on life purpose, values and motivators. Skills and experience are only relevant if the client enjoys using the skill or working in the area in which he has experience, since his main goal at this juncture is usually to obtain increased satisfaction.

Many people underestimate the importance of soft skills in job design - as well as job search - and often believe employers favor a bottom-line focus. But soft skills have become increasingly important in workers as developing and managing effective working relationships becomes more important. In *Working with Emotional Intelligence* (Bantam 1998), Daniel Goleman states:

> "Four in ten [workers] are not able to work cooperatively with fellow employees, and just 19 percent of those applying for entry-level jobs have enough self-discipline in their work habits. More and more employers are complaining about the lack of social skills in new hires."

As many as 67 percent of the abilities deemed essential for effective performance, according to Goleman's review of 181 competence models, were emotional competencies (self-confidence, trustworthiness, initiative, optimism, conflict management, communication and the like), not IQ or expertise.

In a national survey of what employers seek in new workers, specific technical skills are less important than more intangible skills. The three most highly sought-after skills in new hires are a) oral communications, b) interpersonal abilities, and c) teamwork abilities.

(*Working with Emotional Intelligence* by Daniel Goleman and the US Department of Labor, Employment and Training Administration). Thus both soft" and "hard" skills have a place, both in presentation of the client on paper and in person as well as in determining job choice. Figure 10 contains some examples of each:

Figure 10: Soft vs. Hard Skills

Soft/Intangible/Nontechnical Skills	
Team player	Build rapport easily
Good communicator	Reliable
Honest	Flexible
Good time manager	Fair
Adaptable	Hard-working
Detail-oriented	

Hard/Tangible/Technical Skills	
Performance appraisal	Inventory control
Budget development/oversight	Staff supervision
Marketing plan development	Process engineering
Advertising	Recruiting
Cold-calling	Welding
Web site design	

As our clients identify their skills, it is important that we assure them that both hard and soft skills have a role in job targeting and job search. What is the importance of "soft" skills in matching a client to the right job? "Hard" or tangible skills predict what jobs or functions the client can perform. If the client is also good at a particular skill and enjoys it, it becomes a motivated skill and will be important to his Authentic Vocation.™ Often the "soft" skills are more important in predicting the company culture the client will work best in, his ability to get along with others, and his ability to effectively manage.

Skills Assessment Techniques and Tools

There are five primary approaches to skills assessment: checklist, open list, card sort, drawing from Work Experience Stories, and software.

1. **Checklist.** Authentic Vocation™ Worksheet 4 (see Part Five, Career Coach's Toolbox) takes the checklist approach to skills assessment. The client checks the boxes that indicate which skills he/she has education in, direct experience in, has trained others in, or managed others in. Coach and client can then dialog about where the responses cluster and what that means for the client's job targeting and search.

   For another example of a checklist-based skills assessment that is simple and user-friendly, see http://www.adm.uwaterloo.ca/infocecs/CRC/manual/skills.html. This university-generated form divides skills into the categories of specialized, communication/interpersonal, and general and asks the job seeker to identify one in each category.

2. **Open list.** An open list format is illustrated in Figure 11.

3. **Card Sort.** To identify the skills that the person is both good at and likes to use, sorting a deck of cards with various skills typed on them into a two-dimension grid can narrow the field of so-called "motivated skills." Perhaps the best known of these is Richard Knowdell's Motivated Skills Card Sort: http://www.careertrainer.com/instruments.html

4. **Work Experience Stories.** Another approach is to have the job seeker write his/her Work Experience Stories (to be discussed in Chapter 8), then circle key words from them and log them into a matrix which lists key skills (much like those listed in Authentic Vocation™ Worksheet 4). That gives him/her a better idea of which skills he/she has most experience applying in the workplace.

5. **Software and Internet-Based Programs.** There are many skills assessment software programs, many of which over-simplify the categories of skills needed in today's marketplace. The better ones will compare a job seeker's skills with lists of skills required for certain jobs. A free skills assessment is the Motivational Appraisal of Personal Potential (MAPP) tool available at www.assessment.com. One of the best we have found is Careerway (www.careerway.com), which not only explores skills but compares the user's interests, motivators, and daily activities to those required in each of the 900 job types currently listed in the O*Net database (more on this in chapter 9).

Figure II: Open List Approach to Skills

You have developed some skills that you can use in your ideal job. Examples might be the ability to type, set up and maintain a bookkeeping system, run a table saw or similar tools, salesmanship skills, and a host of others, depending on your field(s) of expertise.

List as many of these work skills as you can think of below.

1.

2.

3.

4.

5.

6.

7.

8.

9.

10.

11.

12.

Some of the skills you have listed you have well-developed, but you may not enjoy using those skills. Part of our objective in designing your ideal job is to create a job you enjoy, not just one you are good at doing. To help you in this process, place an "E" next to each skill you enjoy using. These are the skills you will want to focus on using in your ideal job.

We provide you with several tools so that you can tailor your approach to the client's professional level, learning style, and goals. For example, clients in the early stages of their career or in creative fields may find the checklist in Authentic Vocation™ Worksheet 4 intimidating, but they would have the ability to list their skills based on their resume or accomplishments.

Key Coaching Concepts:

1. A "skill" is a "proficiency or ability; expertise; an art, trade or technique."
2. Skills fall into three categories: technical, nontechnical, and transferable.
3. As many as 67 percent of the abilities deemed essential for effective performance require emotional competencies.
4. There are at least five approaches to skills assessment: checklist, open list, card sort, drawing from Work Experience Stories, and software and internet-based programs.

8

FACTOR 5 – WORK AND OTHER RELEVANT EXPERIENCE

"Life is a series of experiences, each one of which makes us bigger, even though sometimes it is hard to realize this."

—Henry Ford

"Experience enables you to recognize a mistake when you make it again."

—Franklin P. Jones

Factor 5 of Authentic Vocation™ asks the client to inventory their work history (and, if applicable, other volunteer or school-related experience) from which they may wish to draw in their next career move. How the client approaches this exercise can tell us several things.

First, the industries in which the client has worked may reveal important elements of the client's personality and style, since often certain industries attract certain personalities (e.g., those who are organized, detail-oriented, and enjoy numbers may be drawn to accounting or finance). It can also reveal the opposite if a client is mismatched to their industry. For example, if a highly creative person has worked in data processing or finance for years and is unhappy, this mismatch suggests a new general direction they will want to investigate next.

Second, the client's work experience and her progression (or lack thereof) may indicate her level of motivation and drive. If she has rapidly progressed through the ranks of her occupation to increasing levels of responsibility, a high level of drive (as well as achievement motivation) is evident. On the other hand, a client who has spent a long time in a job or industry she didn't like for financial or other reasons may have less drive, or may simply not have known what else to do.

And third, a log of work experience can be a launching point for some coaching questions to determine whether the client wishes to remain in the industry she is currently in, return to an industry (or role) she previously held, or do something entirely new. And if the latter, we may ask if there are any aspects of her current industry that she enjoys and would like to continue to experience? (This helps her avoid "throwing the baby out with the bath water" by abandoning both the positive and negative aspects of her last occupation, employer, and industry.) What about the industry or role is particularly unappealing to the client? Would she consider another position in that industry along with some other choices? These questions can clarify for the client and for you, the coach, what jobs and industries are among those to be considered in her next step.

Experience: Limiting Factor Or Source Of Possibilities?

Many people have a kind of "myopia" when it comes to their previous work experience. That is, they have great difficulty seeing how they can transfer their skills and experience from one industry or setting to another. As career coaches, we can help the client open her perspective as to the possibilities that her experience holds.

One way to do this is to think of the client's experience as a set of "building blocks" from which a number of shapes could be created. Working with the client, we can start to experiment as the client tells us what she wants. We can notice where she becomes excited, and where her voice indicates a lack of passion. We can also use our own work experience and familiarity (at whatever level) with various industries to suggest other areas where the client's skills and experience may transfer. (Note: we do not want to go as far as giving advice to the client, for that is outside the scope of coaching. But providing suggestions or ideas for the client to consider along with other possibilities is appropriate at this stage.) We'll explore this idea more in the next chapter.

For clients who are returning to the workplace after an extended absence, whether due to raising children, an illness in the family, or after a sabbatical or other leave, the coach must creatively explore the client's activities. Did they volunteer at a nonprofit, work with United Way, spearhead a fundraising drive for their church, or coach their child's athletic team? All of these experiences can also be relevant as the client seeks to decide what types of jobs to target next.

Work Experience Stories

To market oneself effectively in the 21st century workplace characterized by increasing competition, the candidate must demonstrate to an interviewer or hiring manager his/her ability to do the job in as tangible a way as possible. In addition, many of our clients need to become more aware of what they actually contribute through their work. This alone has created epiphanies among many of my clients: when they realized the many contributions they had made, their self-esteem, which may be battered due to layoffs or other factors, increased dramatically!

One of the best ways to do this is to develop "Work Experience Stories" which demonstrate particular skills being applied within a workplace context. Work Experience Stories have three components, which form the acronym C-A-R:

*   Context, challenge or circumstance encountered when the project began, or what the problem was that was solved.
*   Action taken or accomplishment made to complete the project or solve the problem.
*   Result obtained, quantified whenever possible.

Example:

[Challenge:] When I was promoted to Sales and Marketing Director for Region 5, we were the lowest performing region of the 30 regional territories. My challenge was to bring the sales and overall performance numbers up as quickly as possible.

[Action:] To do so, I met with the 20-person sales staff, jointly established some aggressive goals for the next 6-12 months, and developed a promotional strategy to increase customer awareness of our products, which included incentives for new purchases within a stated length of time.

[Result:] Within 90 days, sales were up by 15%, and by year-end we were second in the nation with $1.2 million in sales.

Most clients should be encouraged to write at least 6 to10 Work Experience Stories to describe their key accomplishments. And they should have at least one story for each skill that is central to their next job target, as well as one to three stories for each position they have held. Using the skill labels on the Authentic Vocation™ Worksheet 4 can help trigger ideas for clients as to what stories to write. The worksheet on which they can develop their stories is Authentic Vocation™ Worksheet 5 in Part Five.

Traditional And New Types Of Career Paths

In the Old World of Work that governed prior to the 1980's, the typical employee moved in a vertical career path through their employer organization. This path was referred to as the "career ladder." As an employee was promoted, he/she (usually he) moved up one rung at a time until, at the top, he retired with the stereotypical gold watch. Sales representative becomes senior sales rep, sales manager, regional manager and ultimately national sales manager in this ladder-like progression.

Though some workers still progress using the ladder-type approach, other career paths have become more common in the new millennium, where 5 to 10 career changes are typical during one's professional life.

1. **Zigzag career path:** The worker's job, career, and educational choices do not follow in a traditional or logical order. For example, someone may begin with a degree in business, and get a first job doing commission sales for a pharmaceutical firm, then study web design and work for an advertising firm doing web-based surveys for a while. After a 6-month parental leave/sabbatical to have a child, the worker may then pursue a home-based business in an entirely unrelated field to allow her the flexibility she needs to be home with her infant.

2. **Portfolio career:** For many people, their divergent interests preclude their being satisfied with just one job or role. The portfolio career allows them to pursue multiple positions at once, one or more of which pay well enough to meet their financial needs, and one or more of which primarily provide "psychic income," meet their desire to contribute to society, or allow them to give back to their profession or community. This model can also be used by the would-be entrepreneur as a transitional strategy, i.e., working part-time evenings and weekends in an entrepreneurial venture and keeping a "day job" either full-time or part-time until the business can support him/her (assuming that their primary employer's policies do not prohibit "moonlighting"). Figure 12 illustrates this approach.

Figure 12: Portfolio Career

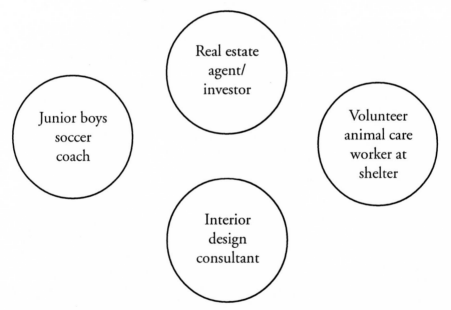

3. **Lateral paths:** Here, the employee moves logically but in a horizontal (vs. vertical) fashion, either through a matrixed organization (where functions cross over and reporting is both horizontal and vertical) or through one or more industries or functions:

> *   *Lateral through industries:* For example, a marketing/
> communications director may work for 5 years in
> transportation company/industry, then move to same
> level position in financial services firm and later to an
> engineering consulting firm, doing the same function
> in each company but changing the "context" to maintain
> his/her interest and professional challenge.

> *   *Lateral through functions:* After 8 years as Quality
> Manager in a multinational lumber products company,
> an employee might be transferred to a position as
> Operations Manager of a troubled region to assist in a
> turnaround effort; two years later after the turnaround
> has been implemented shift to Project Manager for a
> new ISO 9000 manufacturing certification initiative the
> company is implementing. All of these positions are
> within the same corporation, and may or may not
> require a geographical move.

4. **"Pro-tirement"**: Dr. Frederick Hudson, founder of The
Hudson Institute, coined the term "pro-tirement" to define
the active lifestyle of today's retirement-age people. In the
New World of Work, people who are 65 or older (or even
those in their 50's!) are no longer required to retire - in fact,
recent legislation allows seniors up to age 70 to retain their
Social Security income while earning unlimited income from
work. Clients who have accumulated sufficient assets through
work and/or investments to sufficiently fund their post-work
lifestyle, but still desire to be active- whether in paid work or
volunteer activities - may seek out a career coach to help them
plan this so-called "third half" of their life.

Key Coaching Concepts:

1. How the client approaches the exploration and inventorying of their experience can tell us about their personality and drive, and can form the basis for some coaching questions.
2. Experience can best be communicated through the use of Work Experience Stories, using the three elements Context, Action, and Results.
3. The related exercises suggested in his chapter can help shift the client to focusing on achievement, contributions, and strengths, resulting in higher levels of confidence, enthusiasm and energy for taking forward action.
4. In addition to the vertical, ladder-like career path that characterized the old workplace, new career paths include the zigzag path, portfolio careers, lateral paths, and pro-tirement.

9

FACTOR 6 – DESIRED JOB TARGET(S)

"It is not enough to be busy...the question is: what are we busy about?"

—Henry David Thoreau

"Far away there in the sunshine are my highest aspirations. I may not reach them, but I can look up and see their beauty, believe in them and try to follow where they lead."

—Louisa May Alcott

Until now, the Authentic Vocation™ process has primarily involved the client engaging in self-exploration and self-discovery, clarifying life purpose, values, motivators, interests, skills, and experience that they wish to leverage. As we shift from AV Factor 5, Experience, to AV Factor 6, Desired Position and Industry, we may find our clients asking us as their coach to guide them toward job or career options that would be viable for them. This is primarily a career counseling or consulting role, not pure coaching, as we have seen. It is vital that we draw the appropriate balance between offering a few useful tips (drawn from our experience and the resources we will discuss below) and having the client do the work to discover their Authentic Vocation™. Remember: career coaching is all about them, not us!

I like to suggest to clients at this stage that they adopt an attitude of curiosity. "This is an opportunity to think outside the box of what you have done and been so far," I'll tell them. "What larger part of you is being called forth in this transition?" This is also a part of the career discovery journey where the client can feel free to try on different possible jobs or careers, as though they were throwing spaghetti at the wall to see what sticks.

For the client, this phase can feel very scary. Often they will say things like "I wonder if I'm going crazy; I seem to have a different idea every week." Or "Won't I ever figure out what I'm supposed to be when I grow up?" It's the in-between stage of any transition, what I called the "Sorting-Out" phase of transition in *Thriving in Transition*. As career coaches, there are two things we can say to comfort our clients at this stage:

1. Reassure them that this feeling of being scattered and unsure is normal! Just as in quantum physics chaos precedes a new order, in Authentic Vocation™ and QuantumShift!™ coaching trying on new professional roles is a prerequisite to deciding on the one the client will ultimately choose.

2. Encourage them to capture all of the job ads that interest them, notes from informational interviews or books and articles they have read, ideas that occur to them in the middle of the night or in off hours, etc. Whether they stuff scraps of paper into a manila envelope, organize the data in a 3-ring binder, or create an electronic file on their computer, the point is to collect these seemingly unrelated ideas and review them again in 4-6 weeks. It is often quite amazing the patterns that emerge and how obvious the new direction for their career becomes by so doing.

Selecting Job Targets

Remember the "myopia" we talked about in the last chapter that many people have about their experience? Between that and the rapidly changing career paths, clients often feel more limited than they need to about what other jobs are possible for them. There are several approaches you can take to broaden their perspective about their options.

1. **What are the logical next steps?** A beginning point for developing job search targets is to identify the logical options based on the client's prior positions and experience. That is, if they were working in a medium- to large-sized organization and were going to be promoted, what would the next position

up the ladder be (even if the ladder has turned into a spiral, a patchwork quilt, or something else!)?

Example: Mary has been an account representative and sales rep with progressively larger territories and diverse products, so logical next steps would be account rep or sales rep positions with other similar companies.

2. **"Same Raw Materials, New Finished Product."** In addition to the logical next steps, we want to look more broadly about how the client can rearrange her "building blocks" (i.e, her responses to the first 5 factors of Authentic Vocation™) to form new shapes. Let's look at Mary's building blocks and see what other possibilities we can generate.

Example: Mary's building blocks include life purpose - making the world a better place through promoting and selling environmentally-friendly products and services; values - integrity, social responsibility and authenticity; motivators - mentoring, seeing tangible results of her work; skills - working with people, sales, developing marketing campaigns, resourcefulness, and follow-through; experience in consumer products sales and marketing.

Now, given those raw materials and imagining sitting down with a set of toy wooden blocks, what other shapes could they make?

Example: Mary could use her building blocks to be a sales manager or a web designer for consumer products companies, to name two. She might also consider targeting a position as customer relations manager, becoming a self-employed marketing consultant, or an entrepreneur who owns a company with a new socially responsible product.

Most industries have a supply chain: manufacturing transfers the product to the wholesalers who sell to businesses that sell to the ultimate customer as retailers. If a client has experience in the manufacturing of a product, other job/career targets for them can be the distribution or retail side of the business - as well as consulting or working in a government agency that may regulate that industry. So exploring other possibilities along the supply chain is another way to use the same raw material but create a different finished product.

3. **Coaching Questions to Uncover Options.** Throughout this process, since we are coaching the client to discover their answers, we want to ask probing questions to help them generate more possibilities for applying their talents. What questions might you ask to expand or uncover additional options for a client? Here are a few to consider:

   What do you really want to do?

   When you were a child, what were some of your favorite pastimes?

   As a child, what did you dream of being when you grew up?

   What would you do if you didn't care what other people thought?

   What would you do if you couldn't fail?

   What if you had no limits?

   What if money were no object?

   What if that [whatever "that" is for them] wasn't in your way?

   What would it take for you to follow your heart?

   What would you be most excited about?

   What would you like to do if you weren't afraid?

   What are you being called to do now?

   Who are you being called to be now?

   What is your future self [1 year out, 5 years out, 20 years out] doing?

   Who do you want to become?

   Imagine you had a magic wand…what would you ask for?

   What other positions have your colleagues taken after leaving your company?

   When will you do that if not now?

4. **The "Ideal Day" Exercise.** Part Five contains the "Ideal Day" exercise that can be quite helpful as the client strives to fill in the details of their ideal job targets. This exercise can be suggested to complement the more analytical techniques that appear in this chapter.

Useful Resources for Job and Career Information

When clients are looking for ideas about what kind of work to pursue, it is often helpful to begin by perusing the Sunday newspaper (online or in print) classified help wanted ads and noticing which positions sound interesting, or speak to them in some way. If they are looking for a new job within their company, reviewing the internal postings of open positions can also be helpful. It is important for them to realize that the purpose of this exercise is not to apply for the jobs posted, but to notice which ones - in whole or in part - contain the kinds of activities and responsibilities that they want in their next job.

Other helpful resources on the web may include:

Occupational Outlook Handbook	http://www.bls.gov/oco
O*Net	http:/online.onetcenter.org/main.html
Dogpile industry overview	www.dogpile.com
Hoovers industry overview	www.hoovers.com

Also at this stage the client should be gathering names of key individuals (e.g., company managers or CEO's) in the target industries with whom they can conduct informational interviews to learn more. The approach to and format of informational interviews is discussed in detail in chapter 14 in Part Three.

By using these resources and Authentic Vocation™ Worksheet 6, your client should be able to generate a list of 15 to 20 types of jobs he might consider - or at least would be willing to do some further research on to determine feasibility and match with his interests and skills. This is a critical stage to be sure that the client regularly checks in with you so that they don't get overwhelmed or frustrated with the exploration process.

Key Coaching Concepts:

1. When the client feels scared or frustrated about constantly generating new job and career options, reassure them that this is normal at this stage, and encourage them to capture the seemingly random ideas, thoughts, and information that they are noticing at this time.

2. Four approaches to take in helping the client broaden their options for next job or career are: a) logical next steps, b) "same raw materials, new finished product," c) coaching questions to reveal what they really want to do, and d) the Ideal Day exercise.

3. Numerous online resources can be helpful in exploring various jobs and careers, perhaps the most helpful of which is the Occupational Outlook Handbook.

10

FACTOR 7 – WORK ENVIRONMENT

"When two cultures collide is the only time when true suffering exists."

—Hermann Hesse

"I'm a great believer in luck, and I find the harder I work the more I have of it."

— Thomas Jefferson

Why is having the right work environment important in developing a truly Authentic Vocation™? If a client is attempting to apply her talents in a culture that conflicts with her life purpose or does not allow her to use her optimum work style, she will not be as productive or as satisfied as she could be, and ultimately will not stay in the position.

There are 7 key components of work environment (outlined further in Authentic Vocation™ Worksheet 7 in Part Five):

1. **Geographical Location.** Where does the client like to work? In the state and city where he lives — or somewhere else altogether? Perhaps this is a perfect time to explore relocating. Would he like to work in an office or outdoors? In an urban or rural setting?

2. **Pace.** A second aspect of work environment is the pace of the business or office. Does he enjoy an environment that is

bustling and busy, or does he prefer a peaceful, slower pace? How many hours does he want to work each week?

3. **Support.** The degree of support in the work environment is also important. One way to avoid burnout is to surround ourselves with a supportive environment — one in which we have a sense of significance, autonomy, challenge and support, and in which there are relatively few unmodifiable work stresses. This may be provided by the values and culture of the organization (more about this in factor 7 below), through a mentoring program in the company, through new employee orientation, or through a boss that is caring and concerned.

4. **Compensation.** How much money does the client want to earn in his ideal job? What about fringe benefits? What are they? The client may want to complete the Wants/Needs Analysis in Authentic Vocation™ Worksheet 10 to trigger ideas on what benefits and other job factors are important here.

5. **Size.** It is also important to evaluate whether he work best alone, with one or two co-owners, or in a large company setting. To help evaluate the optimal work setting, consider the following profiles of the solo worker, the partner, and the team personality.

Solo Worker Profile

* is independent
* prefers working alone; likes privacy
* is highly creative and contemplative
* has a few carefully chosen friends
* resists authority
* is motivated by opportunity to create and to get credit for creation
* likes to take risks
* biggest fear: loss of control

Partner Profile

* enjoys (and needs) give and take feedback when making decisions and in conversation
* is most creative in context of a close relationship
* has a few long-term friends
* needs equal amounts of time alone and with others

* is an excellent listener
* feels power comes from shared resources
* shares risk-taking with partner
* biggest fear: rejection by partner

Team Personality Profile

* enjoys esprit de corps of large organization, including process of gaining consensus
* wants to be alone about 20% of the time
* is motivated by competition
* forms many friendships easily
* comfortable with authority figures
* is most creative in context of praise from team members and from leader
* enjoys belonging to clubs
* shares risks with team members and leader
* biggest fear: loneliness

If the client is a team personality type, he should also consider how large a company he wishes to work for. Though the team dynamic is present in the 10-person company and a 1000-person company, the day to day experience in those two companies will be quite different.

6. **Primary Function.** The client's next inquiry is whether he prefers to work primarily with people, with data, or with things. His hobbies and past jobs can provide clues here — what activities have given him the most joy: those involving interaction with people, working with data or information, or working on things with his hands?

7. **Corporate Culture.** Culture, or "how we do things around here," is a final factor in work environment. Does the client prefer a company that is conservative or radical, socially conscious or not, employee-oriented or bottom-line/results-oriented? Does he prefer that the company have a clear vision and mission, or that it "go with the flow"?

Evaluating Corporate Culture

Next to the relationship with one's direct supervisor (which author Daniel Goleman, in *Working with Emotional Intelligence,* states is the most important component of employee satisfaction) the culture of a company and the employee's sense of "fit" within it are also critical in both employee satisfaction and retention. In short, if they feel like they fit into the culture, they will stay with the company longer.

Cultures can range from conservative to liberal, bottom-line focused to employee-focused, traditional to radical, and in many other dimensions. By exploring and identifying culture upon starting a job, an employee can make a more sound job choice. As Lloyd Field Ph.D. notes in "How Culture Affects Productivity" (*The Canadian Manager*) "culture should not be confused with climate. Climate is the short-term mood of an organization. Unlike culture, it is fragile and subject to change."

Some of the aspects of corporate culture include:
- behavior patterns,
- standards,
- values,
- overall "feel" of the organization
- everything it does and everything it makes
- telling people what is right and wrong, what to believe and not believe, how to react and how to feel

How can an employee evaluate company climate, either in informational interviews or job interviews? Here are a few ideas:
- The company can ask members of the team the candidate would join to participate in the interview process (if your client/ candidate is a manager or executive, he/she may request this)
- Ask some pre-interview questions to determine the company's culture and whether it appears to be a fit
- Ask to interview 1 or 2 people in the company that are not part of the formal hiring process to ask questions about culture only, not the job itself
- Take advantage of any available software or testing that matches employee values with company values and culture
- Ask hypothetical questions about "what would happen if..." or "what would the company do if...", and listen carefully to both what is said and what is unsaid. What values are apparent?
- Seek out sources that rank companies by culture, such as national and local business magazines that publish an annual list of the "best companies to work for"

- The *Working Mother 500,* in print or on the web, may also provide insights into organizational culture
- Do a "scouting trip" of the company both during business hours and non-business hours - what do you notice about how people appear, their energy, what they are wearing, is the parking lot full on the weekend perhaps indicating long hours?
- Do a web-search on the company to see if they appear in any interesting articles or unexpected places

Entrepreneurship

One of the fastest growing forms of work today is entrepreneurship - owning your own business. By 2010, the U.S. Department of Labor predicts that the number 1 employer will be "self." As a career coach, you may be asked to guide someone who wants to start his/her own business, or at least wants to explore that as one option. You may choose to develop your own expertise in this area (though you will need additional training to do so), or you may partner with a coach who specializes in business start-up and working with entrepreneurs. But initially, you can at least help the client determine whether or not entrepreneurship is a potential fit. Part Five contains an Entrepreneurial Checklist to help clients evaluate whether being an independent business owner is right for them.

Telecommuting and Home-Based Work Options

As people get busier and try to balance the conflicting demands of their life, flexible work options such as telecommuting (aka teleworking) are of increasing interest. Some of your clients may wish to pursue those options. Here are some facts about telework:

- There were 2.8 million new regularly employed US teleworkers, age 18 years or older, in late July 2000, according to the national telephone survey data collected by the Behavior Research Center.
- 39 percent of the workers who do not currently work remotely are interested in teleworking-and 13 percent of those workers would consider the ability to telework an important influence when making a decision to accept another job.

What are the benefits of teleworking? Not only does it increase employee satisfaction, but teleworking fosters increased productivity, according to the survey results. The self-reported productivity improvement of home-based teleworkers averages 15 percent, while telework-center-based employees reported a 30 percent improvement.

If a client wants to consider telework, your coaching inquiry can address the following:

First, telework isn't appropriate for every job. Some job activities don't lend themselves to telework. Organizations need to analyze the job activity, not the job title, to determine suitability to telework. The key is to find jobs with at least a portion of the work that can be done as well or better away from the office - taking advantage of technology and getting away from the distractions and interruptions in the typical office.

Second, telework isn't for everyone. Just as being selective about the job activity is important, it's equally important to limit telework to employees who have the job knowledge/skills, personality, self-motivation, and home setting that will allow them to work effectively at home or elsewhere away from the office.

In short, a person's work environment is perhaps the least considered by job seekers but is a critical contributor to fulfillment as one defines his/her Authentic Vocation.™

Key Coaching Concepts:

1. There are 7 key aspects of work environment to be considered in Authentic Vocation™: a) location, b) pace, c) support, d) compensation, e) size, f) function, g) culture.
2. In evaluating a company's culture, several factors need to be considered including:
   - behavior patterns,
   - standards,
   - values,
   - overall "feel" of the organization
   - everything it does and everything it makes
3. Entrepreneurship is a growing trend, and if a client indicates interest in starting their own business, we must ensure that they are not doing for the wrong reasons.
4. If a client wants to consider telework, your guidance can include the following: First, is telework appropriate for the job? Second, is telework right for this client?

Factor 8 – Business Reality

"Money is a terrible master but an excellent servant."
—P.T. Barnum

Now that the client has identified the kinds of work that will fulfill them emotionally, they need to filter their ideas through "business reality," the tough reality that asks, "Can this occupation support me financially? Does it allow me to sustain the lifestyle to which I am, or would like to be, accustomed?"

Business Reality is placed last in the Authentic Vocation™ model by design. If we allow our clients to become overly focused on income potential and viability of their desired work too early in the process, their creativity will be stifled. In *The Artist's Way*, Julia Cameron points out that many times artists (which can be anyone, not just a gifted painter or musician) become blocked because they are overly concerned about commercial sales potential for their creative output. It is key that the ideas are allowed to flow freely first (in this case as the client explores Authentic Vocation™ Factors 1 through 7) and that only after the creative ideas have been expressed should he/she examine Business Reality. In some cases the "averages" in the statistics will militate against the occupation being able to support a person. This simply calls for further innovation of coach and client: could it become one element in a portfolio career, or could strategic negotiation increase the compensation far beyond the averages due to what the client brings to the table?

We ask four questions at this stage:

- Does the work the client wants to do meet a need in the business/work world?
- Is/are the job target(s) the client has selected financially viable?
- Are there enough potential or actual positions to make the job target(s) viable for a full-scale job search?
- Is the client prepared, both mentally and financially, for the realistic length of their job search?

1. Determining Market Need

For some clients, market need is so obvious as not to deserve conscious inquiry. If a client's job targets clearly fall within one of the ten primary functional areas of the organization we examined in chapter 6, and there are a plethora of help wanted ads for that type of work each week, market need is clearly present. There is always a need for sales representatives, for accountants, for human resource professionals, and for some information technology positions, for example.

Even for these seemingly obvious needs, it is still advisable for the client to check the latest data in the Occupational Outlook Handbook (http://stats.bls.gov/ocohome.htm) to see whether the occupation is expected to grow (and at what pace), remain stagnant, or decline in the coming years. Regional and statewide occupational data from the web sites listed below, as well as the opinions of leaders within the industry can supplement the OOH data and assure the client that they are making a viable choice.

- Career Guide to Industries http://stats.bls.gov/cghome.htm
- National Industry-Occupation Employment Matrix http://www.bls.gov/asp/oep/nioem/empiohm.asp
- Occupational Employment, Training and Earnings http://stats.bls.gov/asp/oep/noeted/empoptd.asp
- America's Career Infonet http://www.acinet.org/acinet/

Clients in mid-career often present a different type of challenge. They don't seem to quite fit into the "boxes" represented by traditional job descriptions. By this point they have completed their formal education and initial job out of college (if they attended college), have some work experience, and have proven themselves according to the external standards of success. That is, they often have a mortgage, family, investments, several automobiles, and other trappings of prosperity. The problem is, these clients have become bored or "fed up" or unchallenged or burned out on doing what has comprised their livelihood so far. There's another part of themselves that wants to emerge, a talent or skill thus far untapped in their professional lives. In my experience working with dozens of midlife career changers, the most satisfying work for the second half of their life often combines, in a creative and many times innovative way, the talents they have exhibited in their first few jobs with the additional part of themselves that is calling to them.

My own career path is one example of this. As I chose my first few jobs, they drew upon my organizational and business skills, which I enjoyed using. My 12 years in the legal field were part of that competency-focused phase which characterizes most people's initial positions. But the time came when merely excelling with those skills became empty. There was something more needed in my work. The creative part of me that had studied music for years, dabbled in art in college, and appeared when I prepared a gourmet meal for a dinner party was not being allowed expression in my work. It was only when I discovered consulting, and later coaching, and began doing that work as an entrepreneur where I fulfilled many different roles (both creative and business) that I found satisfaction. The strategic planning, marketing, writing, and curriculum development satisfied my creative urge, while the financial and business responsibilities fulfilled the analytical side of my talents.

When working with these mid-career clients, the best approach in both articulating a desired career and in evaluating the need in the workplace or business market for it, is to encourage a "both-and" approach. Perhaps, instead of choosing something entirely different than one's prior work as a next step (and failing to draw on the wealth in that experience), there is a way to combine that with the untapped skill set in a new position — and then propose it to a firm who has a need for it. So rather than "either this or that" a client can combine both and create a win-win-win result. Benefits to corporations in these cases can include savings in human capital expenditure, since many times one person ends up filling two roles which would have otherwise required two separate employees. The acid test of whether there is a need is ultimately whether one or more firms respond positively to a proposal submitted by the client to offer that blend of abilities and services to the firm.

2. Evaluating Financial Viability

The second part of Business Reality, once a need is identified, is financial feasibility: will the job provide the salary and benefits as well as growth opportunities to meet the client's needs? Fortunately, there is ample free information readily available on the Internet, as well as through strategic questions asked in informational interviews with people working in the industry, that can provide guidance to the client in this regard.

The following web sites should help the client determine salary ranges for the type of work they are seeking.

www.careers.wsj.com
www.jobsmart.org
www.abbott-langer.com
www.wageweb.com
www.salary.com
http://stats.bls/gov/oes/oes_data.htm
www.rileyguide.com
http://stats.bls.gov/ocohome.htm

In addition, they may want to consult a salary calculator program (for an example, see http://www.homefair.com/homefair/cmr/salcalc.html) if they are seeking employment in a specific geographic location to make any regional cost of living adjustments in the industry averages.

3. Measuring Job Targets For Viability

Once the client has chosen at least three to five target jobs or careers that seem interesting, each needs to be evaluated for viability. The client may find the target is too specialized (and therefore too small), or too large with a lot of openings and options - but too many to strategically pursue.

For each target, determine:

Desired company size: _____
Desired position/job/function/role: _____
Desired geographic area: _____

Size of target market:
a.   Total number of organizations: _____
b.   Number of probable positions fitting
          desired criteria in each organization: _____
a x b =   total number of probable and suitable
          positions: _____

This information and other data to refine targets can be obtained through:
- Industry associations
- Trade publications, magazines
- Hoovers.com
- Labor Market Information for your local area (contact your State Labor Department or State Employment Department)
- US Department of Labor web sites at http://stats.bls.gov/
- ERISS: www.usworks.com; select target city or region
- Local Chamber of Commerce
- State and local Economic Development Department

A rule of thumb (according to Kate Wendleton of the Five O'Clock Club) for viability of a job target is this: "A target list of 200 positions in a healthy market results in seven interviews that result in one job offer." So if there are fewer than 200 potential positions within a client's target, the target may need to be refined.

4. Understanding Job Search Length

Most people just beginning their job search - particularly if it is due to an unexpected layoff - underestimate how long it will likely take for them to become re-employed. While there are exceptions, as a general rule the average length of a job search for a professional or manager is three to six months, regardless of the economy or other factors. Another guideline that is commonly cited is that it often takes as much as one month for every $10,000 of income/salary the candidate was making to find gainful employment.

The following factors can significantly affect the length of a particular candidate's search, however, and may provide openings for coaching to shorten the search:

- **Client's clarity on their job/career target.** If your client comes to you already knowing what kind(s) of work they want to do, the exploration process will be fairly short. In fact, the work can begin with designing a job search marketing plan, one or more resumes, and coaching them in executing their search. The reality is that clients who are that clear about what they want to do rarely seek career coaching; they can conduct a successful search on their own. But market changes such as the recent decline of the information technology and Internet field can test the resourcefulness of even people who know what they want to do.

- **Geographic scope/limits.** This factor includes two scenarios. First, is the client who is open to relocating anywhere within the U.S. or another broad geographical area? The search may be shortened because recruiters with a national scope can more easily place them, and there are more total possibilities available to them. However, conducting the search itself - particularly the aspects that deal with targeted contacts to companies and individuals - can be overwhelming unless the client selects two or three cities or states that are top preferences and focuses there first.

  The second scenario is the client who is absolutely committed to staying where they are - or even more difficult, the client who has moved to a city for lifestyle reasons and now wants a job there. It may be due to having children close to finishing high school, community ties, family in the area, or just a preference to stay there. The effect of this factor on the length of the search is usually to prolong it, since the pool of available possibilities is much smaller for this client. Conversely, however, the execution of the search is more manageable due to this smaller pool. Even this latter type of client can sometimes have delightful results. I worked with an information technology manager in Orange County, California who had just built a lovely beachfront house and did not want to move despite her recent layoff. In fact, she said she wanted a job within 2 miles of where she lived - and this in a part of the country where commutes of an hour or more are not uncommon! Within just three months, she was hired into an IT manager position with a leading Internet firm that needed her exact expertise, and the position was within 2 miles of her home!

- **Searching in same field or career changing.** When clients are seeking a position within an industry in which they have experience, the job search time tends to be shortened for several reasons. First, they know the companies to approach, have a network in the industry and area, and will be favorably considered by screeners when applying for published openings. Career changers, on the other hand, typically need to rely on the unpublished job market for their opportunities, and often also will spend more coaching time clarifying their goals. For these reasons, their job search time is usually (but not always) longer than other clients'.

- **Size of existing network of contacts.** It is not necessarily true that the larger the network, the faster the job search. But if a client has a substantial network of contacts both within and outside of their target industries, it does facilitate the process of getting connected with the right people for both published and unpublished openings.

Even then, however, the client may need to be coached about how to most strategically utilize their network, as we will explore in chapter 14.

- **Marketability of skills.** Are the client's skills and background marketable in the current climate? In other words, is there a demand for what they have to offer? The more demand there is, generally speaking the shorter the search (it can literally be a matter of days instead of months to complete a search in some cases!). Of course, the reality is that when a company downsizes, reorganizes, closes a division, or otherwise eliminates a function from its business that was longstanding, the skills of those workers may be outmoded in today's marketplace. I once facilitated a series of job search workshops for employees of the Forms Division in a major paper-manufacturing firm when that division was eliminated. Many of the men who worked there had 25 or 30 years with the company and literally didn't know what else to do - yet the skills that were desirable to that company for so many years had no real market with other companies. Retraining was an option for some; early retirement for others.

- **Economic and market conditions.** The conditions of the job marketplace and the economy of both the country where the candidate is searching and the global economy all have an impact on the length of the search. During prosperous times, when there are more jobs available than there are candidates to fill them, openings are filled quickly. During recessions or other economic downturns (whether global or limited to one industry or type of work), it takes longer for a candidate to find suitable employment because there is greatly increased competition for each opening.

- **Client's attitude, self-confidence and personality style.** Each client to some extent influences how long their search will take based on whether they are optimistic or pessimistic, confident or unsure, and even introverted versus extroverted. A pessimistic, "poor me" attitude will be unconsciously noticed by interviewers and networking contacts alike, making the candidate less desirable. Conversely, an enthusiastic, "can-do" attitude is contagious and makes people want to hire a person with such an outlook.

Clients who are introverted and have difficulty picking up the phone to contact people they don't know can be successful in their job search, but may find that the search takes longer. We'll talk in chapter 12 about some ways to adjust the job search plan for this variable, but in my experience extroverted, gregarious clients generally have an easier time with the job search and find a job faster than those that aren't.

- **Financial reserves and/or severance.** The ability to sustain oneself during the transition period can make a huge difference in how aggressive the client is in his search. There's nothing like making next month's mortgage payment to stimulate job search activity! But if the client received a generous severance package that affords him the luxury of a few months off, many will take it. And while I wouldn't discourage taking a mini-sabbatical, the client also needs to be aware that he will face a perceived liability when there is a recent gap on their resume. Screeners often jump to the conclusion that the job seeker has been in the search throughout the time gap and has been unsuccessful so far. We will discuss a strategy to counter this perception in chapter 17, but if the client does decide to exercise this option, he needs to be aware of the potential consequences.

- **Support by family and friends.** Are the client's family members supportive of his/her job search, or continually asking when they will get back to work? Does the client have friends or a support group that they can draw encouragement from and share ideas with as they go through the emotional roller coaster of being between jobs? I always became wary when a client's spouse wanted to talk with or meet with me midway through their search; it was usually a clear sign that the spouse was applying more pressure than was appropriate on the client, which even if well-intentioned did not help the client meet his/her goals.

- **Amount of effort and commitment invested.** Looking for a job takes time. In fact, with unemployed clients, their job search is their job until they find a position they like. As a general rule, unemployed clients (or full-time job seekers) should spend four to six hours each day on their search, and employed clients (part-time job seekers) should spend one to two hours each day and at least a half-day each weekend on their search. Clients who apply these levels of effort should fall within the three- to six-month average search time. Those who exert only a half-hearted effort or spend half of each unemployed day playing golf or watching the soap operas on television can extend their search time dramatically.

Failing the Test

You may be wondering what happens if the client's desired job or career target(s) don't pass the Business Reality test. Does that mean they have to give up on the quest for greater satisfaction, even fulfillment, on the job? Of course not. Here again, your coaching skills can make the difference between the client finding a way to pursue their passion and letting it die on the vine.

For example, Dave wanted to leave his job as a production manager to be a stand-up comedian. Comedy, like such fields as acting and musical performing, is a field in which people tend to become highly successful or spend years struggling. The first approach I typically take in such cases is to probe to discover the essence of what appeals to the client about the desired occupation. Does he want to have the opportunity to "work the crowd" and be in the spotlight? Does he desire to lighten up what has been a serious, tedious lifestyle? Does he feel "called" to share his sense of humor with people? These questions often reveal a thread that could be expressed in a number of ways. Dave could become a humorous motivational speaker if his essential goal was to get in front of people and share his humor. He might even be able to bring more humor into his current position and experience increased satisfaction as more of his true self is revealed.

Alternatively, if Dave says that stand-up comedy is truly the occupation he wants, and anything else would be a compromise, we move into what you will learn as Level 1 coaching (see Part Four) and brainstorm possible ways to achieve his goal. Could he start doing stand-up at night while maintaining his production job? Who could he choose as a mentor to help him get started and learn the basics of the business? These and other logistical considerations could allow Dave to make a gradual transition into the job of his dreams and learn as he went how successful he could be. The point is, we as coaches must often be creative and help the client "think outside the box" to create the job of their dreams *and* make a living doing it.

Key Coaching Concepts:

1. Business Reality is the tough reality that asks, among other things, "Can this occupation support you financially? Does it allow you to sustain the lifestyle to which you are, or would like to be, accustomed?"
2. There are four key considerations in using the Business Reality filter:
    a. Does the work the client wants to do meet a need in the business/work world?
    b. Is/are the job target(s) the client has selected financially viable?
    c. Are there enough potential or actual positions to make the job target(s) viable for a full-scale job search?
    d. Is the client prepared, both mentally and financially, for the realistic length of their job search?

PART THREE

JOB SEARCH MECHANICS

THE JOB SEARCH: DEVELOPING A MARKETING PLAN & ALLOWING FOR SYNCHRONICITY

"You are an individualized expression of the creative flow. There is something you can do that no one can do quite as uniquely as you. Somewhere there is a need for that special contribution. You are needed even as you have a need... As you sit thinking, 'If I could only find a job,' some employer is at that very moment thinking, 'If only we could locate the right person for this opening!' Keep that vision of the orderly Universe. It is not a miracle that is needed to create a job for you but an expression of divine order in bringing you together with that which is looking for you."

—Eric Butterworth
Spiritual Economics

In this Part of the book, we enter the realm of job search mechanics. At this stage, your client is wondering: what is the best strategy to use to obtain the position(s) that I have determined to be my ideal? Key steps will include:

1. Help clients think of themselves as a product to be marketed
2. Design a marketing strategy using an appropriate mix of published and unpublished strategies
3. Ensure that clients know how to identify appropriate openings and target companies

4. Make certain clients know how to use the strategies that will get them the best results depending on their goals, role playing as necessary

5. Work with clients to develop one or more resumes that will showcase their qualifications

6. Discuss interviewing techniques, how to answer the most common questions, questions to ask, dress, how to overcome liabilities, and the like

7. Help clients evaluate the job offers they receive

8. Assist clients in negotiating the optimum compensation package

This is an area of career coaching that some coaches love and others dislike. Whether you do this part of the career coaching work or not depends on you. Do you like to see quick results from your work? Do you enjoy pointing to tangible products from your day's activities? Then the job search mechanics work may be a perfect fit. On the other hand, if you prefer the creativity of the career discovery process we have just finished discussing, and don't mind waiting for those QuantumShifts™ to occur, then you may want to leave the job search mechanics to another coach.

One other difference between coaching the career discovery process versus coaching job search mechanics is that your role in the latter phase is often one step closer to a consulting model (see Figure 13). There is a huge volume of information that the client needs to internalize about how the job search process works in order to be successful. Rather than spending the coaching sessions communicating this information in consulting style, it usually works better to take one of the following approaches:

1. Offer regular teleclasses or live seminars of one to three hours in length which paid coaching clients can attend at no charge, as part of their coaching services package, or for a nominal fee, at which you communicate this information.

2. Prepare real-time sessions that can be made available on your web site, or audio tapes you can mail out, for clients to listen to about these topics.

3. Give them a book such as the author's *How to Find the Job You Want* and suggest that they read the relevant chapter(s) prior to broaching the next phase of their search.

Then, the coaching sessions themselves can be spent helping the client apply the job search principles to her specific situation, with both coach and client having a common understanding of how resume design or answering common interview questions or evaluating a job offer should proceed.

Whether or not you decide to directly provide resume writing, interview coaching, negotiating assistance, and job search marketing plan coaching to your clients, you will nevertheless want to have a working knowledge of these topics. At the very least, you will be able to identify why some clients have become disillusioned with their job search, if, for example, they have been relying exclusively on advertised openings in the Sunday newspaper and do not know how to access the unpublished market. And at best, you will want to know enough to spot check the work of any subcontractors so that you ensure your clients are receiving the highest quality work.

Figure 13: Career Coaching Continuum

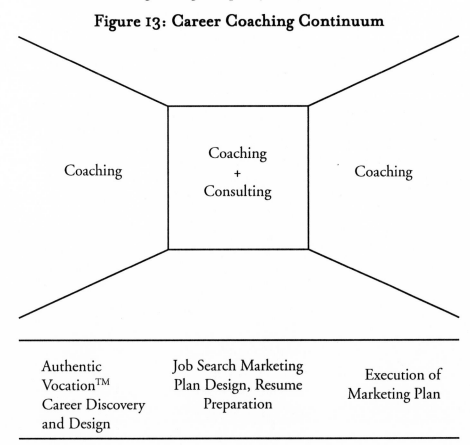

Self as Product

We begin by exploring our mindset. Successful job seekers think one way, unsuccessful ones think another. What's the difference? In today's competitive marketplace, it's no longer enough to think of oneself as a faceless commodity that one hopes someone will purchase for a fair price. That's the approach of the unsuccessful job seeker. Rather, job seekers must think of themselves as a niche product, one which needs to be marketed very specifically to the right target audience in order to result in the right mutual arrangement: the ideal job. Put yourself in the position of a marketer for a moment and imagine you have been tasked with marketing a new software program designed for an industry-specific user group. What kinds of questions would you need to answer to market this product? Many of the same questions need to be asked by the job seeker as she begins her campaign. They include:

- What are my assets?
- How am I different/better than other similar candidates?
- What are my liabilities, and how will I manage them?
- Where are my customers (i.e., prospective employers) located?
- How can I best reach them?

It may be helpful for some clients with whom you work to ask them these questions and have them think carefully about the answers. Perhaps writing out their answers will be useful to refer back to as they conduct their search.

Designing the Marketing Plan: Job Search Strategy Mix

In guiding clients in launching their job search, you'll also need to strategize with them an appropriate mix of unpublished and published strategies that meets the client's goals. In the next two chapters, we will explore in detail how to approach the published market and the unpublished market, including sample approach letters.

Even the idea of creating a marketing "plan" is a foreign concept to most job seekers. See what you already know about job search marketing by completing the quiz in Figure 14.

Figure 14: Job Search Marketing Quiz

Question (answer true or false)	T	F
1. Most jobs are filled through advertised openings.		
2. A job seeker's chances of being hired through an Internet job board are over 75 percent.		
3. Submitting an unsolicited resume is the best way to get hired through an executive recruiter.		
4. The primary purpose of networking is to access published openings.		
5. Every job seeker should use both published and unpublished market strategies in their campaign.		
6. There's no point applying to advertised openings in trade journals; they're overused and usually flooded with applicants.		
7. It will reflect negatively on the job seeker if he/she sends an unsolicited letter requesting a meeting with a manager or CEO to learn more about their company and industry.		
8. Job fairs are a waste of time for people with experience in a targeted industry.		
9. To maximize exposure in the geographic area where the person wants to work, the best approach is to send out several hundred unsolicited resumes in a mass mailing directed to specific human resource professionals.		
10. Once a candidate gets their resume properly formatted with their work history and qualifications, he should use the same resume for each position he applies for, whether mailed, faxed or emailed.		

Believe it or not, every single one of these 10 statements is false. How did you do? As we move through Part Three, each of these principles will be discussed in detail. But in our experience, the typical scenario for a new job seeker works something like this: the candidate updates their resume, looks through the Sunday newspaper and one or two of the large Internet job boards, submits their resume, perhaps attends a networking breakfast, and waits for the phone to ring or the email to arrive. What these people fail to understand is that only 20 percent of jobs filled in a given year are ever published, and the percentage of placements that occur through job boards is significantly lower yet (less than 5 percent at last count). And while people have typically heard that there is something called the "hidden job market," they usually don't know how to access it.

Just to give you a preview of what's coming, there are seven possible components of a diversified job search plan (although not every candidate will use every strategy):

Published Market:
- *Ads (newspaper, trade magazines):* published openings from companies and recruiters
- *Recruiters/employment agencies:* professionals hiring on behalf of companies that have stated needs
- *Internet job boards:* on-line services such as www.monster.com and others that are industry-specific and make published openings available to job seekers
- *Job fairs:* gatherings of employers seeking new staff to which they invite job seekers to attend and distribute their resume

Unpublished Market:
- *Networking (various types):* meeting with individuals in targeted companies and industries to discuss their needs and identify potential unpublished openings
- *Direct targeted mailings:* customized approach letters to specific companies within target markets identifying a potential need and summarizing candidate's background
- *News event-generated mailings:* targeted mailings to companies whose employees or firm are written about in the news media describing recent events within the company that may indicate the need for new employees

Tailoring Marketing Strategy to Client

As your client prepares to initiate her search, it's important to set suitable goals for each marketing tactic to be used so that the client has both a realistic approach and a way to gauge her progress. Part Five, the Career Coach's Toolbox, provides an example of a representative Marketing Plan. You will note that the marketing plan template includes targets for each type of job search tactic and columns for actual activities: letters sent, calls made, interviews generated and offers received. It also specifies the percentage of the client's activity to be spent in the published market versus the unpublished market.

Of course, these percentages and the target numbers for each tactic will need to be customized to your client's situation. Here are a few examples. Note that for the opposite of the examples given, the opposite approach would apply (e.g., an extroverted client, would use naturally the strategies which the introvert may find difficult, so their marketing plan can be more balanced between published and unpublished approaches).

- **Marketing for an introvert:** The natural tendency for most introverted clients is to focus on responding to advertised openings, sending unsolicited resumes to recruiters, surfing the job boards, and writing letters. It is especially difficult for them to pick up the phone and call people they do not know, and to meet with key people for informational interviews. One thing we can do is reduce the number of targeted networking meetings for these clients. But we can also do some scripting and/or role playing with them to increase their comfort level with networking and making follow-up calls to approach letters. Their search will be considerably more effective if they can stretch themselves to make the required calls and get face to face with people.

- **Marketing for the career changer:** When your client is making a change of industry or position, and particularly when it's a wholesale career change, most of the published job market strategies will be of little use. Recruiters and screeners for advertised openings will, as a general rule, only consider candidates that have the requisite experience in the job and/or industry in which they seek to fill the position. Therefore, career changing clients' marketing plans will often consist of nearly 100 percent unpublished strategies.

- **Marketing for the client with a large network:** In career coaching, we meet the client where they are. So if a client is well networked within their industry and/or community, we want to encourage them to use that asset strategically in their search. Their marketing plan, therefore, might have a higher target number of networking contacts to make vis-à-vis responding to advertised openings or submitting to recruiters.

- **Part-time versus full-time search:** When we are working with a client that is looking for a job while currently employed (a part-time job seeker), her targets should generally be halved versus the full-time job seeker who is not currently employed. Some of my clients have also been restricted due to their physical work environment (e.g., open cubicles or company monitoring of employee phone calls) so that they cannot make networking or follow-up phone calls from work. In this case, we can give the client the choice of reducing her target number of calls, or suggest that she consider using / buying a cell phone for this purpose during her lunch hour or before or after work.

Establishing the Ideal Job Vision

In addition to completing the Marketing Plan, the client also needs to initiate her search with a clear vision of the key aspects of her ideal job. The Ideal Job Template and the Ideal Day Exercise in Part 5 begin this process. In addition, the client/candidate should, at the outset of their search, fill in the "Wants" and "Needs" columns of Authentic Vocation™ Worksheet 10 to indicate the items that are non-negotiable and those that would be nice, but not required. Then, when job offers come in, each offer can be evaluated in the right-hand columns against the Wants and Needs to determine which one best fits the individual's criteria.

Organizing the Search

From the very beginning of a client's job search campaign, the client will need a system for managing her contacts. Not only does this allow the client to maintain a pro-active role in the process, but it also puts the information she will need to respond to a call or prepare for an interview at her fingertips. Depending on the client's comfort level with computer-based systems, she may choose a "low tech" or "high tech" approach:

- **Low tech version:** A simple three-ring binder can serve as a lway to organize the search. The client simply creates a tickler file in the binder with index tabs for each month of the year and tabs numbered 1 to 31 for the current month. The binder may also contain subject tabs by area of search, such as "networking contacts," "interviews," "banking industry information," etc. To use the system, each time the client sends an email or letter responding to an ad or approaching a networking contact, she makes a hard copy for the binder and files it under the date designated for follow-up. If desired, a second copy can be filed alphabetically by company (under another set of index tabs) so that it can be located easily if the client does not remember the follow-up date.

- **High tech versions:** A number of software and Internet systems can streamline the contact management process during the job search. Perhaps the most comprehensive is the Job Search Organizer Software developed by one of the Career Coach Institute Certified Career Coaches and available through www.denverjobsearch.com/orgpopup.htm It centralizes all of the client's job search contacts, tracks communications, stores various versions of resume and cover letters, keeps copies of ads or postings, records interview and networking appointments, and provides reminders of important tasks and follow-up (price is just $29.95 at this printing).

    Second, creating and using the "folders" feature in both Word and the email program of your choice (Eudora, Outlook, etc.) will keep job search correspondence organized. Whether one designates the electronic folders by industry ("banking," "insurance," "financial software," etc.), according to marketing strategy ("responses to ads," "recruiter letters," "networking with alumni," etc.) or uses another system that is logical to the client, the information will be more readily retrievable than a long list of documents that are not categorized.

Third, Excel spreadsheets can be extremely useful to track the progress of each "lead," or potential job opportunity. A separate spreadsheet can be used for each strategy, or it can be a long running spreadsheet in chronological order of approach with a column that designates the strategy used ("news event letter," "direct targeted letter," "response to ad," etc.).

Fourth, a contact management program such as ACT, Access, or Outlook will not only track contact names and dates, but can be programmed to remind the client which contacts are ready for follow-up on a given date as the client boots their computer. Notes of each conversation and any related correspondence can also be made. However, ACT and Access may be prohibitively expensive if the client is not in a sales job or other role for which the software could be used after the search is complete.

A final tool is an automated calendar system such as Palm Pilot, a web-based calendar system such as those offered by hotmail.com and yahoo.com, or Outlook. These calendars can be used to track appointments and the client's "to do" list for her job search activities.

Special Tips for Career Changers

If your client is seeking a career change, the one thing you can guarantee is that an approach that asks "Give me a chance. I know I can do the job! You won't be sorry..." will not be successful. This is unrealistic because an employer won't hire someone "on faith"; they have a lot to lose - for example, the employee may lose interest in the new area after hire or the company may need to investment in her training. Alternatively, she may not know enough about the new area yet to know if it fits her goals, or she may fail due to a lack of transferable skills!

A better way to prove interest and capability to a prospective employer in a new job function or industry is to:

- Identify contacts in the industry through trade associations and one's network
- Read the industry's trade journals to learn the terminology and trends in the industry
- Arrange and conduct informational interviews with these contacts
- Request any available industry information from trade associations (Associations Unlimited, available through any public or college library online, can be helpful here, as can Gales Directory of Associations)
- Surf the web for any pertinent information
- Join the local branch of any existing trade associations serving the industry, attend the meetings and chat with people there about the field
- Be increasingly clear about the client's desired work, and why she believes she will be successful
- Re-characterize the client's accomplishments in a more generic format so that they can clearly be shown to be transferable outside the prior industry setting
- Take relevant courses, part-time jobs, or do volunteer work in the new industry/skill area
- Don't hesitate to make a proposal to an employer of interest
- Be persistent!

By taking these steps, your client will be better positioned to make the career change they desire while meeting an employer's need.

Job Seeker Self-Management

For most people, being between jobs raises emotions ranging from fear or anger to denial or excitement. That's normal. Part of our responsibility as coaches is to reassure clients that these are normal reactions to transition, and to befriend (rather than resist) these feelings. Some job seekers will begin their search highly motivated, but will lose momentum after a few weeks. Self-care and proactive self-management can keep them going when it gets tough.

Tips for Workers in Transition

- Remember: doing your job search is your job now, so have a schedule each day which is designed to reach your goals and retain some "stability zones" of familiar routines.
- Know that the "emotional roller coaster" is normal. Develop a positive, resilient outlook so that you can "thrive" during your transition.
- Devise a job search strategy, break it into small, daily steps, and implement one step each day.
- Have at least one goal for each day.
- Practice interviewing and your "one-minute pitch" (see chapter 16).
- Attend at least one networking group meeting each week.
- Avoid hiding behind the computer surfing the Internet - get out and meet people.
- See your job search as your "job," even though your daily activities will be self-generated - you should work 4-6 hours a day on your search if unemployed, 1-2 hours per day if employed, and have a specific schedule for job search activities.
- Eat a balanced diet, exercise daily and avoid excessive drugs and alcohol.
- Program yourself with positive thoughts of your desired outcome: "I am now moving toward the job of my dreams;" "I deserve to be fulfilled," etc.
- Plan your budget for the next 3-6 months, including "what if" scenarios.
- Negotiate reduced payment plans with creditors if needed.
- Avoid using credit cards or increasing debt, which will only increase feelings of pressure and avoid loans from retirement plans if possible.
- Swallow your pride and reach out for support from church, network contacts, family members and friends (and your coach).
- Take one day/week off from the search to keep yourself fresh.
- Remember that you are not your job
- Keep in mind that each "no" (rejection letter or call) means you are one step closer to a "yes" (interview or offer) - a technique commonly used in sales.

Allowing for Synchronicity

"The moment one definitely commits oneself, then Providence moves too. All sorts of things occur to help one that would otherwise never occurred. A whole stream of events issues from the decision, raising in one's favor all manner of unforeseen incidents and meetings and material assistance, which no man could have dreamed would have come his way."

—W. N. Murray,
The Scottish Himalayan Expedition

There is a force at work within the job search that cannot be explained. People and information are brought into the job seeker's life seemingly by accident, when in fact they are a response of the physical world to the candidate's stated goal. Some of my clients have shared with me that a book would literally fall off the shelf in the bookstore and into their hands, or they would suddenly find themselves next to the CEO of their dream employer on the airplane while flying home from a conference. While it's tempting (and might feel more comfortable) to try to control and manipulate the job search process and the people in it to fit our own idea of how it should be, it will have an even better result if we can stay somewhat "open to the flow" of synchronicity.

The term synchronicity was coined by Swiss psychiatrist Carl Jung to describe the "occurrence of a meaningful coincidence in time" that occurs when one is in pursuit of a dream or goal they are passionate about. Joseph Jaworski (son of Watergate prosecutor Leon Jaworski) captures the essence of this idea in his book called *Synchronicity: The Inner Path of Leadership*. He describes the beginning of his own personal awakening and tells the story of taking a spontaneous 7-week trip to Europe when he had a break in his legal caseload. In addition to discovering the freedom of being away from the "oppressiveness of circumstances" of his normal life,

"[A]nother notion of freedom was beginning to make its way into my consciousness at this time, far below the surface - the freedom to follow my life's purpose with all the commitment I could muster, while at the same time, allowing life's creative forces to move through me without my control, without 'making it happen.'"

In a recent issue of *The Career Development Quarterly*, a fascinating article appeared entitled "Coincidence, Happenstance, Serendipity, Fate, or the Hand of God: Case Studies in Synchronicity." In it, authors Mary Guindon and Fred Hanna, both professors at Johns Hopkins University, point out that in the past, "One tenet that has shaped the direction of career counseling is the view that career development is linear, progressive, and rational...However, many counselors [and coaches] are aware that unknowable instances of coincidence, happenstance, and chance factors can play a significant role in career opportunities...We propose that these factors point to the nonlinear and acausal phenomenon of synchronicity."

There are 3 types of synchronicity. The first involves a simultaneous coincidence of subjective psychic content with objective events. The case study given was of Dan, who became dissatisfied with his work as a newspaper reporter, worked with a career coach to increase his awareness of his skills and interests, and coincidentally remembered a long-buried desire to own a small-town press. Then, despite apparently oppressive circumstances such as lack of money to buy such a business and unwillingness to relocate due to his son's ongoing medical needs for a serious illness, he struck up a conversation with an attorney at a parents' night at his son's school. The attorney had just acquired a now-defunct small press in settling a case, had no interest in running it but would allow Dan to do so, virtually eliminating the need for cash to purchase the business. Mere coincidence? Or synchronicity based on Dan's clear and long-standing desire that has just emerged for fulfillment?

The second type of synchronicity is the coincidence of a subjective psychic state with a dream or vision that later turns out to be analogous to circumstances that occur, "at a distance." The case study illustrating this was of Sarah, who was the breadwinner in her family and felt entirely incapable of leaving her job, had a dream of a man dressed in black chasing her with a 2 x 4 board. She ran through a series of unfinished rooms splashed with color. At the same time, through networking she connected with an opportunity to develop programs for a church-affiliated school. The unfinished rooms had 2 x 4's in them and paint cans of various colors.

Thirdly, synchronicity can occur as coincidence of a subjective psychic state with a dream or vision that later turns out to accurately reflect future events. An example is a woman who dreams of horses with riders of different colors, riding along a river, and when the client moves from her current job at a university into a new position at another one, the school colors of both schools coincide exactly with the colors of the riders and horses in the dream.

In working with clients in transition, the opportunities they will explore and pursue may come directly from responding to an advertised opening, from networking, or from a casual conversation which was foretold in a dream. Our job is to be open - and to encourage our clients to be open - to any and all avenues for input that will lead to their next step.

Key Coaching Concepts:

1. Not all career coaches will offer services to assist clients with job search mechanics, but all career coaches should have a working knowledge of the best practices in the job search.

2. Clients need to learn to think of themselves as a niche product that needs a customized marketing strategy to reach the ideal "customer" or employer.

3. The Job Search Marketing Plan will use a carefully selected mixture of published and unpublished job search strategies, and will need to be customized based on the client's personality style and goals.

4. Each client will need a way to track their contacts in their search, whether "low tech" or "high tech."

5. Clients changing careers will need to make the effort to learn more about their target industries and positions as well as other special steps if their search is to be successful.

6. Anyone in transition needs to implement self-care to stay motivated and healthy throughout his/her search.

7. There are aspects of the job search process that have seemingly unknown or "mystical" origins. By being open to this "synchronicity," clients will connect with opportunities they may not have found through more traditional means.

13

PUBLISHED JOB MARKET TACTICS

"Let advertisers spend the same amount of money improving their product that they do on advertising and they wouldn't have to advertise it."

—Will Rogers

"Advertising is legalized lying."

—H.G. Wells

Often, the first thing someone does when he/she is laid off (made redundant) or feels dissatisfied enough to start looking for a new job is to start perusing the help wanted ads in the newspaper. While some people do get jobs through the ads and other related methods, they still represent only about 20 percent of the total jobs filled in a given year.

The "Published Job Market" consists of (1) newspaper ads (print and electronic), (2) recruiters and employment agencies, (3) Internet job banks and (4) job fairs. To guide our clients effectively, we must help them use each of these aspects of the published job market strategically in their overall campaign, devoting an appropriate amount of time to them in view of the typical returns they represent.

Newspaper Ads

Jane, a software engineer, applied for a job advertised in the Wall Street Journal that seemed tailor-made for her. It drew upon her certifications and training in specific program languages, and the company was located in the city where she lived. There was no phone number for follow-up, but when she hadn't heard anything from them in two weeks she called the number in the local phone book and got voicemail. "What's wrong with me?" she moaned. "I know I'm perfect for that job; why haven't they called me for an interview?"

Was something wrong with Jane? No, but many applicants immediately take it personally if they do not hear from the "perfect employer" within a few days of their application being submitted. Let's look at it from the other side of the desk: the Human Resource screener or recruiter. Responses to an ad placed in a local newspaper often number 100 to 500, depending on the size of the metropolitan area covered. A Wall Street Journal or other national ad may draw in excess of 1000 responses for one opening. It takes screeners time to sort through these responses to get to a "short list" to interview. The job seeker must therefore not get discouraged if she does not hear back on a response to an ad, even if it seems a perfect fit.

To obtain an interview from a response to an ad, the hiring manager, screener, or recruiter must view the candidate as a very good fit for the job - but not necessarily a perfect fit. Often, a 70 percent match will qualify a candidate for an interview, especially if the company is having difficulty finding all the skills they desire in one candidate. For example, if an ad requests 5 years of experience in the industry, a Bachelor's degree, good communication skills and experience writing grant proposals, a candidate could apply and expect favorable consideration if they lacked the degree but possessed the remaining qualifications. The degree to which this "70 Percent Principle" is true will vary depending on the number of qualified candidates for the job. The fewer the fully qualified applicants, the more the screener will seriously consider candidates with less than all of the required credentials.

It's important to understand the approach of Human Resources professionals or recruiters in considering the resumes submitted. Their goal is to screen as many candidates out as they can at each stage: initial review of resumes, screening interview, decisionmaking interview, and offer. Our clients must remember the principles of "self as product" and focus on mentioning what is most marketable about them, rather than identifying the flaws that are not pertinent until a later stage of the hiring process.

Tips for Responding to Job Ads:

When a candidate finds an ad to which they want to respond, the following guidelines apply:

- For print ads (e.g., newspaper or magazine), the client should wait 5 to 7 days to submit their resume and cover letter. This prevents them from being rejected simply because the screener is weeding through the initial large stack of responses that typically come in 2 to 3 days after the ad runs.

- For Internet or web-based ads - whether on a job board, company web site posting, recruiter, or on-line newspaper listings - the client should respond immediately, as on-line ads are sometimes closed once a certain number of responses are received.

- In most cases, the best style of cover letter to use in responding to a newspaper ad is the so-called "T-bar" letter (see Figure 15), which clearly compares the job requirements to the candidate's qualifications. This way, if the screener does not have a great deal of experience or knowledge of the technical nature of the job or equivalent competencies - or if the candidate just wants to make the screener's job easier so they don't have to extract the needed information from the candidate's resume - it helps to forward the screening process in the candidate's favor. In responding to an on-line ad, the covering e-mail will not usually accommodate the columnar format of the T-bar letter, but similar information should nevertheless be conveyed to the individual receiving the resume.

- One of the most common mistakes people make in responding to ads is pointing out their weaknesses or areas in which they don't meet the ad's requirements. If there are areas in which the candidate falls short, she should just avoid mentioning them! There will be ample time to address those areas in the interview, and they will only serve to eliminate candidates from consideration if mentioned in the cover letter. Focus should be on strengths, not weaknesses.

- Many ads request a salary history or salary requirements. This is one of the easiest criteria on which to eliminate a candidate from further consideration: if they state a salary range that is

Figure 15: T-Bar Approach Letter for Ads

Date

Decision Maker, Title
Company Name
Address
City, State Zip

Dear Name of Decision Maker:

Your advertisement for a (insert position title) piqued my interest. It appears you have an exciting opportunity for the right individual - and I believe I am that person.

During my _____ years in the _____ field, I have had a number of accomplishments in which you may be interested. They in fact seem to be a perfect match for your opening:

Your Requirements	My Qualifications
1	1
2	2
3	3

I would welcome the opportunity to meet with you, learn more about the specifics of this position and discuss the ways in which I believe I can meet them. *Suggested Phrase for Salary Requests*: I will submit a salary history and other personal information at such time as you indicate serious interest in my qualifications. Please give me a call and we can arrange a time to meet at your convenience.

Sincerely,

Job Seeker
Enclosure (resume)

higher or lower than the (usually unpublished) salary range that is authorized for the position, they will not make the cut of those to be interviewed. From the candidate's viewpoint, they take the ad's warnings seriously and fear that they will not be considered if they don't provide salary data. In a survey of 159 human resource and hiring decision makers nationwide in 2001 by the Career Masters Institute entitled "Revealing Trends in Corporate Hiring Practices," 56 percent of respondents stated that they will consider a qualified candidate even when they don't provide salary information as requested, and another 31 percent said it depends entirely on a candidate's experience. Only 11 percent said they wouldn't consider the application under these conditions. This survey paralleled another larger study completed in 1992 by 3 Vassar graduates in New York City. They reviewed 1352 ads in The New York Times and The National Business Employment Weekly over a 5-month period. Of these, 272 (20 percent) asked for salary history. The researchers spoke with 200 of these employers, and 94 percent said they considered every letter received. The lesson? Don't provide salary history or requirements until asked about it in the interview - and then, see chapter 18 for tips on handling interview questions on this topic.

- Even when the job seems perfect for the candidate and the company is identified, the client will get better results if they use the "Dual Approach" technique. Besides sending their resume and cover letter to Human Resources, using this technique they would simultaneously send a Targeted Letter (see chapter 14 for format) to the hiring manager (i.e., their prospective boss).

- One thing Jane did right was to try to follow up with the company after she submitted her cover letter and resume. In many cases, the ad will be "blind," meaning that the company name is not listed. But if they are identified, some attempt to follow up is recommended. However, I recommend to my clients that they spend the bulk of their follow-up phone call time on the unpublished approaches, since following up on advertised openings does not usually accelerate the step-by-step process they need to undergo to satisfy company standards.

Trade Magazine Ads

One area of advertised openings that is often overlooked by job seekers is the trade magazines. Published as sources of industry information regarding trends, topics of interest, surveys and the like, many of them also include ads for openings within that field. A couple of examples include *Ad Week*, *HowDesign.com*, and *Computer Reseller News* (www.crn.com). Others are available through such sites as www.yahoo.com by clicking on their subject matter categories (Business & Economy, Computers & Internet, etc.). Competition for these positions is often lower than in the newspaper, so the job seeker may have more success responding to these than to newspaper ads. Tips for approaching employers through trade magazines are identical to those for newspaper ads.

Recruiters

If you work with mid to upper level managers and/or executive clients, then executive recruiters will be an important resource for them. To effectively use such recruiters, we must first understand how they work, and counter common misconceptions about them.

How They Work:

1. Most recruiters do not place hundreds of people each year, but rather 1-2 people per month in the executive search firms and a few more among those who focus on other areas (e.g., creative fields, administrative and support staff, technology experts).

2. Executive recruiters' first preference is to identify candidates who are working in companies and very successful - the top performers - and recruit them "away" from the company to one of the recruiter's client companies. So approaching them with an unsolicited resume, though it sometimes generates results, will meet with a wide range of responses.

3. There are two primary types of recruiters: contingency and retained. Contingency recruiters are paid by the company upon placement; retained recruiters are paid monthly whether any openings were filled or not. Most of your clients will

work most with contingency recruiters unless they are at the highest levels of management.

4. Recruiters are not the same thing as employment agencies, which work with people in generally non-management positions in specific industry areas, placing them in temporary or permanent positions. Employment agencies should be used by non-management level clients, along with other strategies in their campaign.

5. The typical fee a recruiter earns for one placement is twenty to thirty percent of the candidate's first year's salary.

Tips for Working With Recruiters:

1. Only include recruiters in the client's campaign if they are seeking a position in an industry in which they have experience - e.g., seeking the same type of position they are leaving in another company, or the next level up. Recruiters are not an appropriate resource for careerchangers.

2. The client needs to state their marketable assets in the cover letter, if used (cover letter with recruiters is optional since recruiters know why the resume is being submitted)

3. Be prepared to document all written and stated facts. Recruiters will check references and educational qualifications, so it is critical that they are accurate.

4. The client must clearly state the industry and position (s) in which they desire to work. This helps the recruiter better match the candidate to their existing openings.

5. All relevant accomplishments must be highlighted, briefly and powerfully, in the Work Experience Story format (see chapter 8) or an abbreviated version of it.

6. Reassure your clients that if they don't hear from the recruiter right away, or they don't return phone calls, not to take it personally. If the recruiter does not have an opening on their desk at that moment that matches the candidate's targets, they will not call to acknowledge receipt of the resume, but they may still have interest in the person's qualifications. The client can feel free to re-contact them in 4 to 6 weeks to see if their openings have changed (and they usually will have by then).

7. As a general rule, don't follow up by phone on the mailing, email or fax. "Don't call us, we'll call you" is the mantra of the recruiter. Most recruiters will store resumes submitted to them for a period of weeks or perhaps months, to match to future openings.

To find the recruiters to target, see the Directory of Executive Recruiters by Kennedy Publications (New Hampshire) and www.kennedyinfo.com.

Internet Job Banks

Answering Internet ads via job banks such as www.monster.com and through other on-line resources can put the job seeker in competition with even more candidates than other ads. Less than 5 percent of job seekers find their new job through a job bank. However, job banks do simplify the search process, especially for those who are open to relocating and can be flexible on the exact responsibilities of the position. A site such as www.careerbuilder.com streamlines the process further by searching multiple job banks simultaneously.

To stand out (in a positive way!) and avoid being lost in the large numbers of applicants through the general job boards listed above, a candidate should also target industry-specific job banks. One example is www.biosphere.com for the biotech industry. To find these, consult an industry association office, network with colleagues, or do an Internet keyword search for the job banks that serve the desired target industry/ies.

Even more so than with newspaper ads, the job seeker should be prepared to contact the company directly or use networking as a supplement to the on-line application. It will also be critical to have an effective electronic resume (e-resume) that meets the requirements of the scanning software many companies are now using. See chapter 15 for tips on composing an e-resume.

One of the critical issues when posting a resume on a job bank is privacy. Once your resume is on the Internet, it can be read and searched for by anyone - including your current employer. Care must be taken to avoid negative consequences (like being terminated) if/ when your employer finds your resume on the Internet. The benefits of making yourself available to job openings must be weighed carefully with the risks of doing so.

To maximize the number of times a candidate's resume is retrieved by recruiters, the candidate should edit some of the information on their resume at least every two weeks. This increases the number of "hits" he/she gets because recruiters will search by date posted, and if it wasn't posted (even if revised) in the last 7 days, it will be overlooked by many searches.

And finally, some job banks offer a "job search agent" technology which pushes opportunities to you. Execunet (www.execunet.com) is one of these, and www.monster.com also offers this feature. This can save considerable time in searching for ads fitting the client's criteria as the software does the work. And it allows clients access to positions when they are posted, eliminating the need to remember to go back and retrieve them. It also precludes being excluded from consideration because the position has been closed to applicants. See page 129 for a list of major job banks.

Job Fairs

A company or, more likely, an industry in a geographic area will periodically sponsor a job fair. This is an event where a job seeker can go, resume in hand, and supposedly meet in person with hiring managers. These are often done when an industry is having difficulty finding enough suitable candidates to meet a growing need. While these can be useful to some job seekers - particularly those who are staying in their existing industry - they can be a waste of time for career changers and others. Talk to others who have attended a job fair sponsored by the same people before if you can, to see what their experience has been.

Key Coaching Concepts

1. Due to the sheer volume of applicants for published openings, the job seeker should not take it personally if the company does not call them right away for an interview.
2. Delaying one's response for 5 to 7 days after the ad is published can improve one's chances of favorable consideration.
3. Trade journals and magazines in the target industries also publish job openings and are often overlooked by job seekers.
4. Recruiters should be used by mid to upper level management candidates seeking another position in the same industry in which they have experience.
5. Internet job banks that are industry-specific will usually contain more relevant positions than the larger, more general job banks.
6. Job fairs can be a useful search strategy when one's industry target is clear.

Online Job Search Resources

JOB SEARCH

4work - http://www.4work.com (specify the state you want to work in and your skills, and this site emails you appropriate listings)

America's Employers - http://www.americasemployers.com

American Jobs - http://www.AmericanJobs.com

America's Job Bank - http://www.ajb.dni.us - Run by U.S. Dept. of Labor (5% jobs in gov't).

Best Jobs USA - http://www.bestjobsusa.com

Brass Ring, Inc. - http://www.brassring.com/

CareerBuilder Network - www.careerbuilder.com (searches multiple job sites simultaneously)

CareerCast - http://www.careercast.com

Career City Jobs - http://www.careercity.com

Career.Com - http://www.career.com

Career Connection - http://www.connectme.com

Career Exchange - http://www.careerexchange.com

Career Index - http://www.careerindex.com (Searches several job databases simultaneously)

Career Magazine - http://www.careermag.com/careermag/

Career Mart - http://www.careermart.com

Career Net - http://www.careers.org

Career Pro - http://www.career-pro.com/index.htm

Career Resource Center - http://www.careers.org

Career Shop - http://www.careershop.com/

Career Site - http://www.careersite.com

Catapult on Job Web - http://www.jobweb.org/catapult/catapult.htm

Contract Employment - http://www.ceweekly.com

Cruise & Maritime Employment Information - www.jobxchange.com/

Dice Online Job Search - http://www.dice.com

Employment Guide - http://www.employmentguide.com

Executive Resources - http://www.executiveresources.org

ExecutivesOnly - http://www.executivesonly.com

Headhonchos.com - http://www.headhonchos.com

International Job Search - http://www.careerpath.co.uk

International-jobs - http://www.international-jobs.org

The Wall Street Journal - http://www.careers.wsj.com

TopHitter - http://tophitter.homestead.com/career.html

E-Span Job Options - http://www.joboptions.com/

Flipdog - http://www.flipdog.com

Helpwanted - http://www.helpwanted.com/

HotJobs - http://www.hotjobs.com

Internet Business Network - http://www.interbiznet.com

Job Bank USA - http://jobbankusa.com

Jobfind.com - http://jobfind.com

Job Hunt - http://www.job-hunt.org/

Jobtrak - http://www.jobtrak.com

Job Web - http://www.jobweb.com

L.A. Times - http://www.latimes.com

Law Careers - http://www.lawcareers.com/

Monster Board - http://www.monster.com

Nation Job Network - http://www.nationjob.com/

NetJobs - http://www.netjobs.com

Online Career Center - http://www.occ.com
Professional Job Search - http://www.professionaljobsearch.com/
QuestUSA - http://www.questusa.com
Six Figure Jobs - http://www.6figures.com
Thingamajob - http://www.thingamajob.com
U.S. Securities & Exchange Commission - http://www.sec.gov/
index.html
Virtual Reference Sites - Jobs - http://www.dreamscape.com/
frankvad/reference-jobs.html
Wall Street Journal Careers - http://www.careers.wsj.com
Wanted Jobs - http://www.wantedjobs.com

TEMPORARY EMPLOYMENT

Net-Temps - http://www.net-temps.com
Interim Executives- http://www.spherion.com/
recruiting_services_intexecs.jsp

RECRUITERS

Recruiters Online Network - http://www.ipa.com
Riley Guide - http://www.jobtrak.com/ - Guide to recruiting
services on the net.

JOB FAIRS

Job Fairs - http://www.careerfairs.com/

14
ACCESSING THE UNPUBLISHED JOB MARKET

"I know of no more encouraging fact than the unquestionable ability of man to elevate his life by a conscious endeavor."
—Henry David Thoreau

"In those days he was wiser than he is now—he used frequently to take my advice."
—Winston Churchill

The unpublished job market (where an opening is filled without it ever being advertised) represents approximately 80 percent of the total jobs filled each year. So it's very important to an effective job search campaign. Yet many job seekers don't pursue it (or at least don't know they are) because either they don't know it exists or they don't know how to access it. It includes opportunities that are revealed through (1) networking with a variety of kinds of people, (2) targeted direct mail campaigns to qualified individuals and organizations, and (3) news event-based approach letters. And as you know from Chapter 12, an integrated job campaign must include a strategic mix of job search strategies.

Determining Whom to Contact

In order to tap opportunities in the unpublished market, your client's first step will be to revisit their desired job and industry targets determined in Authentic Vocation™ Factor 6 and narrow his targets down to 2 or 3 primary ones for a full-fledged search. Not only will he need to determine whether there are enough openings that meet his desired specifications (using the formula in Chapter 9) he will also want to ask himself again whether the occupation still appeals to them, whether it is growing or stagnant (using the Occupational Outlook Handbook) and how well qualified he is for the type of work desired. Of course, networking can be one way to answer some of these inquiries. On page 144 is a list of Internet and print resources that may be helpful to your clients in researching their job or career targets to determine which ones to use as the basis for a full-fledged campaign.

Networking for Unpublished Openings

Networking is a pivotal strategy to use in tapping the unpublished market. We could go as far as to say that developing strategic relationships is the "golden key" to finding an unpublished job. Networking can be defined as the process of meeting with people in a specific industry or career focus area to find out more about what they do and what their current needs are - and to build useful relationships. Informational interviewing is another name for this process, as is holding an "information and referral meeting." Notice that we are not defining networking as "telling everyone I know that I'm out of work and need a new job," which is how many uninformed job seekers approach networking - and then bemoan the fact that it doesn't work for them.

How to Make Your Net Work

To help your clients maximize the value of their networking, follow these key principles:

1. **Remember the objective of networking.** The goal of networking is to gain (a) information and (b) referrals, not (at least initially) jobs. All questions should focus on those objectives. Through the presence the client exudes and the information he gains, this approach will lead to a job opportunity - but if he focuses on that first, it will put the interviewee on the defensive and impair the returns in the process.

2. **Realize the 1:50 Principle.** That is, each person (including you and your client) know at least 50 other people from the various parts of your life. School, work, church, volunteer activities, tennis or golf club, trade associations, neighbors, friends, family - as all of them can become relevant when considering networking. Have your client list as many as they can from these and any other categories. Then, realize that each of them also knows at least 50 other people. The likelihood that several of these people will know an individual that works in one of the client's target industries is very high when we keep this principle in mind. But don't approach them - not yet.

3. **Use a powerful approach letter.** In most cases, the client should mail a letter to the prospective networking contact first, then follow up by phone. Exceptions would include people they already know well, or people to whom a contact is referring them that the contact could call before they even leave the networking meeting. Figure 16 is an example of a networking approach letter.

4. **Follow up by phone to double the response rate.** Encourage your clients to use the phone and email effectively and be politely persistent in reaching the people with whom you want to meet. If they don't, they'll find that their response rate is much less, since a letter from someone the person doesn't directly know can easily be put on the low priority stack of their desk unless a follow-up call is made.

5. **Set a specific time for the meeting - and stick to it.** Ask the networking contact for a 15- to 20-minute meeting, in person if they are within a one-hour drive from where you are, and by phone if they're further away. Incidentally, for clients who have a specific city they would like to move to, we recommend that they schedule meetings with 2 or 3 key contacts in person and either drive or fly to that city for a few days of networking and interviews. This "road trip" puts them in front of the people they need to meet and allows for more meetings to be arranged during their visit based on referrals that they may get while they're there.

6. **Research the company and networking contact prior to the meeting.** The candidate will create a much more positive

Figure 16: Sample Networking Approach Letter

Date

Decision Maker, Title
Company Name
Address
City, State Zip

Dear Name of Decision Maker:

I am currently seeking a more permanent and diverse management role than my current consulting position provides. As I seek to determine a new direction for my future, my plan is to contact a few professionals within the XXXXXX community to get their insights and to network. That is my purpose in writing to you. If possible, I would like to arrange a time to meet with you for 10 to 15 minutes at your convenience. . I am confident that our shared backgrounds in XXXXX will provide a mutually interesting and informative meeting.

As an experienced director of Internet-, software-, and multimedia-based new product development and roll-out, I offer a unique combination of leadership in operations as well as marketing and business development. I have worked with industry leaders such as ABC Company, as well as most recently, Internet start-ups providing cutting-edge on-line services. My Ph.D. in Education, emphasizing Curriculum and Instruction, together with my 10 years of executive level experience, have prepared me to develop, launch and distribute instructionally sound and market targeted products. Among my achievements are managing up to 250 employees, P&L for $18MM, turnarounds, directing 7 highly regarded national technology conferences, and organizing and re-prioritizing 50 simultaneous projects, tripling on-time completion rate.

Because I am aware that many opportunities arise before they are publicly advertised, I realize that getting to know fellow professionals such as you should be an important part of my strategy. The opportunity to exchange ideas and develop contacts with other XXXXXXX professionals would be deeply appreciated.

The opportunity to exchange ideas and develop contacts with other professionals would be deeply appreciated and would be all I ask. I will call your office in a few days to introduce myself and to set a brief meeting. I want to thank you in advance for any assistance and advice you may be able to provide.

Sincerely,

Joe Job Seeker

impression if they have visited the company's web site and otherwise researched the industry and company (and the individual they're meeting with, if they are reported in industry journals or Who's Who publications) prior to the meeting.

7.   **Take only a list of questions to the meeting, but do not take a resume.** If an individual came to a networking meeting with you and started the meeting by laying their resume on the table, what would you think? It changes the tone of the meeting immediately, and shifts the focus to jobs instead of information and referrals. The client will need to have a verbal summary of their background ready to use, but the resume - if it is requested - can be e-mailed to the interviewee after the meeting with the thank-you letter.

8.   **Be sure to ask for referrals to other contacts before closing the meeting.** Whether the meeting has gone very well or has been a bit of a struggle, the candidate should be sure to ask for other people they could talk to (using the interviewee's name) before ending the meeting. This is how the network grows: if each referral generates 2 or 3 other names, the client's network can grow in size within a short period of time.

Format of a Networking
(or Information & Referral) Meeting

The basic protocol for a networking meeting is:

- Introductions and first impressions
- Restate your purpose for meeting
- Brief (1-2 minutes) summary of your background (remember, you didn't bring your resume)
- Ask the most important of your networking questions (see Figure 17 for ideas)
- Ask for referrals ("Who else do you know that I should be talking to?" - schedule the meeting when/where the interviewer is near their Palm Pilot, Rolodex, Daytimer or other source of contact names and numbers)
- Thank them for their time and close the meeting
- Send a Thank-You letter within 24 hours of the meeting in which you emphasize your assets and reiterate the next step in developing the networking relationship

Figure 17: Suggested Questions To Ask In A Networking Meeting

About the Industry
- How old is the industry?
- How large is it?
- How is it changing now?
- Where do you see growth happening?

About the Company
- When was the company started?
- How large is it?
- What products/services does it produce? (ask only if you were unable to determine through advance research, otherwise ask a follow-on question based on your research)
- What kinds of customers/clients does the company serve?
- Who are the primary competitors to this company?
- How would you describe the organizational culture?
- What is the organizational structure?
- What involvement does the company have with technology? Has technology changed how business is done?

About the Job
- What are the key responsibilities of the job/position?
- What are the biggest challenges?
- What is the profile of a high achiever in this job?
- What type of background (education and work) is typical for people entering this job/field?
- What are the advancement or growth opportunities?
- What salary and compensation range is typical?

About the Networking Contact
- How did you get into this field?
- What do you like best about your job?
- What is your least favorite thing?
- Would you recommend that your son or daughter enter this field and/or job now?
- How has it changed in the past 10 to 20 years?
- What advice would you give to someone in my position?

Help for the Introverted Client

If your client is particularly introverted, and resists the idea of networking, here are a few suggestions that may help them become more comfortable:

- Role play a mock networking meeting with them so they know how to conduct the meeting and to respond to rejections.
- Set the process up as a research exercise so that the interviews are a means to the end of gathering more information from which to draw some 'conclusions about next steps; many introverted clients respond very well to this.
- Be sure the client feels very well prepared regarding the above sections: agenda for meeting, questions to ask, etc. This will increase their comfort level.

A Success Story

As we have discussed, networking can be particularly useful to the client who wishes to change careers. It puts him/her in front of potential hiring managers in a non-threatening environment in which the manager can see the talent in the candidate and the candidate can discover the company's needs. In one case, John had become weary of the responsibilities he had as CEO of a software company. He loved working with people, and matching them to the right job, but disliked the other aspects of his demanding job. He came to a colleague of mine for career coaching to explore what other positions might satisfy him. After a handful of networking interviews, he decided that Human Resources management was the functional area he wanted to pursue. Obviously, he would have little success approaching published openings since his change would be viewed as a downgrade from the high level of responsibility he had previously had.

John conducted a campaign that relied exclusively on networking. He met with dozens of HR managers and hiring executives over a period of 12 weeks, and due to his diligent research on each company, his positive attitude, attractive personality and his increasing clarity about his goal, he received no less than 12 offers for positions as HR Director from companies with whom he had networked.

Targeted Mail Contacts With Companies

Perhaps the most under-utilized strategy of all is the targeted letter. Such a letter simply describes the candidate's current situation and background, is addressed to a hiring manager of a target (or potential target) company, and can be an excellent way to gain inroads into a firm. The company may or may not have published job openings; that is irrelevant to this approach. What the client will be doing is approaching companies within their target industry and geographic range that may have a need which matches his/her areas of expertise. Once the client has decided to target a specific industry, and determined the leading firms within the industry they would like to approach, the targeted letter introduces the candidate to the firm and opens the door to further conversation.

A targeted letter:

- Is no more than one page in length
- Is addressed to a particular individual in a hiring capacity (2 to 3 levels above where the client would be working)
- Does not focus on jobs, but on potential contribution the candidate could make to the firm
- Highlights the key relevant accomplishments of the candidate in which the firm may be interested
- May (but need not) include the name of a mutual acquaintance who has referred the candidate to them
- Should be sent by snail mail, not email (too easy to erase or may not be opened)

Figure 18 illustrates the Target Letter. The candidate should follow up directly with the hiring manager by telephone or email 5 to 7 days after the letter is sent to pursue a face-to-face meeting, if practical, or alternatively (for a long-distance search) a telephone appointment for a networking interview.

Figure 18: Sample Direct Targeted Mail Letter

Date

Decision Maker, Title
Company Name
Address
City, State Zip

Dear Name of Decision Maker:

Many high tech companies are coping with these difficult times by hiring the best production and R&D people available. While this may help to "shore up" a company's competitive position, many organizations find that nevertheless their bottom line is slipping. Their usual response? Send in an accountant!

These companies, and perhaps you or some of your subsidiaries, need more than mere accounting help. As VP of Operations for a $100 million hardware manufacturer, I directed the turnaround of a company that was on the verge of closing. As a result, 2000 was the most profitable year they had ever had, and 2001 looks even better.

This experience, and my prior work within the industry, has given me a great deal of insight into how a company can get into trouble - and more importantly, the danger signs to watch out for. Once I enter a firm, I'm able to assist its management team in identifying ways in which they can run their financial systems more efficiently and economically and I have a proven track record of success in improving both revenues and profitability:

* Improved cycle time by 25% within 1 year through re-engineering key processes
* Established a Management Information System that linked management strategy to actual production results, further improving both profitability and internal communications
* Upgraded the hardware and software systems used to manufacture components of the company's key product line, allowing production to triple within 2 years

I have an M.B.A. as well as 15 years of progressively responsible management responsibility in operations, strategic planning, MIS, finance and project management.

I would appreciate the opportunity to meet with you to discuss the contribution I could make to your organization. I will call you in a few days to follow up on this letter and see when a convenient time might be. Or if you prefer, please feel free to call me at (123) 456-7890.

Sincerely,

Job Seeker

News And Company Events As A Vehicle For Job Search Contacts

In addition to referrals and targeted mailings, tying an approach letter to a recent event in the industry or company can improve its chances of leading to a meeting. New product launches, receipt of venture capital or other investment or grant funds, relocation, expansion and the like are all appropriate types of events for this purpose, as well as "people on the move" sections in business publications. News of such events can be found by perusing the local Business Journal, the *Wall Street Journal*, the business section of the client's local paper, and trade magazines (all available in the Internet resources in this module and the prior one). The question to keep in mind while reading these articles is, "What job opportunities might this event lead to?"

Example: If a company announces that it just received venture capital, it may need R&D people to develop or refine a product, marketing and sales people to sell it, operations people to manage production, and finance people to account for the production and sales. On the other hand, if a company announces a merger, some redundant jobs may be lost, but the company may also need people to manage the newly formed staff, to assist with the consolidation of two cultures and sets of processes into one, and to re-evaluate the financial aspects of the new company.

Figure 19 provides an example of a news event generated approach letter.

Keys To Getting A New Job Created

Though it may sound farfetched, it's not uncommon for people to persuade a company to create a new job that perfectly meets their needs. There are several keys to getting this to happen:

- Determine what you want to do.
- Find a company/industry who could benefit
- Conduct one or more informational interviews with one or more hiring managers within target companies to learn more about their needs
- Identify a need they have that you could fill

Figure 19: Sample News Event Approach Letter

Date

Decision Maker, Title
Company Name
Address
City, State Zip

Dear [Decision Maker:]

I read with interest the article about your firm in the (insert Newspaper or whatever source) regarding with the probability of your expanding your (insert related skill or whatever). (Discuss the parts of the article that you feel particularly well-qualified to address) As I read this article, I found myself particularly interested in [Company Name] and in being part of your new expansion. That is why I am writing to you directly.

As an experienced director of Internet-, software-, and multimedia-based new product development and roll out, I offer a unique combination of leadership in operations as well as marketing and business development. I have worked with industry leaders such as ABC Company, as well as, most recently, Internet start-ups providing cutting-edge online services. My Ph.D. in Education, emphasizing Curriculum and Instruction, together with my 10 years of executive level experience, have prepared me to develop, launch and distribute instructionally sound and market targeted products. Among my achievements are managing up to 250 employees, P&L for $18MM, turnarounds, directing 7 highly regarded national technology conferences, and organizing and re-prioritizing 50 simultaneous projects, tripling on-time completion rate.

I would appreciate having the opportunity to discuss your plans to develop further insight into a possible association. I will call your office early next week to arrange an appointment. I look forward to talking with you.

Sincerely,

Job Seeker

- Submit a proposal for a job you could do for them
- Persuade them to accept it and start work

Remember: a job is simply a match between a need and someone who can fill it at less cost than the return (or expected return) from the employee's services. As may be apparent from this discussion of the unpublished market, it requires a greater initiative, creativity, and "out of the box" thinking than the published market. But it pays high dividends: when a job is found in this way, it can be customized to the individual's needs and will often pay more than a generic published opening would. It's well worth introducing our clients to this key portion of the job market.

Key Coaching Concepts

1. Networking is simply the process of meeting with people in a specific industry or career focus area to find out more about what they do and what their current needs are - and to build useful relationships.
2. By following several tips on the networking approach and honoring the typical agenda for a networking meeting, the process may generate multiple job opportunities.
3. An under-utilized strategy is addressing a direct targeted letter to a hiring manager in a target company outlining what the candidate can offer to the company.
4. News events are another basis on which to approach a company to suggest applying the candidate's services to solve problems or leverage opportunities raised by the news event.
5. It is possible to have a company create a job for a candidate if they can prove that they will add more value than the cost of the job.

INTERNET RESEARCH RESOURCES

OCCUPATIONAL INFORMATION

O*Net (replaces the Dictionary of Occupational Titles) http://online.onetcenter.org

Occupational Outlook Handbook http://stats.bls.gov/ochome.htm

COMPANY & INDUSTRY INFORMATION

AltaVista - http://www.altavista.com

Annual Report Gallery - http://www.reportgallery.com

Business Journals - http://www.amcity.com and www.bizjournals.com

Career Mosaic - http://www.careermosaic.com

CEO - http://www.CeoExpress.com

Dogpile.com - http://www.dogpile.com (metasearch engine)

Employment Guide - http://www.careerweb.com

Hoover's Online - http://www.hoovers.com

Infospace - http://www.infospace.com

Job Journal - http://www.jobjournal.com

Jobs & Careers - http://jobscareers.com

News articles & industry information - http://www.individual.com

Securities & Exchange Commission - http://www.sec.gov

Sleuth - http://www.sleuth.com

U.S. Department Of Labor - http://www.dol.gov

US News & World Report - http://www.usnews.com

Vault - http://www.vault.com (profiles 3000 companies in 40 industries)

Wet Feet - http://www.wetfeet.com

15

RESUME
DESIGN SECRETS

"Never try to tell everything you know. It may take too short a time."

—Norman Ford

In this chapter, we will introduce the "do's" and "don'ts" of resume preparation so that your clients can compete successfully for the positions they are interested in. As with any of the aspects of Job Search Mechanics, you may wish to establish a strategic partnership with a professional resume writer for this part of the process. For a more complete treatment of this rather large subject, see the Resource List in Part Five.

Ten Principles for Powerful Resumes

The "do's" of resume preparation include heeding the following principles:

1. *Remember that a resume is a marketing tool, not a complete chronology of a lifetime of work.* Content should be selectively chosen using the "self as product" mindset. If in doubt as to whether to include a hobby, award, accomplishment, or skill description, ask, "Will this make me more marketable for this position if I include it?" If not, leave it out!

2. *Realize the primary purpose of a resume: to get an interview, not a job (directly).* Remember that the job search is a two-part process. The first part is marketing oneself sufficiently on paper (or through networking) to get the interview. Then, the second part is selling oneself in person at the interview to ultimately get the job. (More about that in the next chapter!)

3. *Lead with client's best tangible skills.* Many job seekers make the mistake of putting their "soft" skills in the first half of their resume. This is not what screeners are most interested in. And since most recruiters and screeners will only review a resume for 30-60 seconds before making an initial "yes" or "no" decision, the critical information must be contained in the first 1/3 of the first page! In Figure 20 is a roadmap of the selection process and where to emphasize which type of skills:

Figure 20: 3 Phases Of Selection Process Determine Which Skills To Emphasize

Stage	Question Recruiter/Screener is Asking	Skills to Emphasize
1	"Can you do the job?"	Tangible skills
2	"Will you do the job?"	Tangible/intangible skills
3	"Do you fit into the position and company?"	Intangible skills

4. **Customize the resume for each opening applied for.** In the pre-1980's workplace, it was common to prepare one resume and use it for all purposes. That no longer works, since employers need to see the specific ways in which the applicant's qualifications meet the job requirements. Aspects of the resume to be changed (or at least evaluated) in customizing include the job title (if used), accomplishments or Work Experience Stories used, and whether or not to include education or recent training.

5. **Use a chronological resume (especially with recruiters) unless the client fits one of the categories of exceptions.** There are two basic types of resumes: chronological, in which the person's work experience, accomplishments, and education are listed in reverse chronological order (see Figure 21), and

functional, in which the person's background is organized in clusters of skills or types of accomplishments drawn from their positions over a period of time (see Figure 22; both samples courtesy of Certified Career Coach™ Meg Montford.) Figure 23 also provides an alternative format for managers and executives to use.

The exceptions where the functional format is preferred are:

- The client is changing fields or careers
- Work history is very long or has gaps in it
- A wide range of skills needs to be more effectively showcased
- Diverse accomplishments from a long career at one company needs to be emphasized
- Record of frequent job changes needs to be de-emphasized
- Lack of work experience, as with new worker moving into the workplace, needs to be de-emphasized

6. **Begin the resume with "Summary of Qualifications" instead of an Objective.** In general, job objective statements are out of favor unless the resume is for a recent graduate, and can unduly narrow the scope of positions for which the client would be considered. The Summary should include a brief overview of the applicant's background and a couple of very short bulleted representative accomplishments.

7. **Continue with applicable sections of the resume, depending on client's background.** Other sections include experience, if relevant to this job. If client is new to the job market, education and accomplishments during school would precede experience. Other optional sections at the end include any publications authored, awards received (when relevant to the job), and any professional associations (avoiding political or religious affiliations as this is legally prohibited information).

8. **Use references strategically; avoid listing them on the resume.** Including references' names on a resume is akin to handing a perfect stranger your business plan or financial statement at a cocktail party. You wouldn't do it! In fact,

Figure 21: Sample Chronological Resume

TAMMY GRANT

9219 Land Oak Drive
Home: (816) 555-1212
Kansas City, Missouri 64138
TGrant881@email.com

SUMMARY OF QUALIFICATIONS

Self-motivated Customer Service Specialist with excellent interpersonal skills. Creative problem solver and team player focused on coordinating efforts to meet customer needs. Fast learner assessing customer complaints and then assuming responsibility to ensure customer satisfaction. Ability to balance accounts. PC proficient / 50 WPM typing skills.

EXPERIENCE

HOME ENGINEER
1997 to Present

CUSTOMER SERVICE CLERK
1997
Associated Cable Television Company, Osceola, Missouri

> Performed administrative functions in this temporary office position. Answered inbound customer calls. Coordinated service requests from subscribers. Logged cable outage reports and dispatched service repair representatives. Marketed cable television services and promoted benefits to phone customers; explained policies and regulations.
> - Resolved two customer complaints to result in cancellation of disconnect requests.
> - Earned recognition of supervisor by working overtime on several occasions.

CUSTOMER SERVICE REPRESENTATIVE
1987 to 1997
Missouri Gas Company, Osceola, Missouri

> Answered phones and responded to customer inquiries for assistance with new hook-ups, change in service, billing complaints and technical service requests. Recorded work orders and assigned service technicians. Set up customer accounts in computer database. Received customer payments, posted to accounts and deposited in bank. Collected delinquent accounts and issued disconnect notices. Sold floor appliances to independent contractors and to the general public. Acted as relief receptionist.
> - Reduced number of technician field trips by clarifying customer requests and solving basic problems by phone.
> - Saved company $3000 by negotiating payment arrangement with past due account.

EDUCATION

Liberal Arts Degree Program, University of Missouri, Kansas City, 1981

Figure 22: Sample Functional Resume

9219 Land Oak Drive
(816) 555-1212
Kansas City, Missouri 64138
TGrant881@email.com

TAMMY GRANT

SUMMARY OF QUALIFICATIONS

SALES.....CUSTOMER SERVICE.....COLLECTIONS
- Establishing rapport quickly with varied personality types
- Calming irate customers by assisting with billing problems
- Interpreting and explaining policies and regulations
- Negotiating payment arrangements with past due accounts
- Collecting delinquent accounts, issuing disconnect notices
- Promoting and marketing services to phone customers
- Selling appliances to independent contractors, plus general public

DISPATCH.....CLERICAL
- Answering inbound customer calls
- Coordinating service request calls from subscribers
- Communicating by radio with service technicians
- Dispatching service technicians to sites of field problems
- Preparing accurate work orders, assigning to field technicians
- Performing administrative functions of office personnel
- Setting up customer accounts in computer database
- Processing payments, posting to accounts
- Balancing cash receipts, making bank deposits

SKILLS PROFILE

Excellent interpersonal skills

Customer service expertise

Creative problem solver

Computer proficiencies

Type 50 wpm

Fast learner

EXPERIENCE

HOME ENGINEER	1997-Present
CUSTOMER SERVICE CLERK Associated Cable Television Company, Osceola, Missouri	1997
CUSTOMER SERVICE REPRESENTATIVE Missouri Gas Company, Osceola, Missouri	1987-1997

EDUCATION

LIBERAL ARTS DEGREE PROGRAM   1981
University of Missouri, Kansas City

Figure 23: Sample Executive Resume

Joe K. Jobseeker

Address, City, State ZIP   Phone   Email address

Senior Vice President, International Operations
Business Expansions / Acquisitions and Mergers / Sales and Marketing Strategies
Distribution Channel Management / Start-Up Management

Held successful leadership roles within such companies as Big Company 1, Fortune 500 2, and ABC Corporation. Increased revenues in each position of responsibility by improving distribution channels, restructuring sales and marketing functions, strategizing successful business expansions and management of mergers and acquisitions.

* **Quadrupled sales in 3-year period through effective distribution of new products into Latin America**
* **Integrated Latin American operations following company's acquisition of $450 million distributor**
* **Created leasing program that penetrated a market previously controlled solely by Fortune 500 company**

Awarded an MBA in International Business, University of Arizona (1999). Bachelor of Science in Business, XYZ University (1994). Strong multi-cultural exposure, fluent in Spanish and possess a strong knowledge of international finance and import/export regulation.

Professional Achievements

Transitioned Mexican, Brazilian and Argentine Operations Following $450 Million Acquisition - Integrated Big Company 1's newly acquired operations in Mexico and Venezuela following acquisition. Reduced annual operating costs $13 million by combining the South American operations into one entity, consolidating back room operations and combining all Mexican backroom operations into a newly formed service company.

Led Successful Business Expansion into Latin America - Achieved a 28% return on capital as leader of ABC Company business expansion into Latin America. Formulated a three-year strategy that included opening a distribution facility in Miami to service this market, segmenting the existing brands and creating separate distribution channels.

Career History

Vice President, Latin America Operations, Big Company 1, 1994 to 2001. Held P&L responsibility and directed growth strategies for $24 million in electronic security technology for this company. Served on the strategic planning board and worked directly with the President to determine both long and short term financial and management goals and strategies.

Fortune 500 2, 1987 to 1994. Increasingly responsible roles throughout a seven year tenure with this $1.6 billion industry leader in the distribution, sales and servicing of software technology included:

> **Regional Manager, 1992 to 1994.** Held P&L responsibility for the $52 million Northern Latin American Division that encompassed Venezuela, Colombia, Peru, Ecuador, Central America and the Caribbean. Also oversaw an additional $12 million in sales through more than 200 outlets in a non-affiliated distributor network market.

> **Regional Financial Controller, 1987 to 1992.** Controlled financial functions and reporting for the Latin American Region with operating companies in Mexico, Venezuela, Brazil, Argentina and Puerto Rico.

Vice President, International Banking, ABC Company, 1982 to 1986. After being charged with expanding chartered banks into the Latin American market, expanded correspondent banks from 20 to 95 in a two-year period. Assisted in expanding the international deposit base from $1 to $3 billion.

---

you'd have to work up to giving them your business card, right? The client should be prepared with three to six references, listed on a separate sheet with the job seeker's name and contact information. Ideally, one or two of the person's former supervisors should be included, as well as subordinates (if the person is or seeks to be a manager) and peers. Personal references are optional.

9. **Consolidate client's background into no more than two pages.** Even the client with 25 or more years of experience can selectively include information that will position them for the job in one to two pages. This is the standard in virtually all hiring except (a) academia, (b) government positions, (c) scientific research positions, and (d) executive biographical narrative resumes.

10. **Avoid any unnecessary information, but include all that's required.** Resumes in the old workplace included personal information such as health status, race, gender, religion, and age information that is now prohibited - leave it out! On the other hand, be sure that client's name and phone number appear on both pages of the resume and on the reference sheet (in case the pages get separated), and double check to be sure that all information is complete.

Common Resume Errors

For the "don'ts" of resume writing, be sure to avoid these errors:

- Using nonstandard size paper (8 1/2" x 11" is standard)
- Folding the resume instead of sending it flat in a 9" x 12" envelope (folding is optional)
- Stapling or clipping the pages together
- Printing double-sided (this appears unprofessional and can become distorted when being scanned)
- Printing in colored ink (unless you're in graphic arts or advertising)
- Including a photo (provides illegal information)
- Laminated or glossy finish (looks like you're trying too hard!)
- Using dark or nonstandard color paper (should use cream or white unless you're in advertising or a creative field)
- Using nonstandard fonts (should use Times Roman or Arial/Helvetica)
- Including incomplete information
- Burying accomplishments in long paragraphs (boil them down to bullets instead)
- Failing to customize the resume to the job applied for
- Education listed before experience (unless you just graduated, experience is more important than education)
- Objective listed at the top (use a summary of qualifications instead)
- Including personal information such as height, weight, health, religion, etc.
- Inserting too much detail (street address/phone number for employers, months of employment instead of just years, etc.)

Creating An Electronic Resume ("e-resume")

Electronic resumes are different from standard (hard copy) resumes in several ways: they must avoid any bold, italic, bullets, borders or other formatting that will be lost when pasted into an email. They must also be brief and to the point! And they must use simple, standard fonts such as Arial, Courier or Times Roman. Margins should be narrow: flush left and about 2 inches on the right to facilitate cutting and pasting.

Certified Career Coach™ and professional writer Meg Montford suggests this process to convert a standard resume to an e-resume: Use the "select all" feature in the Edit menu of Word, and remove all bold, bullets, italic, and underlining. Then, change the margins to 1 inch on top, bottom, and left, and 2.5 inches on the right. The goal is to have no more than 65 characters across one line. Save the document as a text only (*.txt) format in Word. Close the document, then reopen in Notepad to make the changes and reformat with keyboard-only document enhancements as all bullets, lines, etc. will be distorted. Test the document by sending in email to yourself before sending it to a prospective employer.

1. **Put the most important information at the top of page 1.** Employers search for their most important criteria first - the same way they write job listings. In addition, many search engines base their hits on the top half of page 1. And notice that the first half of the page is one screen full of information, so it's everything the viewer will see when they first access your e-resume. Critical content for this section are: your contact information, keywords pertaining to your target jobs, representative achievements (briefly stated!) and a listing of the 10 most recent years of work experience.

2. **Be sure to include a keyword list at the top.** Include hard skills first, beginning with technical knowledge or training you have. Then, use key action words as required by the job (implemented, created, managed, etc.). Any pertinent soft skills such as communication skills or organizational abilities would go third in the keyword list.

3. **Use multiple forms of critical terms.** Internet "spiders" (as well as systems relying on scanning) look for both the verb and noun form of a key word. So in addition to "managed" you will want to include "manager" in the first half of page 1 - or somewhere else in the resume if the skill is of secondary importance.

SAMPLE KEYWORD LIST for Production Manager: "Fortune 500 experience. ISO-9002 implementation. Managed production of hardware components. 500-person production team manager. Organizational skills. Team builder. Budget development and management. Meets or exceeds production deadlines."

4. **Be redundant to get more hits.** Mentioning each critical skill at least three times triples the odds of an employer finding and selecting your resume.

Figure 24 is a sample electronic resume.

Figure 24: Sample Electronic Resume

TAMMY GRANT
9219 Land Oak Drive
Kansas City, Missouri 64138
Home: (816) 555-1212
TGrant881@email.com

SUMMARY OF QUALIFICATIONS
Self-motivated Customer Service Specialist with excellent interpersonal skills. Creative problem solver and team player focused on coordinating efforts to meet customer needs. Fast learner assessing customer complaints and then assuming responsibility to ensure customer satisfaction. Ability to balance accounts. PC proficient / 50 WPM typing skills.

EXPERIENCE
HOME ENGINEER, 1997 to Present
CUSTOMER SERVICE CLERK, 1997
Associated Cable Television Company, Osceola, Missouri
Performed administrative functions in this temporary office position. Answered inbound customer calls. Coordinated service requests from subscribers. Logged cable outage reports and dispatched service repair representatives. Marketed cable television services and promoted benefits to phone customers; explained policies and regulations.
** Resolved two customer complaints to result in cancellation of disconnect requests.
** Earned recognition of supervisor by working overtime on several occasions.

CUSTOMER SERVICE REPRESENTATIVE, 1987 to 1997
Missouri Gas Company, Osceola, Missouri
Answered phones and responded to customer inquiries for assistance with new hook-ups, change in service, billing complaints and technical service requests. Recorded work orders and assigned service technicians. Set up customer accounts in computer database. Received customer payments, posted to accounts and deposited in bank. Collected delinquent accounts and issued disconnect notices. Sold floor appliances to independent contractors and to the general public. Acted as relief receptionist.
** Reduced number of technician field trips by clarifying customer requests and solving basic problems by phone.
** Saved company $3000 by negotiating payment arrangement with past due account.

EDUCATION
Liberal Arts Degree Program
University of Missouri, Kansas City, 1981

Resume Screening Software

Most large employers use software to scan and/or screen incoming applicants' resumes to streamline the screening process. If the ad identifies the company, you can contact them by phone to ask whether they scan incoming resumes. And if they do, you can send one copy for scanning and one for review by a live person (being careful to specify which one is for which purpose).

To ensure proper scanning by the software, follow these guidelines:

1. First line must contain only your name. Otherwise, the scanner gets "confused." So use a separate line for your address, phone number and email address.
2. Plain is better. Avoid italics, bolding, and underlining, as well as fancy borders.
3. Columns and graphics. Since scanners and screening software are programmed for simple alphabetical letters and numbers, "fancy" features tend to make the letters run together or otherwise not come through clearly when scanned. This is a very unfortunate reason to be rejected from consideration!
4. Make sure the image is crystal clear. Print on a high-resolution laser printer if possible, and submit an original, not a photocopy.
5. Use a keyword section. Just as with an e-resume, be sure to include a keyword section that will allow the computer to sort you into the "qualified" stack of candidates.

Resume Distribution Services

In addition to submitting a resume in response to a specific opening, candidates can also use one of the resume distribution services that will send the candidate's resume (or a targeted letter) to companies meeting certain specifications. The advantage of such services is that it broadens the client's exposure within the industries they have targeted. Typically, the candidate can choose the geographical areas, industries, size of companies, salary and positions to whom their qualifications are sent. One that we recommend is www.yourmissinglink.com.

If you decide to use one of these services, two things are critical: (1) be sure you are provided with the names of the individuals to whom your materials were sent, so that you can follow up by phone, and (2) avoid the services that charge substantial fees ($3000 to $10,000 or more) for this type of service, as you can obtain comparable results by working with a coach and using the suggestions in this book!

Web Portfolios

A new way of letting prospective employers know about a candidate is through the use of a "web portfolio," which draws from the information in the electronic resume ("e-resume") and includes multiple web pages such as:

- Highlights
- Resume
- Certifications
- Special Projects
- Related Work History

The job seeker can then include the link to his/her web portfolio in cover letters in lieu of, or in addition to, a resume attachment or enclosure. Candidates who should consider this medium would include those who want to create a more "personal" or "innovative" image to their prospective employer, or who wish to show technological expertise. Certainly, a web site designer should have online samples of his/her work as well.

Employment Applications

Except for entry level positions, employment applications tend to be a mere formality (if used at all). However, a note on them is appropriate in case your clients raise questions on completing the application. Tips for success:

- Bring a summary of all the details you will need for the application with you. Dates, names, phone numbers, and other information that will be required to complete the application should be on a sheet to which you can refer as needed.

- Be honest. Expect that the information you provide will be verified.

- Describe your accomplishments positively and with enough detail. Let the screener have a "snapshot" of your past work experience. Instead of "Fulfilled all job requirements," say "Successfully completed daily data processing for a 100-item chart of accounts; initiated new system to organize reports for ease of access."

- Don't be afraid to omit salary/wage information. Just as with cover letters, information about your past pay may be used to screen you out before the screener becomes familiar with what you offer.

- Don't answer illegal questions. If the application asks about personal disabilities, sex, race, religion, health issues, marital status, or other legally prohibited information, leave it out and, if necessary, discuss it tactfully in the interview.

Key Coaching Concepts

1. Remember that a resume is a marketing document, not a complete chronology of a lifetime of work.
2. Realize the primary purpose of a resume: to get an interview, not a job (directly).
3. Lead with your best tangible skills.
4. Customize your resume for each opening for which you apply.
5. Use a chronological resume (especially with recruiters) unless you fit one of the categories of exceptions.
6. Begin your resume with "Summary of Qualifications" instead of an Objective.
7. Continue with applicable sections of the resume, depending on your background.
8. Use references strategically; avoid listing them on the resume.
9. Consolidate your background into no more than two pages.
10. Avoid any unnecessary information, but include all that's required.
11. When preparing an electronic or scannable resume, include a keyword section, avoid anything other than plain text, and put the most important information on the first half of page 1.
12. Use a resume distribution service if you believe it will enhance your exposure among target employers.
13. Also consider a web portfolio if you want to present more of your unique qualifications and/or show technological savvy to your prospective employer.
14. Approach employment applications, if used, as strategically as you would any other part of the job search process.

16 INTERVIEWING STRATEGIES THAT GET THE JOB

"I think the person who takes a job in order to live - that is to say, (just) for the money - has turned himself into a slave."
—Joseph Campbell

"You must always do the thing you think you cannot do."
—Eleanor Roosevelt

The next step in the job search process is usually a job interview. And no matter how favorably the client has presented themselves in writing through a powerful cover letter and customized resume, the interview can "make or break" their chances of being hired.

Job interviewing in today's workplace is much more of an art than a mere skill. While there are aspects of it that can be learned and practiced, the unique dynamics of interviews also require the candidate to observe and respond to the nonverbal cues of the interviewer. That is, listening between the words that are being spoken can often provide invaluable insights into what the interviewer is really looking for and how he/she is evaluating the applicant.

The interview is actually the beginning of creating a new relationship with the staff in the new company - the prospective employer. So both candidate and interviewer want to make a good impression! Company policies and practices regarding interviews vary widely, and interviews also vary at different stages of selection and at different levels of the organization (e.g., an interview for an entry level employee will be less complex and involved than one for a CEO). So for all these reasons it will be helpful to think of interviewing as an "art" - a canvas to which all parties involved are contributing to make a unique image that constitutes the relationships and roles of both applicant and company.

To be successful at interviewing, we need to work with our clients in several areas:

- Pre-interview strategies that get them through the screener and help them be prepared for the interview
- The logistics of interviewing, including first impressions, dress, and scheduling
- Two types of interviews, and how one's approach is different with each
- How to answer the most commonly asked questions
- Ways to avoid becoming defensive when shortcomings are raised
- Key follow-up tactics

Pre-Interview Strategies

When does the interview start? Many people would answer, "When I walk into the reception area of the hiring organization." Wrong! The interview actually starts when the prospective employer responds to the applicant's letter, resume, or other approach - i.e., in the first responsive phone call. If the client mishandles this call, there will be no interview. Some helpful hints prior to the interview include:

1. **Handle the phone professionally.** Have a line dedicated to your job search if you can (especially if you have young children or teenagers in the house). The voicemail message should be simple, professional, and in your own voice, e.g., "You've reached the voicemail for Sam Smith. I'm sorry I've missed your call, but will return it as soon as possible if you leave your name, phone number, and message." Consider letting all calls go to voicemail (even if you are there) to ensure that you have the information you need in front of you when you return the recruiter's call. And if you are conducting your search while employed, you may want to use your cell phone as your job search line so that you can receive (via

voicemail) and return calls during breaks in your work day - e.g., lunch hour.

2. **Handle the callback strategically.** When you call the recruiter back (even if it's just 5 minutes later!), your goal is to set an appointment for a screening interview. To give you some time to prepare for the interview and learn more about the company, avoid getting into a screening interview during the callback. Even the next day gives you more preparation time. And after the day and time for the interview is set, don't forget to ask these key questions to help you with research, scheduling, and positioning:

   - Who will I be meeting or talking with at this interview? (so you can check on their background if any information is available online)
   - How long do you expect the meeting(s) to last? (so you allow ample time)
   - What can you tell me about the position in addition to what the advertisement or posting indicates? (helps you choose Work Experience Stories that are relevant to the full range of requirements)
   - Was there anything in particular about my qualifications/ background that interested you? (what they say may surprise you!)

3. **Do your homework prior to the interview.** Gather background information on the industry, company and interviewer through their web site and other source material referred to in prior chapters:

   a. Research the industry:
      - historic trends
      - recent rends
      - noteworthy companies in the industry
      - geographic area job trends
   b. Research the company:
      - history, growth rate, any changes in structure (e.g., going public)
      - current size, structure
      - products and/or services offered now, and history of development
      - financial history, current status and profitability

- top management people, including backgrounds, philosophy, tenure with co., age, etc.
- culture, dress code, communication patterns (can gather these if picking up marketing materials in person)

  c. Research the interviewer and key people in organization and/or department you'll be working in. Use your network for this. Also check "Who's Who" in your industry, Standard & Poors Register of Corporations, www.hoovers.com, and similar publications.

    Part Five contains a sample Pre-Interview Research Data Sheet that clients can use to summarize their pre-interview research findings.

4. **Know how to answer the common interview questions and handle any shortcomings you may have** (discussed below).
5. **Prepare questions to ask the interviewer during the interview. Choose from the following list in Figure 25.**

Figure 25: Sample Questions to Ask at an Interview

- What has led to this position coming available?
- Is this a new position?
- Why have you gone outside the company to fill this position?
- How long was the person I'm replacing in the job?
- How many times has the job been vacant in the last 5 years?
- What are the strengths and weaknesses of the person I'm replacing?
- Assuming I'm offered the job and take it, what benchmarks does the company expect to be achieved in the first 6-12 months?
- How are performance reviews conducted?
- What is the number one priority for the person who takes this job?
- What do you see as the main strengths a person needs to have for this job?
- What are some of the longer-term objectives you have for this job? For your department?

- What is the number one challenge in this position?
- How has the company been successful over the last few years?
- (If your research didn't answer it) What is the company's current market share or position in the industry?
- In what areas do you see the company's primary strengths?
- What 3-5 traits would the ideal candidate for this position possess?
- CLOSING QUESTION (ALWAYS ask this): What are the next steps in your selection process? (Clarify, follow-up, and leave with permission for recontact.)

Logistics of Interviewing

First Impressions

Whenever we meet someone for the first time, we form a first impression based on a combination of factors. Researchers tell us that up to 90 percent of our communication is nonverbal: tone of voice, dress, posture, facial expression, and physical appearance. So in preparing for an interview, creating the right first impression is a vital part of success.

A recent survey of interviewers found that the most influential factor in the interview is (contrary to common understanding) not experience or qualifications, but personality and personal presentation. The full list of the top 10 factors is listed in Figure 26.

Figure 26: Influential Factors Scale (In Order of Importance)

1. Your personality — how you present yourself during the interview (including your dress)
2. Your experience
3. The qualifications you show for the job
4. Your background and references
5. Your enthusiasm regarding the company and job
6. Your educational and technical background
7. Your growth potential

8.   Your compatibility (ability to get along with co-workers)
9.   Your intelligence and capacity to learn
10. How hard a worker you appear to be

As part of that first impression, our clients need to:

a)   Greet the receptionist warmly, ask him/her a few questions about what it's like to work there, and get his/her name for later follow-up and acknowledgement (they're the one that will help the candidate get through to the hiring manager on the phone!)
b)   Have some "chit chat" prepared to use when the interviewer comes out to greet the applicant
c)   Make direct eye contact with the interviewer
d)   Shake hands firmly, but not too vigorously with the interviewer
e)   Be the first one to make a statement or ask a question to position the client as a proactive participant in the interviewing process

Dress for Interviews

In the old workplace, dress for interviews was easy: the rule was to wear a three-piece suit. Now, with casual dress codes much more common and dress varying by industry, company, and area of the country, it is more difficult to predict what will be appropriate. As a rule of thumb, applicants should dress just a little nicer than they would for day-to-day work. If unsure, best practice is to err on the side of being conservative. This is another question that the client can ask during the interview scheduling phone call if they are unsure about appropriate dress.

In addition, clients need to be sure their grooming is impeccable. Keep jewelry, perfume, and accessories to a minimum, but pay careful attention to such details as the condition of one's shoes (polished, heels not worn down); women should carry only a briefcase or purse, not both; and basic hygiene should be observed. For additional information on dress for interviews, see *The New Dress for Success* by John T. Molloy. Finally, the applicant should bring a list of their references to the interview to present if/when it is asked for.

Scheduling

Certainly there are times when the client has no choice as to the time or day for their interview. But in many cases they are given a choice. Research has shown that Monday is the worst day to interview, with Friday a close second. And if the client has some options regarding timing of the interview, the most positive impression will be made in a mid-day timeframe. A few other hints: for management/exempt positions, don't be in a hurry to be the first one interviewed - the first person interviewed is three times less likely to be hired than the last one, though the rule is reversed for nonmanagerial level positions. And keeping an interview appointment during bad weather gives a significant advantage - assuming the interviewer was able to make it in! This shows eagerness and dedication.

Types of Interviews

There are two primary types of interviews, and a few variations on each. The client's role and approach will vary with each type. Screening interviews are usually done by trained human resources staff who are skilled in interviewing. They will make the interviewee feel comfortable (unless a stress element is part of the criteria of the job, in which they may do just the opposite!). They will proceed through a prepared list of questions, logically and systematically. The purpose of the screening interview is to screen out all candidates who do not meet all of the basic job requirements. Job seekers should understand each question that is asked, and only provide the information requested. Volunteering more than is asked for will usually do more harm than good in this type of interview.

Screening interviews are often done over the telephone. The advantage to this method for the client is they can have their notes in front of them regarding their company research, answers to interview questions, and the like. However, since the screener does not have the visual input of their appearance and other nonverbal cues, it is critical that the client's verbal presentation be flawless (or as close to it as possible!).

The second type, the decisionmaking interview, is usually done by the manager or person who will actually make the hiring decision. These people are usually not skilled in interviewing, and the job seeker may feel more awkward than in the screening interview. In many cases it will be necessary that the job seeker take a more proactive role in the interview and its direction and content to succeed here. For example, the candidate may be the one that asks many of the questions or suggests what needs to be covered.

The primary style of decisionmaking interview has changed from the old skills question-and-answer style to "behavioral interviewing." This means the candidate needs to be prepared to not only answer the question asked, but illustrate the answer with a story or respond to a hypothetical situation by illustrating his/her reasoning process. If the client has prepared his/her Work Experience Stories, he/she will be well-prepared for this common type of interview.

Variations on the decisionmaking interview are the group interview, the serial interview, the interview that includes a meal, and the so-called blessing interview.

- **Group interview:** Here, several managers or other company representatives interview a candidate simultaneously, usually around a conference table. Coaching tips for this type of interview include making eye contact with each person in the group while answering a question, addressing the candidate's questions to more than one of the interviewers, and following up with each interviewer individually after the interview by letter.

- **Serial interview:** This approach has the candidate undergo a series of interviews with various company representatives one after the other, often lasting as long as a full day. It can be grueling! The challenge for the applicant is to be as fresh and spontaneous with the last of five to eight interviews as they were for the first one. From the company's standpoint, this approach allows the interviewers to compare notes about what they observed, and often one will notice something that the other(s) missed.

- **Interviews over a meal:** Another whole set of issues are added to the situation when food is involved: whether or not to order a cocktail, what kind of food to order to create the right impression (and not be too messy), how to balance answering the interview questions with finishing one's food, and learning to follow the cues of the others present to show that the candidate fits in. Common sense goes a long ways here: avoid smoking or ordering cocktails (even if others do) so that your mind remains clear to answer the questions. Order something simple and easy to eat so that you can concentrate on what's most important: the interview. And avoid telling off-color jokes or otherwise creating a less than professional impression.

- **Blessing interview:** At the conclusion of an interviewing sequence in many medium- to large-sized companies, there is a "blessing interview" with the CEO or General Manager of the firm. The purpose of this interview is not to review your qualifications; the interviewer assumes you have met the job requirements through the prior interviews (of which there may be two or as many as six or seven). Here, the CEO generally wants to see if your style and personality are a good fit with the organization. Some rather informal or casual conversation is characteristic, and if the candidate is successful the CEO puts his "blessing" or stamp of approval on the decision to hire the applicant. The offer would then follow.

The 10 Most Commonly Asked Interview Questions – and Best/Worst Answers

Question	Best Answer	Worst Answer
1. Tell me about yourself.	Often the first question in an interview. Assume they want a summary of your work-related qualifications and have a 60-second "personal commercial" prepared that includes a) overview of work done during last 10 years only (not entire career), b) degree(s) - ONLY if related to the position, c) a few of your specific skills that relate to the job requirements. See sample in Figure 27.	"What would you like to know?" Talking about where you were born and raised, how many children you have, personal/non-job related information

Question	Best Answer	Worst Answer
2. What are your salary requirements?	(See chapter 18 for details) Defer: "I don't know enough about the job yet to respond; can you tell me about the expectations for the first 6 months?" Turn it around: "I'm sure you pay a competitive salary, and I'm negotiable. What is the range you've budgeted for the position?" Give a broad range: If you have to give a number, state the range of compensation AND value of benefits, bonuses, etc. over past 5-10 years (in chapter 18 under "broad range" you say 3-5 years)	"I wouldn't consider less than $100,000. What do you pay?"
3. What are your greatest strengths?	This question is used in the behavioral interviewing style which is most common today. The answer should include a) concrete/tangible job skills (e.g. increasing sales, managing a turnaround or merger, written communications, teambuilding, software programming) and b) actual stories or examples of how the candidate used those skills to achieve a specific result.	"I'm really a great person, a team player, and I'm sure I'd fit right into your organization." [the problem: these are subjective or intangible traits, not concrete job skills]
4. What are your weaknesses?	Response should cite an area which may have been a challenge in the past but which they've worked to overcome.	"I don't really have any." "Well, I know you want someone who knows the computer, and I really don't have any experience with that." [This is a job search shortcoming, not a weakness - and you certainly don't want to volunteer it!] "I tend to be a perfectionist." [overused]
5. What are your career goals?	"I'd like to become increasingly valuable to your firm by consistently exceeding the performance standards and learning new skills." [Has the candidate thought past the next paycheck?]	"I'd like to have your job." (intimidating)

Question	Best Answer	Worst Answer
6. What did you like most about your last position?	Tie the answer into the company's needs and/or show your initiative or outstanding performance - e.g. if interviewing with a growth firm, you could say "What I liked best was the opportunity to grow the sales in our region by 50% over 5 years."	Most people answer this without thinking about the interviewing company's needs. So if they say they liked the independence of their last job and the interviewing company wants people who fit into the established "company-think" and stay within the boundaries of their job, that could disqualify the candidate.
7. What did you like least about your last position?	"Though I liked most of the aspects of the job and company, the one limitation was lack of growth opportunities." [shows initiative]	"Well actually, I'm suing my former employer for unethical practices." "I disliked the bureaucracy" (when interviewing with a large, highly structured firm or agency)
8. How quickly do you think you will be ready to contribute to our firm?	"I believe I can contribute pretty immediately. In past positions, I've had to learn a lot of [terminology or whatever] in a short time, and did quite well. For example... [tell a story]"	"Since I don't have experience in your industry, it will probably take 3-6 months before I am really valuable." [And we're supposed to pay you for this??]
9. Why did you leave your last position?	"The company reorganized and my position, along with a number of others, was eliminated." "I had achieved as much as I could within that company and felt the need to seek another job to continue to grow."	"I was forced out because I didn't get along with my coworkers." "My boss was out to get me."
10. Why do you want to work here? Or: Why should we hire you?	Strut your stuff! Summarize the answers you've given to their questions as they relate to the job requirements, in a concise 1- to 2-minute response. (And reiterate this when you do your thank-you letter, within 24 hours of the interview.)	"Well, it seems like a pretty good place to work." "I understand you pay above market wages, and money is the most important thing to me."

There are literally hundreds of interview questions that could be asked of a candidate during either a screening or a decisionmaking interview. However, those listed below are more common than others and, once a client knows how to answer those listed below, the strategy for other questions follows suit.

Figure 27: Sample One-Minute Summary

"I have 15 years of progressively responsible management experience in the graphic arts field, including both Internet and print media. Most recently, I was manager of a franchised operation in a major metropolitan market and grew the business from start-up to $40 million in sales. I have an MBA degree and continuing education in various desktop publishing software programs. My strengths include innovative marketing, building rapport with a variety of customers, and building effective teams within a deadline-driven environment."

Dealing with Shortcomings

Nearly every candidate has some shortcoming vis-à-vis the job for which they are applying. Whether they lack the specific education or experience the company desires, or face such potential issues as age, frequent job changes, or a termination for cause, the one thing a candidate must avoid is becoming defensive regarding that issue - or worse, finding themselves spending the majority of the interview trying to overcome it. A "shortcoming" is simply a perceived liability or deficiency in the job seeker's qualifications or background

A powerful technique to use in addressing shortcomings in the interview is to use the "Acknowledge and Redirect" technique. What this requires is, when the applicant is asked a question about the shortcoming, to simply acknowledge it, redirect the conversation to a common area, and illustrate how that area bridges the perceived shortcoming. For example:

Employer asks candidate whether they have a Master's Degree. They answer:

> "I appreciate your raising that issue; I know it was one of the qualifications you listed for the job. From what you've shared with me today, you're looking for someone that can work well with people and knows the terminology of your industry. If I could demonstrate how I have used those skills in several previous positions, would that help relieve your concern?" [Job

seeker then tells story here of past accomplishment(s) that illustrate these skills, thus demonstrating equivalent value despite lack of stated requirement.]

Handling Specific Issues

- **Termination:** Frame it in terms of a business decision, mention that other positions were also eliminated (if they were)

- **Long time with one company:** Highlight different positions within the company, different duties and staff to show that it was more like having different jobs (shows you're adaptable despite long time at one firm)

- **Frequent job changes:** Point to any commonalities (same industry, same size company, significant amount of tangible results produced, etc.) between past jobs and this one and state why you're committed to a more permanent position now (if you were)

- **Age - too old:** Focus on your fitness and vitality, desire to work indefinitely, and the advantages of being a mature worker such as loyalty, stability, etc. - while showing you have an open mind to new ideas. Of course, this usually won't be raised directly due to employment discrimination concerns.

- **Age - too young:** Focus on outstanding accomplishments in school and anything that shows maturity, including clear longer-term goals.

- **No experience in target industry:** Point out accomplishments in similar functional roles, characterizing them generically to show transferability. For example, when interviewing for a position as Chief Financial Officer at an aerospace firm after years in banking, instead of "At XYZ Bank I was responsible for overseeing accounting and financial analysis of commercial and retail (individual) accounts and reduced error rates in our FDIC reporting from 5% to 1% in 6 months," say "At a Fortune 300 corporation, I oversaw accounting and financial analysis for business customers in various industries including aerospace, and reduced error rates by 400% within 6 months."

- **No degree:** Highlight any continuing or professional education, skills learned on the job, and demonstrate openness to lifelong learning; also emphasize job-related experience to offset lack of formal education.

- **Degree not in area of target job:** Focus more on experience as it relates to the job and on any continuing education that has equipped you to do the job, as well as familiarity with technical concepts, customers, or other aspects of the target industry.

Following Up After the Interview

Whew! The interview is over and your client feels like they did well. Perhaps the interviewer even told them they would be called back for a second interview. Now is the time to acknowledge and congratulate the client for another part of the process well done!

Before the client even leaves the parking lot of the interviewing company, you may want to suggest that they spend a few minutes debriefing the interview on a notepad. This is especially important if they avoid note-taking during the interview - which we recommend - so that they can focus on the nonverbal communication and be perceived as more attentive. The debriefing would answer such questions as these: What appealed to the applicant about the position? The company? How do they feel they did in the interview? What are the next steps in the hiring process? What were the names of the interviewers, receptionist, and others they talked to? Any drawbacks to this position compared to others for which they have interviewed?

Upon return to his home or office, the client can further position himself favorably by sending a thank-you letter reiterating the highlights of the interview, his accomplishments as they relate to the company's stated needs, and any follow-up that was agreed to at the interview, such as a next interview (see sample in Figure 28). This letter should be sent within 24 hours of the interview. If he met with multiple people, he should send a customized letter to each. Hard copy letter is preferred to emailing to avoid it being deleted or overlooked. Simply sending this letter gives the client an advantage because less than ten percent of applicants bother to send a thank-you. We know of situations where between two equally qualified candidates, the one that sent the thank-you letter was hired primarily because the letter showed initiative.

Figure 28: Sample Follow-up Letter (send within 24 hours)

Date

Interviewer, Title
Company Name
Address
City, State Zip

Dear [Name of Interviewer]:

Thank you for your time in discussing the [position] [day]. I am excited about the possibilities of working with you!

Just to recap, we discussed that the following accomplishments lend support to my ability to confidently meet any challenges related to this position:

      1.
      2.   WES's!!!
      3.

(Select Work Experience Stories that support the key areas of need that emerged during the interview)

I am convinced that my proven track record of [summarize skills being emphasized], can provide both the immediate and long term results you desire. The environment at ABC Co. appears to provide the challenges I am seeking and in which I have always been successful. I look forward to speaking with you again on _____.

Sincerely,

Joe Job Seeker

One of our Certified Career Coaches™ did interview coaching with a media manager who had been out of work for 12 months. After this roleplay session, he successfully interviewed for and got a position as broadcast manager for a national television sports network. Interview coaching can make a difference!

Key Coaching Concepts

1. Interviewing is an art, not just a skill.
2. The interview begins with the first call-back, not when the candidate appears for a face-to-face meeting at the company premises.
3. For pre-interview success, one needs to handle the phone professionally, handle the callback strategically, do research on the company and position prior to the interview, prepare to answer common questions and deal with shortcomings, and prepare their own list of questions to ask the interviewer.
4. It is important that a job seeker understand how to make the best first impression, that they dress appropriately for the company and position, and that they schedule the interview (if given a choice) at a time when they are most likely to be selected.
5. There are two types of interviews, screening and decisionmaking.
6. Of all the interview questions that can be asked, 10 are most common. A "one-minute commercial" as well as carefully thought-out answers to all 10 interview questions is a critical part of interview preparation.
7. The "Acknowledge and Redirect" strategy will help candidates overcome shortcomings and avoid becoming defensive when shortcomings are raised.
8. After the interview, the candidate should debrief what has happened and send a thank-you letter within 24 hours of the interview to everyone with whom he/she talked.

Evaluating Job Offers: Wants vs. Needs

> "Life is a progress from want to want, not from enjoyment to enjoyment."
>
> —Samuel Johnson

If a client's search has been successful, he/she will begin getting offers anywhere from one week to six months after he/she starts the search. Three common mistakes at this stage are:

a) accepting the first offer received,
b) failing to evaluate the offer against desired criteria, and
c) neglecting to seek improvement of the offer.

Coaching suggestions for the first two situations are discussed below; improving the offer will be covered in Chapter 18.

Accepting First Offer Received

Clients are often tempted to accept the first offer received, either because they are afraid there will be no other offers, because they have been in the search a long time and need to get back to work, or because they doubt their own abilities and marketable skills.

To help them avoid making this mistake, we can first let them know that multiple offers are quite common, particularly when they use the suggestions given here regarding a diversified marketing approach. If their financial situation from lack of an income is becoming severe, it may be unwise to wait for other offers. But if the client has reached a similar stage in the interview process with several companies and expects other offers soon, it is best to use those multiple offers as they come in, to optimize the compensation package of the job the client really wants.

If the client is ready to jump at the first offer due to lack of confidence in her own abilities and skills, then coaching around that issue will help her overcome it.

Failing To Adequately Evaluate The Offer

When an offer is received, it becomes very apparent that if the client has not considered what her ideal job should include, it is much more difficult to determine when she has found it! Some types of people make decisions about accepting or rejecting job offers based solely on an intuitive hunch; others analyze the opportunity to excess.

The best guide in considering job offers is to notice one's intuitive reaction to the offer - but not let that be entirely determinative. The client can then turn to Authentic Vocation Worksheet 10 (see Career Coach's Toolbox in Part 5) for a comprehensive list of criteria that can be analyzed and evaluated. Several offers can also be compared against each other and the client's Authentic Vocation, either to validate an intuitive "yes" to the offer or to reveal shortcomings in it that weren't immediately apparent.

The categories of criteria to evaluate include:

1. **The compensation package:** Here, the client will be analyzing not only whether the salary falls within a desired range, but also whether the benefits include those that are critical ("needs" versus mere "wants"). Also, if benefits such as computer allowance, flexible scheduling, child care allowance or facilities, or other non-standard offerings are desirable to the client, she may need to specifically request them.

2. **Authentic Vocation™ criteria:** Next, the client can ask herself (or you can ask her) questions to determine whether the job offered satisfies all 8 elements of her Authentic Vocation™ as she has defined it in the first half of the coaching process.

3. **Career development considerations:** To be a career self-

manager and to remain challenged, most people also need to know that there are growth opportunities in the position they take and in the company for which they work. Is this important to your client? If so, is she looking for an occasional training provided by the company, a full tuition reimbursement program, or a comprehensive organization-wide commitment to employee development?

4. **Work/life balance issues:** As individuals' lives become more complex and stress increases, there is a virtual outcry for balance between work and personal life. For employees with young children or ailing parents - or just an unwillingness to continue working unhealthily long hours in a demanding environment - this factor will be very important. Does the job require significant commuting time? Travel as part of the job? Are there policies which encourage flexibility to deal with family issues? These are a few of the considerations in this regard.

5. **Company soundness and position:** Finally, even if a candidate finds the "perfect" position, it can soon become anything but perfect if the company goes out of business, is acquired soon after hire, or has a poor reputation in its industry. These final factors investigate the risk involved in the company itself (i.e. is it a start-up or well established?) as well as its reputation, turnover rate, competitive pressures in the industry, and the like.

Using this combination of intuition and analysis, a client will make a much more well-rounded and better informed decision whether to accept one offer versus another.

Finalizing The Employment Arrangement In Writing

Offers are often made verbally - and unfortunately for the prospective employee, candidates often accept verbally too. Later, if there are misunderstandings, the candidate has no basis on which to enforce what they understood the terms of the job to be. Therefore, it is highly recommended to get the offer reduced to writing. That way both parties are clear on its terms. Some of the items to be included in the written offer are:

- Starting date
- Job title
- Responsibilities/job description
- Benefits (in detail - not "as stated in employee manual") including company holidays, vacation policy, insurance, retirement benefits if any, and other relevant topics
- Relocation package, including all aspects (real estate commission, moving expense limits, procedure for reimbursement, whether tax on relocation package is included, temporary lodging if any, house hunting trips if any, storage if any, transportation of any special items such as boats, etc.)
- Transition of 401k and medical insurance benefits (e.g., reimbursement for COBRA if there is a waiting period for company medical insurance)
- Stock options or bonuses - check for detail here: is it clear enough so that reasonable minds would interpret the language the same way?
- Severance benefits, if any

Some executive clients may want a formal employment contract to memorialize their employment arrangement. Others (including many executives) will be adequately served by a letter of offer, signed by the new employee upon acceptance to acknowledge its terms. This written document should be signed before the client moves to the new location or begins work so that there are no misunderstandings.

Key Coaching Concepts

1. Three common mistakes at the offer stage are: (a) accepting the first offer received, (b) failing to evaluate the offer against desired criteria, and (c) neglecting to seek improvement of the offer.

2. The categories of criteria to evaluate in reviewing offers include:
   - The compensation package
   - Authentic Vocation™ criteria
   - Career development considerations
   - Work/life balance issues
   - Company soundness and position

3. Verbal offers need to be reduced to writing for the client to adequately consider them.

18

NEGOTIATING THE OPTIMUM
COMPENSATION PACKAGE

"When I was young I thought that money was the most important thing in life; now that I am old I know that it is."
—Oscar
Wilde

At this stage the client may have one offer or ten, but they will benefit in any case from coaching to strategize the negotiation stage. Common misconceptions about negotiating in the context of a job include:

Myth	Truth
The offer as stated is the "best they can do," i.e., there is no room to improve the compensation	There is usually at least 20 percent more compensation available; we have seen packages be increased by as much as 100 percent in rare cases.
This is an "arms-length" negotiation, just like selling a house or car.	It is a unique kind of negotiation because you will be working with these people for some years and this is the beginning of the relationship. It's more like negotiating a prenuptial agreement.
It is best to maintain a policy of full disclosure when asked what your salary history or requirements are.	Salary is not a relevant issue until the offer stage; until then, use one of the three strategies discussed below to postpone the discussion until it is pertinent.

Myth	Truth
When you have a long list of items to be negotiated in the offer (and which you want changed), it is best to just raise a few first and see how the employer responds.	Wrong! This can alienate the employer and, in some cases, result in the offer being withdrawn. Instead, raise all of your "discussion points" at once so that both parties know what is on the table.
The most appropriate term for the document outlining the changes the candidate wants made to the offer is a "counteroffer."	No, this sets up an adversarial dynamic that will not further a win-win outcome. Instead, just call it a "responsive memo" to preserve the cooperative spirit of the discussion.

Negotiation Tactics For The Three Key Phases Of The Interview

Just as in interviewing we discussed pre-interview, interview, and post-interview strategies, there are three stages of negotiation. The final post-interview stage is referred to here as the offer stage. Throughout the process, the savvy negotiator will operate by the tenet that they can ask for anything (the worst the person can say is no, right?), but they cannot demand anything. "He who becomes demanding loses" in the negotiating game.

Negotiation Tactics for Pre-Interview Stage

Thorough preparation prior to the interview is essential to negotiating as well as successful interviewing. Not only will the candidate need to research the company, but they will also want to do some preliminary research into what market salaries are for similar positions. The resources listed below provide free salary data for this purpose:

www.careers.wsj.com
www.jobsmart.org
www.abbott-langer.com
www.wageweb.com
www.salaryexpert.com
www.salary.com

The client may also want to use a salary calculator to calculate the difference in salary between different geographic locations if the position he/she is interviewing for is in another city, state or country. See http://www.homefair.com/homefair/cmr/salcalc.html for an example.

In a stable economy, the client will be well within market standards to seek to improve their prior compensation by ten to twenty percent. That amount will go down during economic downturns and up when the economy is booming.

Negotiating During the Interview

The topic of compensation can come up anywhere in the interview process. The first rule is: let the interviewer raise the issue! If the candidate brings it up before the interviewer does, it makes the candidate look overanxious and more concerned about money than about achieving the right fit between him/herself and the job/company.

The second rule of negotiating is that the applicant's goal is to defer the discussion of salary and compensation until the offer stage. Why? Because the only reason an interviewer will raise it earlier is to find a reason to screen the candidate out, and until an offer is made there is nothing to which the candidate can respond (other than market salary ranges, which are just general information).

The following three techniques will help defer the compensation discussion until a appropriate time:

1. **Deferral:** Here, whether the issue is raised for screening purposes early on or because the company has a custom of asking about salary in the first interview, the candidate can defer discussion of compensation by a response like this: "I don't really know enough about the job yet to say what a reasonable salary would be. Can we discuss the job requirements a bit more and come back to this question?"
2. **Turnaround:** This tactic turns the question around to the interviewer by asking "What salary range did you have budgeted for the job?" Often, they will tell you!
3. **Broad range:** If the interviewer won't disclose the range, says it's "negotiable, depending on the qualifications of the candidate," or demands a specific answer, the broad range is

an alternative tactic. If the candidate can total the full compensation package as it has ranged over the past three to five years, the response can be "My compensation packages over the past 5 years have ranged from the low $60's to around $80,000, depending on bonuses, benefits, industry, responsibilities and other variables." This approach doesn't say that any specific range is acceptable, but avoids the candidate getting locked into a number that's too high or too low.

Recruiters and hiring managers will use an applicant's prior income, if they know it, as a basis for an offer in the new position. This is not in the client's best interest if they are trying to better their situation! So a response like this may be appropriate:

"My [function/role/industry] was different there than here, though I know the skills I used will transfer easily to this position. Therefore, my prior income is not really representative of my value to you in this role." Or,

"My compensation focused a significant amount of [stock options/equity, etc.] and not as much on base salary, so I'd like to explore with you my value in this role regardless of how we structure our package."

Negotiating at the Offer Stage; Improving the Offer

As mentioned above, most offers have the potential of at least 20 percent more salary as well as additional benefits if they are important to the candidate - but the candidate must ask for them! At the offer stage, remember our key principle: ask for anything, demand nothing. Here's a strategy for requesting an improved package using this approach:

- Get the offer in writing as explained in Chapter 17. Ask for some time to consider and respond to the offer. Anywhere from two days to a week is reasonable, depending on the level of position, whether relocation is involved, and the like.
- Review the offer carefully, analyzing it against the Wants and Needs in Authentic Vocation™ Worksheet 10. Also compare

it with market salary rates in the salary data web sites listed above, through trade association data, and any other resources available to the client (or to you).

- Rather than making a counter-offer, develop a list of "discussion points" to discuss with the hiring manager. All points which the candidate wants to raise or improve should be included in this list, instead of "piecemealing" the negotiations. Also include points with which the candidate is in agreement.

- Work with the client, if desired, to write a responsive letter or memo in which they again acknowledge the offer, state the terms with which they agree, and list the discussion points together with reasons they want those aspects of the offer to be improved.

- The client should then call the hiring manager (hopefully working directly with the manager, who has authority to change the offer, instead of human resources). They will essentially tell the manager that they appreciate the offer and agree with much of it but have a few points to discuss, and offer to email or fax the list to them for later discussion.

- Fax/email the list and call back at an agreed time to discuss (let them review the list first).

- Have a phone conversation about the items you want to discuss.

- Ask the manager to help find a mutually acceptable option if they won't accept the initial proposal.

- If salary is too low, consider expanding job responsibilities or adding a bonus element to justify a higher compensation amount.

- This process may go on for several rounds before final agreement is reached!

- Memorialize the final agreement in writing, signed by both parties.

Post-Job Search Coaching Opportunities

Just because the client has accepted their position does not mean that your coaching is necessarily over! Whether the client has made a career change, a shift from office- to home-based environment, or obtained a promotion, or another situation, there is a need for further career coaching in many cases. The first 3 months in a new position are often a "trial period" in which both employee and employer are verifying that the employee is a good fit for the job and organization. In addition, there is the process of learning the written and unwritten rules of the company culture, of which coaching can increase the client's awareness and effectiveness in navigating.

In one case, I coached a woman following her move from a large corporate environment to a home-based executive position in a smaller company. Part of her goal in taking the position was to have more time with her two young children, but learning to actually take that time - as well as more time for herself -took some shifts in her thinking that the coaching helped to implement. And of course, after a client has been in a job for a few months or years, they will often begin thinking about another job change, so you want to maintain contact and be their "coach of choice" when that time comes.

Key Coaching Concepts

1. The negotiation process, like the interview, begins in the pre-interview stage and continues through the offer stage.
2. The first rule of negotiating is to let the employer raise the issue.
3. The second rule of negotiating is to ask for anything but demand nothing.
4. Pre-interview, research into the company as well as market salary rates is the key strategy.
5. During the interview, one or more of three tactics can be used to defer the discussion of compensation: deferral, turnaround, and broad range.
6. Post-interview, during the offer stage, the offer should be reduced to writing, analyzed versus the Wants/Needs Analysis and market rates, and a list of "discussion points" developed. Often, there is at least 20 percent additional compensation available - if the client asks for it! The client should then discuss the list of discussion points with the hiring manager and a mutually acceptable arrangement reached, which in turn must be reduced to writing.
7. Coaching can continue after the client has taken his/her new position to help him/her with the adjustment to the new job and environment.

PART FOUR

QUANTUMSHIFT!™ COACHING

THE QUANTUMSHIFT!™ COACHING MODEL

"Change comes to our lives not only from shifts in our inner needs, but also from shifts in our external circumstances... When we respect the natural cycles of life, we find that each of life's stages has a spiritual dimension."

—Jack Kornfield
A Path With Heart

"When an electron is about to make a quantum leap to a new orbit, 'it puts out temporary "feelers" towards its own future stability by trying out - all at once - all the possible new orbits into which it might eventually settle, in much the same way as we might try out a new idea by throwing out imaginary scenarios depicting its many possible consequences.' These temporary feelers are called 'virtual transitions,' and the actual transition of the electron into its new, permanent home a 'real transition.' 'Virtual transitions "are often of the greatest importance, for a great many physical processes are the result of these so-called virtual transitions."

—Danah Zohar,
The Quantum Self;
David Bohm,
Quantum Theory

Now that coaching as a profession is coming into its own, growing at more than 20 percent per year, a plethora of coaching models exist. At this writing there are more than 75 coach training schools, each with their own approach to coaching. So, you may be wondering, why do we need yet another model? And where does QuantumShift™

coaching fit into the mix? The answer: it provides the structure, methods, and techniques by which we help our clients access their Authentic Vocation.™

In talking with colleagues and company representatives about their coaching styles and experiences, one thing is apparent: what some people call "coaching" is not actually coaching. It is instead an individualized version of a group training, interpretation of an assessment tool, consulting repositioned to catch the latest trend in business services, or even therapy or counseling masquerading as coaching. In fact, many "coaches" are not using a model at all, but a compilation of ideas from personal experience that they hope will pass for coaching. This confuses the public as well as prospective coaches, and is one reason why we at Career Coach Institute use the International Coach Federation coaching definition (which you saw in Chapter 1), ethical standards, and competencies as the standards governing our coach training.

Adhering to the ICF's universal definition and standards, however, still does not delineate a specific coaching approach or model. Many of the commonly used models of coaching today work at the level of "effects" or behavior only. For example, if someone brings an issue of not knowing how they'll pay next month's mortgage to the coaching session, many coaches would address the issue by exploring possible issues at the "surface" only. They would brainstorm with the client about their budget, where they could cut expenses, how to get a raise in pay or bring in more income from other sources, and the like.

While this approach may be useful, it does not address deeper systemic issues within the client's belief system which, if addressed and transformed through QuantumShift!™ techniques, would automatically solve the problem of paying the mortgage - and conceivably every other financial challenge the person has faced! So QuantumShift!™ Coaching ("QSC") is a deeper, more lasting, fundamental and broad reaching transformation than merely problem-solving to find a solution to the current issue. The immediate situation, we believe, is usually a symptom of a belief-based coaching issue, and working at the deeper level will create higher impact for the client. And when the client "gets it," the shift that occurs (a "quantum shift") is immediate and usually permanent. After that, if it's still necessary, the surface-level brainstorming and problem-solving can be done (we call it "Level 1 coaching") but it has more meaning because it is within the context of the larger change.

"Quantum shifts," also called "quantum leaps" by physicists, refer to unexpected sudden moves to another state of being - or in the case of particles, to another orbit. As the quote at the beginning of this chapter illustrates, the behavior of particles as they "try on" new orbits and then make a sudden leap parallels our human behavior in exploring options prior to making a dramatic shift in our behavior or beliefs. The discovery of quantum physics completely turned the former paradigm - Newtonian physics - on its ear. And QuantumShift! coaching does that with existing coaching paradigms too.

The model is deceptively simple in theory: it outlines three key coaching competencies, each of which is used during a complete coaching session. We begin by establishing rapport with the client (whether a new client or a continuation of an ongoing client relationship) and establish the agenda or issue to be discussed in the coaching session. That done, the majority of the session will be spent using the second competency: exploring and elaborating upon the issue the client has raised, using a wide variety of techniques. Finally, the third competency or phase of the session is eliciting action, in which the client determines at least one step they are going to execute in the coming week.

There are three levels of QuantumShift™ coaching, each of which will be explored in detail in its own chapter later in this Part. Level 1 deals with behavior, performance, and the "surface" level of effects we mentioned above. Level 2 works at the level of beliefs, motivation, and other thought systems which undergird our daily activities. And Level 3 operates at the level of our identity, our views of our inner self, and who we are.

Figure 29 illustrates the elements of the model:

Figure 29: QuantumShift!™ Model

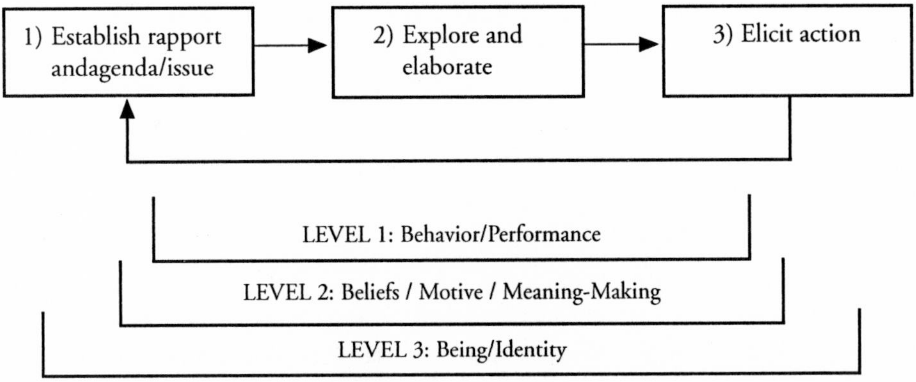

Adapted from Chris Argyris

Perhaps the difference between QSC and other methods of coaching will become more apparent with an example. John was a member of a project team, but at team meetings sat quietly, did not offer ideas, folded his arms and looked away during the discussions. A coach using Level 1 would try to change his withdrawing behavior, train him in communication techniques and body language. A QuantumShift™ coach using Level 2 would explore his beliefs about being on a team, see if anything is demotivating him about being on the team or how the team is approaching the project, and perhaps administer an assessment which deals with team dynamics, styles of interacting, and the like. Going even deeper, a QuantumShift™ coach using Level 3 coaching would probe how John views himself vis-à-vis the team, what kind of person he perceives himself to be, perhaps use a 360-degree assessment or other personality evaluation tool to increase his awareness about his own natural strengths and weaknesses, and ask, "Who do you need to be in order that your involvement on the team is engaging for you?"

If this does not seem perfectly clear yet, don't worry! It isn't as simple as it initially appears, and the following chapters should help you greatly by isolating specific elements of the model for individual treatment.

The Role and Results of QuantumShift!™ Coaching

Perhaps the real proof in effectiveness of QuantumShift!™ Coaching lies in its results. Both personally and in the organizational setting, QuantumShift!™ career coaching can have a dramatic effect, especially as part of a blended learning approach in a corporation.

What do people and companies do when faced with an issue that could benefit from coaching? If an individual is in dilemma about a career move, he may ask his friends and family, read books on careers, and/or surf the Internet for information and leads before seeking out a coach. If the coach does his work well, the coach will help the person clarify his goals and streamline his job search process, resulting in a career that is more satisfying.

If a company is considering implementing coaching, whether through external coaches or an internal manager-as-coach or coaching staff approach, it is often because they are having performance problems. Productivity is off, morale is lower than desired, error rates are up in the production line, or they want to increase the amount of claims processed or widgets produced per employee dollar paid. Fortunately, research tells us that there are other reasons for bringing in coaches. Fully 86 percent of companies hired coaches to sharpen the leadership skills of high potentials, and another 72 percent hired them to correct management behavior problems, according to recent industry research.

In our experience organizations frequently make one of the following three mistakes when considering using coaching, whether to enhance the high performers or address performance problems:

1. **The Training Approach.** They send the involved people to a training session, thinking content provided in a classroom setting will "fix" the problem. No follow-up intervention is used.

2. **Failing to Identify "Strengths."** They fail to assess the "strengths" or natural abilities of their employees and match them to the best job to maximize their contribution to the firm. Instead, they use training to improve weak areas in the individual - which, as Marcus Buckingham et al point out in *Now Discover Your Strengths*, will never create strengths but rather compensatory skills.

3. **Surface-Level Performance Coaching.** They bring in coaches that use "performance coaching," one form of the surface level coaching we described above, and even if that coaching resolves the current situation, others crop up in its wake. Each situation requires separate coaching, resulting in higher costs for the company and a never-ending stream of coaching needs. (Can you see how QuantumShift!™ coaches tend to obsolete themselves faster than others?)

The QuantumShift!™ alternative to mistake number 1 is to combine training with coaching. A research study written by Certified Career Coach™ Denise Bane, Ph.D., and published in *Public Personnel Management* magazine, found that when training is combined with coaching, individuals increase their productivity by an average of 86 percent, compared to 22 percent with training alone. That's quite a difference!

Regarding mistake number 2, QuantumShift!™ coaching draws on the concept of "strengths" and, using an appreciative approach inquiring into what's working well, what the employee likes in their job, and what they would like to do more of, helps match natural abilities with a fulfilling job.

And of course, Levels 2 and 3 of the QSC model directly address mistake number 3 by probing into beliefs, motivation, and identity when appropriate to facilitate systemic change.

Three Principles of QuantumShift! Coaching

The QSC model draws on three key principles from quantum physics. In this new world of physics, like some Eastern philosophies such as Buddhism, the relationship between cause and effect is not always linear. For example, the Buddhists talk about "not doing" as sometimes being the best type of action to take. In *Zen Mind, Beginner's Mind*, Shunryu Suzuki writes, "In calmness there should be activity; in activity there should be calmness. Actually, they are the same thing." This does not make sense to our Western minds, but if we practice meditation, martial arts or similar disciplines, we discover its meaning. With that in mind, let's examine the three QSC principles.

1. **Change occurs discontinuously, and its source is unpredictable.** As you learn coaching techniques and begin working with clients, you may expect that the client's most significant change will come from your brilliant coaching question, or from the client doing a certain activity that you have suggested. And that may happen! But just as often, the change they need may actually occur due to an offhand comment they hear while carrying out their daily tasks, or a thought that occurs to them while they are driving to work. That is not to say that you did not have a role in their transformation, just that the path to change is not linear. It is in fact often cumulative. When a person sets their intention toward change, a series of events and people are drawn into their life because of that intention (as the W. Murray quote in chapter 12 points out). Yet it is not just one of those people or events that causes the transformation, but the combination of them - or something else seemingly unrelated - that causes the client to shift.

An example from my own life a few years ago was the transition that led to my founding Career Coach Institute. I had spent the year prior to doing so feeling "lost" in my professional life. Though outwardly successful, I was no longer challenged by what I had been doing as Senior Vice President in a career management firm. I needed something more creative, more flexible (since my husband had just retired) and over which I had a greater sense of ownership than the salaried job offered. After attending many personal growth workshops, reading dozens of books, and becoming enrolled in a business coach training program, I still felt unclear about what was next for me. I also took a teleleader training course that equipped me to lead classes over the phone.

As my husband and I drove back from our Thanksgiving holiday with my family, I was trying to develop topics to offer as teleclasses to complete my certification. Suddenly, like a bolt of lightning, it struck me: I could combine my years of experience in career development with teleclasses and coach training and have a one-of-a-kind career coach training school. I knew instinctively that it was the kind of inspiration that constitutes a "calling," as Gregg LeVoy describes it in his book by that name. Yet it wasn't anything my husband said, anything my coach at the time did, or anything else that was causally related in time that led to my epiphany; it was a combination of those and some quiet time to think and reflect. This is an example of principle number 1 in action.

2. **We create (or at least heavily influence) our own reality.** In quantum physics, scientists actually found that a particle would change its entire nature and turn into a wave when an observer began watching the activity of the microscopic particles. The observer is somehow connected to the particle in a way not previously understood. This applies in coaching in that by our merely coming together with a client, a third space which we refer to as the "coach space" is created - and that is where our interaction occurs. It is co-created by the coach and client as the session proceeds. New ideas, insights, and results then emerge which would not have occurred by just sitting and thinking about the issue, journaling, or other individual activities without a coach.

3. **Be open to synchronicity!** Just as we need to be open to synchronicity ("meaningful coincidence") in the job search (see chapter 12), we also need to expect it to be operating in our work with clients. In doing so, what appears impossible becomes possible by combining the power of dedicated intention with an openness to how it manifests. Joe Jaworski points this out in *Synchronicity: The Inner Path of Leadership*:

    "It's critical that you focus on the result and not get attached to any particular process for achieving the result. When we are in the process of creating something, we must have the flexibility of mind to move with what needs to be done. What allows this to happen is precisely the fact that we're not attached to how things should be done. It's a little bit like sailing. If you're focused on your course rather than your destination, you're in big trouble. If you were to be blown off course, you would never simply return to the course you were on. No one would sail that way. Rather, you would focus on the destination and set a new course. But that's the way we live our lives. We get attached to our assumptions about how things should get done."

We will explore how to get behind assumptions as we delve further into the model.

Desired Outcomes of Successful Career Coaching

As we use the QSC model in our coaching with career clients, we seek to achieve four ultimate outcomes:

1. **Enhanced self-awareness.** One goal is to facilitate the client's process of knowing themselves better, particularly vis-à-vis other personality styles (e.g. through one or more assessments) and regarding the unconscious beliefs, motivations, and principles that would otherwise keep them on "automatic pilot" in making decisions. Greater self-awareness leads to more conscious choices in every aspect of life, including career.

2. **Clarity of purpose and goals.** As you know from Part Two, life purpose is the foundation of Authentic Vocation,™ and

we believe is also the secret to finding fulfillment in one's work. QuantumShift!™ coaching is in part designed to increase the client's clarity regarding their purpose. In addition, it leads to clearer long- and short-term goals as we use it as an Organizing Principle (see Figure 5 in chapter 4).

3. **Increased career self- management.** In today's turbulent work climate, each worker must manage his own career as though he was self-employed. This is the only kind of "job security" that exists today. QuantumShift!™ career coaching is the equivalent of "teaching someone to fish, rather than handing them a fish" so they can manage their career for a lifetime, not just during this transition.

4. **Overall betterment of one's quality of life.** As one's fulfillment at work increases, it is certain to spill over into other areas of life. And as life purpose is used as a filter to determine which life roles to increase and which to decrease (see chapter 4), work/life balance improves and with it quality of life. So in a very real sense, participating in QuantumShift!™ career coaching betters the quality of one's overall life experience.

Key Coaching Concepts

1. The QSC model includes three competencies: (a) Establish rapport and agenda, (b) Explore and elaborate, and (c) Elicit action.

2. There are three levels of QSC: Level 1 - behavior; Level 2 - beliefs; and Level 3 - identity.

3. Companies seeking to bring coaching into their firm often make one of three mistakes: (a) The Training Approach; (b) Failing to Identify "Strengths," and (c) Surface Level Performance Coaching.

4. QuantumShift!™ Coaching is based on three principles: (a) Change is discontinuous, and its source is unpredictable; (b) We create (or at least heavily influence) our own reality; and (c) Be open to synchronicity!

5. Career coaching should achieve four desired outcomes: (a) Enhanced self-awareness; (b) Clarity regarding life purpose and goals; (c) Career self-management; and (d) Overall betterment of one's quality of life.

20 INITIATING THE COACHING RELATIONSHIP

"Success usually finds you before you're ready."
—Barbara Sher
Wishcraft

So it's happened: a client prospect has called you to inquire about your coaching services. While this is not a primer on sales skills, it is about handling the client from inquiry to commencement of coaching. The best coaches don't "sell" their skills per se, but instead develop a sense within the client/prospect that the coach understands the client's needs and can help them meet those needs or solve their problems.

Let's explore some common reasons a person would call a coach. Your job at this point is to both understand and identify the client's needs and to dig deeper (yes, it starts here!) to help the client see either underlying issues or broader solutions than they may initially anticipate.

- They have been laid off (or "made redundant")
- They dislike their job
- They dislike their career and want to explore a change
- They want to make more money
- They need a new resume
- They have a job search liability with which they need help in overcoming
- They have never conducted a job search ("fell into" each job or have been with one company their entire career)
- They want to advance/get a promotion

- They want to start their own business
- They're over-stressed and want some relief

In each case, we want to ask more about their stated need, how they believe coaching will benefit them, and whether our services are appropriate for their stated need. The ICF competencies require that we not misrepresent our services, and that if the client is not appropriate for us that we refer them on to another coach or service provider. Figure 30 illustrates the process that we go through as we decide whether or not a match exists.

Figure 30: Determining The Match Between Prospect And Coach

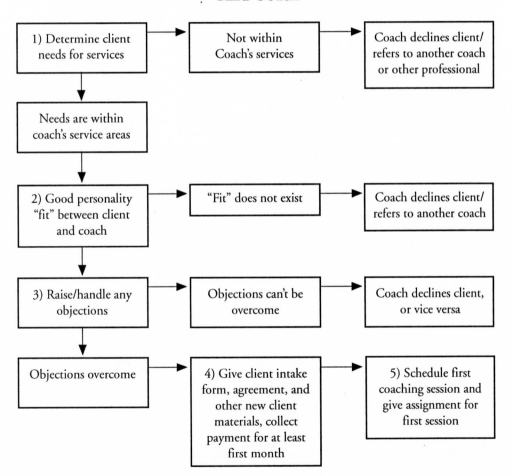

It is during this initial conversation with the new client when we need to define coaching, simply, and clarify how it's different from other roles such as therapy, career counseling and consulting (see chapter 1 for more details here). It is also a good time to outline the respective roles of coach and client, to be further elaborated in the written Coaching Agreement.

The prospective client may have questions to ask and what in sales jargon are called "objections" (too much money, not sure if I have the time, is now the time to do it, do I need to interview other coaches too, etc.). The professional career coach simply addresses these objections one at a time and suggests a coaching program or package that will meet the client's needs for a reasonable fee.

Most career coaches charge on a monthly basis, no less than US$300 per month and upwards of US$2500 per month if working with executive clients or in a technical specialty area. That fee can include three or four half-hour coaching sessions (once a week; some coaches work a three-week month), as well as assessments, workbooks or books with relevant information to the coaching process, access to a networking group if the coach offers one, email between sessions, and the like. Most coaches (regardless of specialty) request a 90-day minimum commitment from the client. The work may go longer or shorter than that (and if shorter, a prorata refund is appropriate in most cases). But that gets both client and coach into a committed relationship and gives enough time to work through the stated issues and their implications from a belief/motivation/identity standpoint.

The New Client Materials Packet

Once the prospect has agreed to become a client, some type of written agreement and other initial forms should be provided. With corporate clients, a written agreement will be required. With individual clients, it is recommended both to memorialize the arrangement and ease their foray into the coaching relationship. In addition, written agreements facilitate resolution if there is ever a misunderstanding any aspect of the engagement.

One special note at this stage for corporate clients: when hired by a corporation to work with employees within the organization, special care must be taken to clarify who the client is and to whom you owe confidentiality. The Career Coach's Toolbox provides several forms of Coaching Agreement that can be customized to your needs. CAVEAT: please have an attorney in your state, province or country review the form before using it to ensure that it satisfies the legal standards of your jurisdiction. Several states in the U.S. have much stricter standards than others regarding how coaches must represent themselves to the public.

In addition to the agreement itself, you may have a welcome letter, a set of policies or guidelines your firm uses (if not outlined in the agreement) in the event a session must be postponed, is missed, or when other situations arise. An explanatory article such as "What Career Coaches Do" in the Career Coach's Toolbox or perhaps materials you have authored yourself can also be included, and the Coaching Intake Form (to be discussed next) with instructions for the client to follow. Finally, if any assessments are to be administered at the outset of the coaching, instructions to fill those out online or a paper form if applicable can be another item in the new client packet.

The most professional career coaches will provide their new client packet, as well as other client materials, electronically for ease of transmission and response. So if the forms you've been using are not electronic (or you've been printing them out to send to clients), begin emailing them instead to modernize your image.

The Intake Session

One of the initial issues you will need to decide as a policy for your practice is how you will structure the intake session with your new clients. There are no hard-and-fast rules on this now; however, there are a few protocols that most coaches follow.

Length. Most coaches do one of the following here:
1) Discuss the coaching process as the client signs up and ask them to review the contract, if any, as well as complete the intake form and review any other materials prior to a first session; the first and subsequent sessions are each 20-30 minutes in length. No additional charge is made for the intake session in this scenario.
2) Hold a one- to two-hour intake session in which they explain the coaching process, get the coaching agreement signed,

review any initial intake forms and/or assessments the client has completed, and set goals/desired outcomes for the coaching interaction. This session is typically charged at a rate equaling 50 percent of one month's coaching in addition to regular coaching charges for the balance of the sessions that month.

Coaches who prefer option 2 believe that the longer session creates a more solid rapport at the outset. They also will frequently discuss the results of an assessment here to give the client an immediate experience with the coaching process. Those who use option 1 may find that clients are resistant to paying an additional fee for the intake. They may simply prefer to start with the standard session length, using the first session to discuss the intake form (see below) and again give the client an immediate coaching experience.

Virtual or face-to-face. Another decision for you to make here is whether to hold the intake session face-to-face or over the phone. If the client is local, you may prefer to hold an initial face-to-face session so that you get more of a sense of the person, their presence, etc. And if it is a corporate client where you need to establish rapport with both the client/employee and his/her manager (who may be paying your fees), a face-to-face meeting may ease the process and facilitate an effective interaction. The logistical issue with meeting face-to-face with an individual client is that you will need a professional space to hold the meeting. While some coaches meet new clients in a coffee shop or restaurant, privacy is limited there. And the expense of office space - even in an executive suite - may be prohibitively expensive for the new coach.

If you either prefer not to find space to meet in person or the client is in another city, state or country, you may wish to request a photo of them (and share yours with them) so that you both have visual images to complement the audio images you get through the tele-coaching. (Of course, if you do the face-to-face meeting, you can charge more for it!)

Hopefully, during your initial pre-coaching meeting with the client (the one where they committed to embark on the coaching journey), you have gained a sense of how coachable the person is. That is, are they mentally healthy, open to the process, presenting coaching (versus therapeutic) issues, and the like. The Career Coach's Toolbox contains a worksheet called "Are You Coachable?," a tool you can use to help the client decide with you whether coaching is the appropriate intervention at this time and for the issues they are facing.

The Intake Form

As you begin coaching with any new client, you will want them to complete an intake form. This form gives them a chance to tell you about themselves, and to communicate the most important issues on which they want to focus during the coaching interaction. A sample intake form is provided n the Career Coach's Toolbox, which you are free to use with your clients if you wish.

One way to automate your intake process so that you have an easily accessible record is to use client-tracking software such as that of www.clientcompass.com. This software is affordable and offers not only automated client intake, but also invoicing, client session preparation forms, payment history, marketing and practice building activity tracking, and credential tracking if you are working toward certification. It interfaces with Outlook, Palm, and mail merging through Word as well.

Benchmarks for a Successful Intake Session

When you've finished an intake session, how do you know it has met the client's needs? What skills do you need to apply to be effective in this part of the coaching interaction? Here is what our coaches have noticed:

- Client feels excited about moving forward - and may express it
- You as coach are a bit more directive than in a regular coaching session because the issues are coming from the client's written work
- Rapport is established and the client feels comfortable sharing their issues with you
- The client has had one or more "tastes" of coaching throughout the intake session and looks forward to more
- You have a better sense of the client's primary issues and their personality
- Both you and the client come to agreement at the end of the intake on the goals which you will be focusing on throughout the coaching interaction (a kind of informal Coaching Plan)

The Coaching Plan

One final part of building the initial relationship is the development of a Coaching Plan. Listed as a specific competency in the ICF Coaching Core Competencies, a Coaching Plan is an agreed set of goals and objectives, based on the client's stated needs and desired outcomes, which coach and client will work on jointly throughout the coaching relationship. It can be formal or informal, depending on whether you are working with individual clients or within an organization, where a reporting mechanism may be required.

There are a number of advantages of having a coaching plan. First, it provides a bridge and a structure to go from where we are to where we want to be. "If you fail to plan, you plan to fail," as the old adage goes. It is a point of reference at the beginning, middle, and end to remind the client what their goals are/were, update them as they go, and see what they have accomplished when the coaching is completed.

A Coaching Plan differs from the intake form/process in several ways:

- It integrates the goals, desires, concerns and perceived barriers stated on the intake form into a specific plan for development
- It may draw on the results of one or more assessments and the results of them
- For clients within a corporate engagement, the Coaching Plan may be articulated at the outset of the coaching process; for individual clients, it may come after 2-3 sessions, once the rapport is clearly established and the client's most important goals become clearer
- It states specific outcomes to be achieved through the coaching interaction (reaching certain goals, overcoming perceived barriers such as fear or self-doubt, etc.)
- It is shorter than the intake form, usually just a page in length (see sample Coaching Plan in the Career Coach's Toolbox)

Benchmarking Client's Current State

To formulate a Coaching Plan, the client must first have a sense of their current state of being. There are numerous tools to do this, which may include our own Ideal Job Exercise, in which the client imagines that they are watching two movies, the first of their current job and lifestyle, describing a typical day from awakening to bedtime; then the second of their Ideal Day, including work and personal aspects. From this narrative, two contrasting wheels can be developed that are divided proportionately by time spent on each type of task or activity during the day, now and in the ideal scenario.

Current Job/Life   Ideal Job/Life

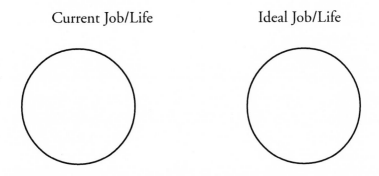

Another exercise that specifically addresses work is the Work/Life Balance Wheel in the Career Coach's Toolbox.

Key Elements of a Coaching Plan

There are 3 critical elements of a Coaching Plan:

1. **Goal(s)**: Goals are the desired changes the client would like to make during the coaching interaction.
   - Goals must meet 4 criteria:
      a. *Specific:* The goal should be specific enough that you know what you will do, when you will do it, and it should be quantified as much as possible
      b. *Realistic:* Are they "just out of reach, but not out of sight"?
      c. *Measurable:* Is there a specific result that the client can point to to know that the goal has been achieved?
      d. *Rely on your own responsibility:* People will sometimes set goals that depend on others for their achievement. For example, if the goal is to get a promotion within your department or company, that goal depends on someone giving you good performance reviews,

another person vacating their job, and someone deciding that you fit that job.

If your client sets this type of goal, inquire into the essence of the goal and reformulate it that way. The essence of the goal above may be more money, more responsibility, getting away from a co-worker they don't get along with, or any number of things. If the goal is set in those terms, it has more than one possible way to be achieved.

· This element answers these questions:
    a. What do I want to change in my life in the next 3-6 months?
    b. What do I want to improve?
    c. What is in my way? Or what do I want to overcome?

2. **Action Steps:** Once the goals are clarified, we then help the client describe the action steps to lead to their achievement. For example, if the goal is to move to a coastal town and have viable work there, initial behaviors might include listing the criteria for the ideal location (size, east vs. west coast - or abroad, demographics, etc.) list 3-5 towns that fit the stated criteria, inquiring of the Chamber of Commerce (via Internet, phone or "snail mail") about the towns, and identifying the web sites that include job openings and company information for those areas. This second element answers these questions:
    a. What specific actions will I take to achieve my goal(s)?
    b. What action steps are most urgent (i.e. must be done first) and which are less urgent?
    c. If I need more resources, information or contacts to achieve my goal, where will I find it?

3. **Results:** There is a third critical aspect of the Plan, Results. It is critical because without it, there is no evidence of success. This is the payoff for achieving the goal! Some of the possible types of results might include measurable changes in behavior (e.g. instead of avoiding making phone calls to contact prospective employers, the client makes 5 phone calls per day); specific dates for completion; numbers of interviews, letters sent, resumes submitted, etc.

Example: If a client's goal is to find a job that pays them $10,000 more per year, the result may be more financial ease, ability to save for retirement, etc.

This final element answers the question, "What is the payoff for completing the Action Steps?" The Coaching Plan is co-created by coach and client, with the client (ideally) being the one who takes notes, using the form provided in the Career Coach's Toolbox, and providing a copy to the coach after the session.

Implementing the Plan

Of course, once the Plan is formulated, the next step is its implementation. One goal or action step should be immediately identified as the first thing to do. After a week or two - or several months later - the client may find that his/her goals have shifted and that, as a result, the Coaching Plan needs to be changed. That's fine as long as the client is not avoiding making the changes they initially stated! One of the ICF coaching competencies asks that we adjust the Coaching Plan as appropriate as time goes on.

Your role as coach in implementing the Plan is to:

- Be supportive
- Encourage the client to "go for their dream"
- Help guide the client to the people, resources, and information they need to implement it
- Hold the client accountable for the results they have stated they want
- Depending on your coaching style, keep minimal or more detailed records of the client's progress (you may want to use the Client Compass software for this purpose - see www.clientcompass.com)
- If need be, confront the client with the fact that they did not take the actions they agreed to

Key Coaching Concepts

1. When a prospect calls to inquire about coaching, the coach's first step is to determine whether the prospect is a good fit for the coach, and vice versa. To do so, the coach (a) determines the client's needs, (b) assesses the fit between coach and client personality, (c) addresses any objections, (d) provides the client with a new client information packet, and (e) schedules the first session.

2. Two initial decisions the coach will need to make regarding their intake sessions are length and whether they are to be done over the phone or face-to-face.

3. Using a tool to determine whether the client is coachable is an optional step at the outset of the coaching relationship.

4. It is advisable to use a written Coaching Agreement so that both parties are clear on their roles and responsibilities.

5. Following the intake session, client and coach should co-create a Coaching Plan which outlines the goals, action steps, and results to be obtained from the coaching work.

6. The goals set in the Coaching Plan should satisfy four criteria: (a) specific, (b) realistic, (c) measurable, and (d) rely on their personal responsibility.

21

LEVEL 1 COACHING

"Insanity is doing the same thing over and over and expecting a different result."

—Albert Einstein

We continue our discussion of coaching skills with Level 1 of the QuantumShift!™ Coaching model. You may have had the impression from our overview in chapter 19 that Level 1 is undesirable as a coaching style. In fact, it is quite useful. And it is the simplest coaching technique, which is why we begin here. However, the old adage, "if all you have is a hammer, everything is a nail" applies here. If you have no other tools in your toolkit besides Level 1, your coaching will fall short in many situations.

Level 1 coaching works at the level of behavior and performance to effect change. Each place the behavior appears must be separately addressed at this level. This is the first rung of Chris Argrys' ladder of inference, which we'll explore further in chapter 23.

What Level 1 Coaching Does:
- Works to change behavior
- Solves problems
- Tries to improve performance
- Focuses on observable data
- Leads to specific action steps
- Prioritize goals and actions to be taken

Level 1 coaching is easiest because many of us are accustomed to doing problem solving, goal-setting, and prioritizing for ourselves. Consultants who enter our training program to become coaches are often experts in this style! The shift for them - and for each of us - is to learn to be neutral and unattached to any ideas we may submit to the client. In the coaching environment, we are not "experts" in the subject matter the client is raising - no matter how much experience we may have with it! This is where our role as catalyst and facilitator, from our coaching definition, is particularly applicable.

What Level 1 Coaching Doesn't Do:
- Address motivation
- Inquire into interpretation
- Explore beliefs
- Question identity
- Ask about why something is important

The contrast between Level 1 and Levels 2 and 3 will become more apparent as we progress. But these are a few "off-limits" issues at Level 1.

Premises of Level 1 Coaching

Each level of coaching is based on a series of premises. In the case of Level 1, its philosophy can be described as follows:
- The objective is changing behavior, eliminating "problems," and/or resolving a dilemma at the behavior level.
- Performance improvement is a focus.
- No mention is made of beliefs, assumptions, motive, meaning, or interpretation of situations; they are irrelevant to behavior change.

Level 1 Coaching Techniques

When coaching at Level 1, we need to not only know the appropriate questions to ask (samples of which are listed at the end of this chapter) but also have other coaching techniques to help the client resolve their issue.

1. **Cartesian Coordinates:** To be able to fully address all aspects of a problem that the client wants to solve, the Cartesian Coordinates method assures that "no rock remains unturned." Otherwise, we will have "unintended consequences," or things which follow from the client's actions that they neither anticipated nor intended.

Figure 31: Cartesian Coordinates

THEOREM AB Example: What would happen if you did?	CONVERSE -AB Example: What wouldn't happen if you did?
INVERSE A-B Example: What would happen if you didn't?	NON-MIRROR IMAGE REVERSE -A-B Example: What wouldn't happen if you didn't?

For example, Sue couldn't seem to decide whether to leave her job as a financial analyst despite feeling drawn to become a consultant to companies who were analyzing merger or acquisition targets. A coach using the Cartesian Coordinates would first ask Sue "What would happen if you left?" and invite Sue to list the answers. Second, "What wouldn't happen if you did?" In other words, what would you miss out on if you didn't start your own business now? If the business climate were such that mergers and acquisitions were on the rise and she was well connected in her industry, which would cause her to lean in favor of the decision to leave. But perhaps she would have to give up profit-sharing, bonuses, or stock options at her current employer by leaving at this time. Those factors must also be considered.

The third coaching question in this method is "What would happen if you didn't?" That is, if you stayed in your job, what would the benefits be? And finally, "What wouldn't happen if you didn't?" What risks would you not have to take, what tough decisions could you avoid, etc.? This way, the client has all the relevant criteria before her. She can then evaluate those criteria, consult her inner sense of which option is right, and make her decision.

2. **Draw on past successes.** Help the client access past situations where they have successfully managed a similar issue and leverage that success here. For instance, if a client was finding it hard to become self-motivated to make the contact calls they needed to make in their job search campaign, the coach could ask whether there was any other time in their past when they were motivated to take necessary steps toward a goal. If so, how did they find that motivation, and is there any parallel they can draw or skill they can build upon from that experience in the current challenge?

3. **Find an expert.** Ask whether the client knows anyone who has successfully solved a similar problem that she could contact for advice or input.

4. **Shift perspective.** Though a somewhat advanced skill, this can be used skillfully at Level 1. For example, the coach might ask the client, "what if you were the coach? What would you ask now?" "What if you were someone else in the scenario? How would they see the situation differently?" More on this in chapter 26.

Traps in Level 1

Since most of us have some experience with problem solving, we often make assumptions or fall into certain traps when learning the coaching technique. Some common ones are:

·   **Gathering information to solve the problem yourself.** Information-gathering questions to elicit details about the situation are common among new coaches. What's key to remember here is that you don't have to know all the details or fully understand the situation to coach the person about it. Even if you have a lot of experience with similar issues, you can't see through the client's eyes. Coaching is all about the client and helping them come to their own answers. Instead of gathering information, simply ask neutral questions to lead the client to their next insight. Contrast the two examples in Figure 32.

Notice how the client stays more neutral in the coaching column

Figure 32: Information Gathering vs. Coaching

Information Gathering		Coaching	
Coach:	What would you like to discuss today?	Coach:	What would you like to focus on today?
Client:	I'm having trouble with my supervisor at work.	Client:	I'm having trouble with my supervisor at work.
Coach:	What kind of trouble is it?	Coach:	What makes this an important issue for you?
Client:	She supports other employees in going "over my head" in getting things approved.	Client:	I'm feeling undermined by him.
Coach:	Give me an example.	Coach:	On what evidence do you base that statement?
Client:	Well, yesterday Mary went to my boss and asked my boss, Dan, to approve the new course she wants to teach next term. Dan did so, even though that is my responsibility because I'm Mary's direct supervisor.	Client:	He approves requests from employees who report directly to me.
		Coach:	What do you want?
		Client:	To have my authority recognized.
Coach:	What kind of course was it?	Coach:	What if authority wasn't so important to you?
Client:	Organizational Development Principles for the Pharmaceutical Industry.	Client:	[Pauses to think.] I might feel less resentful.
		Coach:	What else?
Coach:	What are some of the main points the course covers?	Client:	I would be able to concentrate better.
Client:	How to set up an OD plan, things to watch out for, who the key players are, stuff like that.	Coach:	So would you like to work on authority being less important, or your relationship with your supervisor?
Coach:	What kind of paperwork should Mary have done instead?	Client:	Both. I think it has to do with how I communicate with him.
Client:	She should have filled out a Request for Course Approval, Form 101A, and submitted it to me in due course.	Coach:	And what do you want to be different in your communication?
		Client:	I need to be more assertive.
Coach:	Could you suggest that she do that next time?	Coach:	So what step would you like to take between now and next time to move in that direction?
Client:	Yes, I guess so.	Client:	I'll script out what I'd like to say to him.

and how the topics discussed go an entirely different direction than when the coach feels the need to get all the details as in the left column. (For future reference, this also illustrates the impact of Level 2 coaching in the right column.)

- **Giving advice or assuming a consulting role.** A second trap in Level 1 is giving advice. No matter how intelligent or well-informed or even well-intentioned we are, advice has no place in coaching. We are subject matter experts or consultants, but coaches. Giving advice is telling the client what you would do, or what they should do, or otherwise submitting an idea that you want them to implement. The dynamic therefore shifts to your best answer, rather than the client's. And even if the idea is brilliant, the client has less ownership than if it were the answer they came to through your provocative questions. In the above example, if the coach began to tell the client that they "should" take an assertiveness class, told a story about a similar situation and what they did and suggested the client do the same, or something similar, that would be inappropriate advice.

Level 1 Coaching Questions and Techniques

- What do you want to resolve today?
- What are your choices?
- How do you see your options in this situation?
- What have you tried already?
- What has worked for you in the past?
- What would you like the result to be? Or look/sound like?
- What's the best possible outcome here?
- Could someone else do it [whatever the client is challenged with]?
- Do you know anyone who has done this that you could talk with?
- You have mentioned two opposite choices; are there any others?
- What will your first step be toward your desired result?
- What's missing?
- What are you going to do to make that happen?

Key Coaching Concepts

1. Level 1 coaching works at the level of performance and behavior to facilitate change.

2. Level 1 coaching does not inquire into motivation, beliefs, meaning, identity, or similar issues.

3. Coaching techniques to use at Level 1 include Cartesian Coordinates, drawing on past successes, finding an expert, and shifting perspective.

4. Traps in Level 1 coaching include gathering information to solve the problem yourself, and giving advice.

22 THREE CORE COACHING COMPETENCIES

"The difference between what we do and what we are capable
of doing would suffice to solve most of the world's problems."
—Ghandi

"The secret of success is making your vocation your vacation."
—Mark Twain

You will recall that in the QuantumShift™ Coaching model, there
are three core coaching competencies, which also constitute the
three phases of a successful coaching call:

1. Establish rapport and the agenda or issue to be discussed
2. Explore and elaborate on the agenda or issue
3. Elicit action

In this chapter we will examine each of them in depth.

Phase 1: Establish Rapport and Agenda

This first competency or phase of the coaching session (usually the
first two to five minutes of your coaching call) is critical to the success
of the session overall. It sets the tone for the rest of the interaction
and can determine whether it will be focused or unfocused, effective
or not.

You must be fully present as the call begins and use strategies that will successfully help the client determine what they want to focus on. Otherwise, the call can end up being a mere "conversation" instead of a "coaching interaction." (Remember the difference? A coaching call has one or more specific goals, coach is neutral catalyst with focus entirely on client, etc.)

Preparing for the call

To establish this "presence" with your client - meaning you are undistracted, focused, and centered on them — you will probably want to develop some practices that will help you prepare for your coaching calls. Here are a few ideas that have worked for other coaches:

- Close your eyes and take a few deep breaths
- Light a candle in your work area
- Have a picture of a peaceful nature scene in your work area that you can look at before you take a call
- Have an object such as a special stone, container, or crystal on your desk that you can physically touch to center yourself
- Repeat a simple saying or thought such as "I open myself to serve my client" or "I now prepare myself to access my Inner Wisdom" just before the call
- Consciously put aside any mental distractions from events that have just happened (including your last client call!)
- Ensure that your work area is quiet and free from noise that would detract from the quality of the coaching session
- Have a glass of water nearby
- Clear your desk of everything except the client's file (if any) and a pad and pen (or a clean screen on your computer) to jot down any notes - and your calendar, if it is not on your computer (to schedule the next session)
- Turn off any music that you may have been listening to, as well as the television
- If you have children, be sure they are being cared for in another room
- Put a smile in your mind that carries through your voice as you answer the phone

- Get off the Internet!
- If it is difficult to become centered for a particular call, close your eyes as you pick up the phone to eliminate all visual input and concentrate on the client's voice
- Visualize an image that is calming for you: floating in warm water, sitting by the ocean, walking through the woods, etc.

You may think of others. But however you do it, become focused so that you can concentrate on the coaching session. (Some new coaches find that they want to avoid too much preparation because it makes them anxious - that's fine too!)

1(a) Establishing Rapport

Both you and your client will immediately pick up verbal and nonverbal cues from each other as the call begins (if you're listening for them!). Imagine yourself starting a coaching call. Would you act any differently if the client was talking quickly, seemed excited, appeared depressed, or was distracted? Talking quickly is observable data that could mean many things; but "seemed excited, appeared depressed, or was distracted" are interpretations, aren't they? If you sense behavior in the client that may indicate excitement, depression, etc., ask them about it in a neutral way! For example: "I notice you're talking very quickly today. "What is happening?" or "What do you attribute that to?"

Once any initial issues are addressed, the following questions are other ways to establish rapport:

- How are you doing?
- How has your week been?
- What has been happening in your life that you'd like to share?

In the first coaching call, establishing rapport may feel different than in subsequent sessions because you do not know the client, their personality and sense of humor, etc. This will particularly be true if you do not do an extended intake session (see chapter 20). You may feel the need to make a "good impression" since you are setting the tone for your entire interaction here (though of course the process actually began when you had the initial conversation with the client in which they committed to coaching). In subsequent calls, you have an ongoing relationship with the client (which grows with each session). You may need to catch up a bit on the past week's activities, how the client has done with their assignment/action steps, etc. But the rapport-building may take less time in the subsequent sessions because you have the relationship established.

Indicators That Rapport is Established

How do we know that rapport has successfully been established? We notice the following:

- Client is receptive to coaching
- Client lacks defensiveness
- Extraverted clients begin processing out loud, talking through the issue and possible solutions
- Client seems eager to share what's been happening
- In subsequent sessions, they have completed the work they promised last time
- You feel a flow with the client

What If Rapport Isn't There

There may be some calls where you immediately sense that something is unsaid, or you find it difficult to create rapport. Perhaps the client is facing a challenge, has an issue they want to discuss with you, or is just plain distracted by children, an ongoing event at work, or their commitments. Despite our natural tendency to the contrary, avoid taking it personally. Most likely, the client's issue is not about you. And even if it is, you now have a forum to discuss it. (It's worse if the client just stops keeping their appointments but will not explain why!)

What you can do in this situation is to:

- Ask the client if there is something they wish to discuss
- Say something like, "It sounds like you're a bit distracted right now. Is this a good time to talk, or should we reschedule?"
- [If client isn't following up/doing their work] "What would make this valuable for you?" Or "What's in the way of your following through?" More on this in chapter 26.

1(b) Establishing Agenda

The second objective of Phase 1 of the session, establishing the agenda or issue to be discussed, may involve nothing more than asking a question. Or in other cases it may require isolating one issue out of a long series of initial statements the client makes.

One way to ensure that the issue is isolated before the session begins is to use a Pre-Session Worksheet such as that found in the Career Coach's Toolbox. You would provide this form to the client prior to the session, asking them to complete and email it to you 24 hours before the session. Of course, something more urgent than the issue that seemed most important 24 hours ago may arise, and you can feel free to shift the focus when that happens. But it gives the client an opportunity to recap their week's activities and determine what they want to discuss during the current session. This can be particularly helpful for clients who have a tendency to ramble and not stay on one topic during their coaching sessions.

Following are some suggested questions to ask to identify the agenda or issue:

- We have about ___ minutes today; what would you like to focus on?
- In the time we have today, what's the most important thing we could talk about that might make a big difference in the next week?
- (After the client shares what's been happening) You've mentioned several possible issues for us to discuss. Which one would you like to focus on first? Or, Which one seems most urgent now?
- What would be the best use of our time today?
- How would you like to spend our time today?
- What issue did you bring to the session from your prework?
- How can we use the time we have to make a difference for you?

What To Do If Client Doesn't Have An Issue

The Pre-Session Worksheet may minimize the number of times this happens. But if it does - and sometimes the client just may not have a pressing issue - you may need to generate some questions to stimulate more ideas. And once you have been coaching a client for a few weeks (or months), there are times when it's helpful to recap, summarize, and otherwise recognize progress - as well as take the coaching to a new level. Following are some questions that might help in this situation. (Granted, some of them are somewhat leading, but they can take the client into areas they may not go on their own.)

- "Is there an area of your life in which you would like to have bigger results?"
- "Have you had any random thoughts or fantasies about how your life could be better?"
- "Would today be a good time to summarize what we've accomplished in our coaching so far?"
- "What are 5 things you'd like to accomplish in the next 6 months?"
- "How is not having an issue a good thing for you right now?"
- "Is there anything you have been wanting to say [to me or another person] but haven't?"
- "Is there anything you've been wanting to do but haven't yet?"
- You could also administer an assessment and use that as a basis for some future goals, a new Coaching Plan or other developmental objectives

Phase 2: Explore and Elaborate

The second phase or coaching competency, Explore and Elaborate on the agenda set by the client, usually constitutes the largest amount of time spent during a coaching session. Though of course you will want to begin by exploring the issues as stated by the client, there will usually be underlying issues that will be rich for exploration, particularly as you move into coaching at Levels 2 and 3. These may include:

- What is motivating the client - in this situation and in their life overall?
- The client's assumptions about their current situation and/ or how the world works
- What the client sees as "just the way it is" and therefore is not open to question
- Priorities among competing issues with the client
- Beliefs the client holds about behavior, situations and themselves

- The client's intellectual models, derived from multiple beliefs and conclusions: How do they view the world? Where did those views originate? Do they serve the client now? What needs to change?
- Client's awareness of their behavior - and of other styles of learning and behavior (which can be derived from administering various assessments as well as through coaching and observation)
- Client's values, and their awareness of whether they are conscious or unconscious

"Blind Spots"

What happens if you see a coaching issue and the client doesn't want to explore it? We call these "blind spots" because both client and coach aren't aware of the issue. One of our coaching competencies is to "demonstrate respect for client's perceptions, learning style, personal being," and to "ask permission to coach client in sensitive, new areas" B(3)(d) and (f). So if the client is reluctant - or downright unwilling! - to discuss an issue, it is our responsibility to honor that. However, there are some coaching techniques that can open such a door:

- Ask the client, "Are you willing to explore your resistance to this issue?" or "Do I have your permission to ask a few more questions on this topic?"
- Use the "Reflective Model" outlined below and ask the client if they hear the issue as you restate it to them
- Say, "You may not be tracking with me on this, since I think it is a blind spot for you, but what else might be going on here?"

This kind of "blind spot" can be uncomfortable for the client until they too can see the issue. What's important is that the client understands. If you feel the need or think you need more clarity, beware of the trap that you may be trying to solve the problem yourself. Let the client do it! A good question to ask here is: what do you [client] need to be more clear about to resolve this issue?

The Reflective Model of Elaboration: Hear, Restate, Inquire

Active listening is one of the ICF core competencies. This simply refers to the ability to listen to more than the words, "to focus completely on what the client is saying and is not saying, to understand the meaning of what is said in the context of the client's desires, and to support client self-expression," to quote the competencies.

The Reflective Model is a variation of active listening in which the coach takes an active role in fleshing out what the client has shared. The coach:

(a) listens ("hears") what the client says, then

(b) restates it back to them (hopefully offering a deeper or different perspective on the statement), and finally

(c) inquires as to any inconsistencies the coach notices or other areas in which the coach senses the need to further explore the issue.

Figure 33 illustrates how this works.

Figure 33: Coaching Example - the Reflective Model in Action

Client is trying to decide what to do as part of a team doing a corporate consulting intervention but it is one of a series that management authorized but did not act on. Client is concerned about reaction of the employees "in the trenches" to the information she will be delivering.

Coach: How could you as a person helping on this assessment get this information to upper management?

Client: That's what I've got to figure out. Working with VP of construction, you have me working on this, what kinds of things could we do/avoid for the people in the trenches to make sure you don't have to deal with this again.

Coach: Is that likely to happen?

Client: Yes, one agreement on front end is that if I see something where they're shooting themselves in the foot, I can raise it. I have unofficial license.

Coach:	So you've already asked that permission up front. What would keep you from doing it?
Client:	I guess I do now that you say it.
Coach:	Sounds like you have the answer.
Client:	I got off track on the emotional issues.
Coach:	What will you do in the next week?
Client:	Talk to the HR manager and tell him my thoughts because I know him better, then I'll follow his lead.
Coach:	OK, please let me know how it goes.

Coaching Questions to Ask to Explore/Elaborate on the Issue

In exploring and elaborating, the precise questions used will depend on whether the coach takes a Level 1, 2 or 3 approach.

Level 1:
- What have you tried already?
- What else could you do?
- Of those two possibilities, which one is most critical now?
- Say more about that
- Which is most important?
- Is anything in your way?
- [If they say they don't know] If you did know, what would it look [or sound/feel] like?
- What would you be doing differently if...?
- Has this ever happened before?
- What has to happen for x to occur?
- If you could not do x, what other options are available?

Level 2:
- What is important about that?
- What really matters to you in this situation?
- How can you do it better?
- Why does it matter?
- What's your intention?
- How does that serve your purpose?
- Is there any part of you that feels [scared, uncertain, etc.]?
- If there were one thing you could anchor to, what would that be?

- What is that connected to?
- What would you need to know to x?
- What's underneath the [stress]?

Level 3:
- If you were to achieve this state, what would be happening in you that would be [irresistibly compelling]?
- Why do you think you'll be successful?
- What kind of a person would you have to be to achieve x?
- What beliefs would a [successful] person hold about themselves?
- Is there something that makes a [successful] person fundamentally different than you?
- What if this was the perfect environment for you to learn what you need to know about yourself - what is the lesson?

Remember: You don't have to understand the client's situation to help them unless you're problem-solving, so avoid "fact-finding" or "information-finding" questions.

Avoiding "Interrogation"

One danger of spending the entire second part of your coaching interaction asking one question after another is that the client can end up feeling like they're being interrogated. This does not further your rapport, and can raise defensiveness (or worse!) in the client. To avoid this, try mixing up your coaching techniques: along with asking questions, give them some feedback, state your observations, solicit (or give, on select occasions) ideas, reaffirm what they're saying, restate what they've said, etc. This actualizes the coaching competency of "dancing in the moment," being present yet flexible as the situation requires.

Indicators that Exploration/Elaboration is Successful
How do we know that we have explored and elaborated enough on the issue?
- Client seems "complete"
- Client has an "a-ha" experience
- Client knows what to do next

- Client has resolved the issue they came with (or others that arose during the session)
- Client understands themselves and/or the situation better and can move forward
- Client reiterates what they're going to do
- Client exhibits excitement

Phase 3: Elicit Action

After we have helped the client amplify the issue they wished to discuss, we then need to draw the session to a close. They may not be finished processing the issue, but it is up to you to keep your sessions within the stated time limits so that other client appointments do not start late!

"Eliciting action" does not always mean the client will take physical action. If they are wrestling with a Level 2 or 3 issue, it is often not resolved in one session (though when they "get it," the aha! experience creates a QuantumShift! that stays with them!). So the step you and the client agree on may be to notice situations in which a problematic behavior shows up and see what thoughts or beliefs are going through their mind at that time. Or perhaps they'll reflect on an idea. Or like one of my clients recently did, to avoid spending time on issues that are petty and not related to her strategic goals, she put a sign in her work area that said "Think Big!" to remind her to keep her thoughts on what was important.

This coaching competency cannot be underemphasized, because the client will take with them the tone and feeling of this phase of the coaching call as they go into their next week. Will they leave the session excited or lackadaisical? Energized or depressed? Action-oriented or overwhelmed? The way you handle this aspect of the session will contribute substantially to this part of the client's experience.

Testing Action for Viability

It is critical that the action agreed upon be one or more steps that the client is not only planning towards, but prepared to do, capable of doing, and willing to do (we call this "PCW" for prepared, capable and willing). If a client is reluctant to state or commit to an action step, many times it is because one or more of these elements is absent.

And as a result, they are unlikely to follow through.
- **Prepared:** Client is clear on what they will do, excited to do it, and the timing is right. They are prepared to get into action immediately.
- **Capable:** Client has the necessary skills to do the agreed action, or if not, they know what resources (people, books, courses, etc.) to consult to gain the needed competency.
- **Willing:** To be willing is to freely choose a desired action, more than wanting to do it; at least, to have given themselves permission, and at most, to have established a highly motivated commitment to move forward.

One aspect of preparedness that can create reluctance in the client is simply lack of clarity about how to take the issue you have discussed during the interaction to a next step. They may want you to suggest an action step, or may say "I don't know" when asked what they're taking with them from the session to do in the next week. To coach someone who presents this situation, you might ask, "If you did know, what would it be?" - a great question to shift perspective. Or, "Have you considered doing x?" - which is not the same as saying "I think you should do x," but still helps them past a blind spot or area of unknowingness, can also help you bring the session to a successful conclusion.

Remember that the client's sense of what's a reasonable plan of action may be bigger or smaller than your own comfort level! It is usually best to let them assume the level of commitment they believe is realistic, and if they either far exceed it or don't make much progress, the scope of the next week's action can be adjusted accordingly - or the barriers explored.

Coaching Questions to Elicit Action

The following questions can bring the session to conclusion and forward the client's action:
- Based on our discussion today, what's your next step? [Let them clarify/summarize]
- With all this being said, summarize what will happen next.
- What's one thing you could [or will] do...?

- If there was one thing you could do right now that would make a difference, what would it be?
- What are you going to do next week? or, What specific actions are you going to take?
- Could you summarize what you're taking away from our session?
- Can you set a time frame for that?
- What will you take away from this call?
- Is there anything to prevent you from...?
- Is anything in your way?
- Do you need to know or learn anything new to implement this plan?
- Based on our discussion, are we on the right track? How do you know?
- How would you like to end our session today?
- Do you have any final questions that I might help you with before we end our session?

If you're running short on time, a great question to ask is: "If there were one thing you could do in the next week to take this issue further, what would it be?"

Our coaching competencies require that we help the client "do it now" when appropriate. So in suitable situations, immediately starting to role-play or do what they've suggested can begin the shift during the session.

Indicators the Eliciting Action is Successful

How do you know the third phase of the coaching session is successful? Here are a few indicators:

- Client knows what to do next, and is prepared, capable and willing to do it
- Client is excited!
- Client wants to end the session so they can get started
- Client seems complete

Key Coaching Concepts

1. Prior to a coaching call, the coach must become focused, centered, and prepared for the call, using one or more techniques from the suggested list.

2. Phase 1a, establishing rapport, occurs in the first few minutes of the coaching call, and sets the tone for the rest of the session.

3. If rapport seems to be difficult to establish, it can help to ask the client whether there is something they need to say.

4. After rapport is established, the issue or agenda to be discussed should be determined during phase 1b. The Pre-Session Worksheet can help if the client tends to ramble.

5. Phase 2, exploring and elaborating, constitutes the bulk of the coaching session.

6. The Reflective Model of Elaboration can help clients through blind spots.

7. One trap during Phase 2 is interrogating the client; mixing up coaching techniques can help.

8. In Phase 3, eliciting action, the session is drawn to a close. This phase is critical because the client takes the feeling that the session ends with into his/her week.

9. To test action for viability, we need to inquire whether the client is prepared, capable, and willing to do the action suggested.

23 LEVEL 2 COACHING

"Sometimes I've believed as many as six impossible things before breakfast."

—Lewis Carroll
Alice in Wonderland

"The essence of belief is the establishment of a habit."
—Charles S. Pearce

Level 2 coaching takes us one level deeper than Level 1 to the underlying beliefs, motivators and unconscious programming that drives our clients' behavior. It can be described as working with a client to help him access his unconscious programming. As a result, that programming may be consciously changed when desired so that behavior and other effects of this programming change automatically. Note that we do not impose this change on our clients; we ask a question that invites them to go there and honor their response, whether "yes" or "no."

Often, Level 2 issues underlie stated Level 1 issues and cause impacts in the client's life that he does not understand. For example: a client has a series of unsatisfying jobs, his boss berates him and he makes less than market salary. Inquiring into this pattern may reveal a Level 2 issue such as a low level of deservingness, i.e., that he believes only a certain amount of income is acceptable. This may originate in childhood socioeconomic circumstances, messages that have been internalized from other significant influences in his life, or from another source. If the client can consciously change these beliefs through coaching, he will inevitably avoid repeating this undesirable pattern in his next job choice.

What Level 2 Coaching Does:
- Ask what the client's motivation is (directly or indirectly)
- Inquire into the client's interpretation of events
- Explore client's beliefs about a situation
- Challenge or test assumptions the client has made for validity
- Ask about why something is important

What Level 2 Coaching Doesn't Do:
- Work to change behavior
- Solve problems
- Try to improve performance (at least not directly!)
- Focus on observable data
- Prioritize goals and actions to be taken
- Question identity

Premises of Level 2 Coaching:
- The purpose is to change beliefs, assumptions and the person's models of the world.
- Through changing the "program" by which the person runs, performance and behavior will change automatically.
- Level 2 questions explore beliefs, assumptions, motive, meaning and interpretation of situations.

As we have discussed, attempting change at Level 1 (the level of behavior) requires multiple interventions, because changing a behavior in one situation will not carry over to another. It's like an old container that is too full and begins to leak; plugging one hole will simply force the liquid to come out another, and the process of keeping the liquid in the container is endless. So it is with Level 1 coaching.

Please note that we are not saying never to use Level 1 coaching. There can be a place for so-called "problem-solving" in the coaching process. But usually, it is after the Level 2 work has been done. Then the client is conscious of his motivation, choosing his assumptions and beliefs (vs. being driven by them), that Level 1 coaching can have the best impact.

Traps: What is Not Level 2 Coaching

In Level 1 coaching, we must be careful to avoid giving advice or answers, which is the role of consulting. Different traps occur at Levels 2 and 3. Here, the distinction between coaching and therapy can be most evident, depending on how skillfully the coaching is done.

Remember, in most therapy the therapist:

- Inquires into the past more than the present or future
- Works with what was to change what is now
- Focuses on the client's feelings and emotions
- Leads the client through psychotherapeutic techniques — the therapist directs the process

By contrast, a skillful Level 2 (or 3!) coach:

- Inquires into the present and future more than the past
- Works with what is and what could be, not what was
- Focuses on the client's motivation, beliefs and assumptions, helping the client test and examine them to bring them to conscious awareness
- Lets the client set the agenda for the session, asking skillful questions and providing provocative feedback to help the client broaden his/her awareness to implement change

Principles of Level 2 Coaching

Ladder of Inference

Noted business writer Chris Argyris has articulated a model for problem-solving and understanding human behavior which he calls the "ladder of inference." Each of us climbs the ladder each time we interact with another person or have an experience in life. It is a frequently used mental pathway that, with each step up the Ladder, creates increased abstraction and distortion, and the person becomes more removed from the initial experience. The result? Often, misguided beliefs and significant misunderstandings occur which become more and more complex as they are applied within an organizational or family system.

Figure 34 illustrates the steps in the Ladder of Inference.

Figure 34: The Ladder of Inference

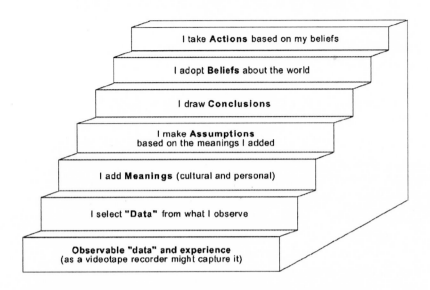

Beginning at the bottom of the ladder, we have an experience, from which (second step) we select some data from the experience to focus on. (Of course, it is almost never the entire or an accurate picture of the event!). We then add cultural and personal meanings to what we have observed, make assumptions based on those meanings, and draw conclusions. Those become our beliefs about the world, on which we take actions as we live our daily life. See Figure 35 for example.

Figure 35: Coaching Example: The Ladder of Inference at Work

[DATA:]You are making a presentation to a group of colleagues.

[MEANINGS:] Most of them are engaged and alert, except for Ann, who seems to be bored.

[DATA:] She turns her eyes away from you and puts her hand to her mouth. She doesn't ask questions until you're done, and then suggests that the group should ask for a more expanded report.

[MEANINGS:] In this group, such a comment usually means the group should move to the next item on the agenda, and

[GROUP CONCLUSIONS:] everyone starts to do so.

[YOUR ASSUMPTIONS:] You think, "Ann must think I'm incompetent, which is a shame, because my ideas are just what she needs in her business."

[CONCLUSIONS:] In fact, she has never liked my ideas...she must hold a grudge against me for something."

[BELIEFS AND ACTION:] By the time you sit down again, you have decided you won't include anything in the report that she can use, justifying your behavior by the "fact" that she wouldn't read it, or even if she did may even use it against you.

The Ladder of Inference is a powerful tool in coaching. We (and our clients) move up the Ladder with lightening speed, usually unconsciously, and without questioning the assumptions we make and the meaning we attach to otherwise neutral behavior. And we are often reluctant to release our conclusions because, to us, they are based on "real data" and the "truth" is obvious, right?

As a Level 2 coach who understands the Ladder, we can inquire about and challenge assumptions by asking such questions as:
- [very direct approach] Ann, do you think I'm stupid?
- On what data do you base that conclusion?
- Have you noticed this behavior (in yourself or another) before? If so, did it always mean the same thing?
- What meaning did you attribute to the event or behavior when it first occurred?
- What other meanings are possible for this behavior?
- What conclusions did you draw about your meanings?
- What other conclusions could you draw?
- What beliefs do you hold (or need to hold) to keep this conclusion in place?
- What beliefs would you need to have in order to view this situation differently?
- Even if your belief was true, do you have other options for action steps here?

Espoused Theory vs. Theory in Use

An important aspect of Argyris' theory is the distinction between an individual's "espoused theory" (what they say is important to them) and their "theory-in-use" (what they actually do). Bringing these two into congruence is a primary focus of Level 2 coaching. The easiest way to think of this concept is to contrast someone you believe has integrity (what they say is the same as what they do) versus a hypocrite (what they do and what they say are two different things. Here are two examples from Argyris (1976, p. 16).

Example 1. A teacher who believes that she has a class of "stupid" students will communicate expectations such that the children behave stupidly. She confirms her theory by asking them questions and eliciting stupid answers or puts them in situations where they behave stupidly. The theory-in-use is self-fulfilling. (This principle has been referred to in psychology as the Pygmalion Effect.)

Example 2. A manager who believes his subordinates are passive, dependent and require authoritarian guidance rewards dependent and submissive behavior. He tests his theory by posing challenges for employees and eliciting dependent outcomes. In order to break this congruency, the teacher or manager would need to engage in open loop learning in which they deliberately disconfirm their theory-in-use.

What are the implications of these examples in career coaching? Quite simply, our beliefs about our clients, and their beliefs and assumptions about us and about the people and situations they encounter, greatly affect our coaching interactions. If we can get "unstuck" from those underlying conclusions and the beliefs they form, we can more consciously direct our mental energy to have more of what we want in our lives.

Figure 36 offers an example of Level 2 coaching from a real-life situation.

Figure 36: Coaching Example —Level 2 Coaching at Work

Jenny discussed with her coach her anxiety about an upcoming campaign meeting. She very much wanted to convey an attitude of power and confidence despite her slight appearance. In prior meetings with the campaign committee, her input as campaign manager was ignored. The meetings got off track as everyone put their own ideas on the table. To avoid a repeat occurrence, she planned to wear her power suit to the meeting, arrive early, and sit at the head of the table to be in control at the meeting.

Her coach noticed that the underlying issue was one of power and self-confidence, and asked Jenny "What's important about being in control and powerful here?" Despite feeling like the behavioral issues of what to wear and where to sit were the place to focus, Jenny agreed to reflect on the question. But instead of that question, she turned it around and asked, "What if power were not so important to me?" She determined that:

- She wouldn't have to stress about finding a clean blouse to wear with her power suit

> - She wouldn't care about control but instead would focus on working together to obtain positive outcomes, and
> - She would be much less stressed about the meeting and in general.
>
> The outcome? She wore jeans to the meeting, arrived late (not intentionally, but she didn't obsess about it), sat in a side chair instead of at the head of the table, listened to other people's suggestions and took notes, accepted constructive criticism of the plan she created, made adjustments to the plan and left the meeting with a smile! And as a post-script, her candidate won the election!

Level 2 Coaching Questions

- What's important about this to you?
- Where is your energy regarding this?
- What matters most to you?
- What's the meaning or significance of this for you?
- In what way are you attached to this?
- If there were one thing [you could do] to make a difference here, what would it be?
- How could you change the way you view this situation/ behavior?
- What are some other possible meanings/interpretations?
- What would have to happen for things to change?
- What am I unwilling to change?
- What would you have to believe in order to...?
- What do you have to let go of to...?
- If money [or time or the kids or...] weren't an issue, what would you say/do?
- What if that weren't The Truth?
- What's your motivation?
- What decision have you been avoiding?
- What choice have you been making that you could change now?
- What are you not willing to look at here?

Additional Level 2 Coaching Techniques

When we're working at Level 2, we are bringing the unconscious beliefs to consciousness. It's as though we're establishing a new habit or pattern of thinking. And like learning any new habit or skill, we need to marshal all of our mental, physical, emotional, spiritual and social resources in order to implement the change. Marshall Goldsmith, designated the Nation's #2 executive coach, refuses to work with an executive unless the entire team surrounding that executive will also give input at regular intervals and will fully participate in supporting the executive in making the changes he/she desires. We can learn from this principle!

The following techniques will augment our powerful questions and help move the Level 2 coaching process into a QuantumShift!™ in our clients:

1. **Visualization.** Most work in corporate America today draws primarily on the left brain: analytical processes, thinking (vs. feeling), logic and objectivity. To make changes in our beliefs and foundational assumptions, we need to invite the right brain (our creative, intuitive aspects) to participate too! An exercise we can suggest to our clients is for them to visualize themselves as though they have achieved their goal. Visualization is simply forming a mental picture (as though we were watching a movie) of our desired state and reinforcing it frequently (at least daily; hourly is better!). The most effective visualization is done when we are undistracted, quiet, undisturbed and focused. Sitting quietly with our eyes closed is best. Whether it is a guided meditation such as the Symbol Meditation in the Career Coach's Toolbox or reflecting on a positive image for the future in which the client embodies a desired state, visualization is one way of directing the mind to work with us to create change.

2. **Role Modeling.** Related to but slightly different from visualization is role modeling in which we find someone who exhibits the trait or who has made the change that we want to make. We then pattern ourselves after this person. He can be dead or alive, someone we know personally, have read about or have seen on the movie or television screen. What's

important is that in every respect, he embodies the change we want to make. Then, we can visualize or imagine that he is standing in front of us and as he turns his away from us there is a zipper down his back. We unzip the zipper, step into his skin, and experience the world through his eyes, ears and mind. What do we notice? This is a powerful exercise - be sure your client is ready for it!

3. **Affirmations.** Psychologists tell us that that it takes at least 21 days of consecutive repetition of a new behavior before we can say it has become a habit (that is, it has reached the level of unconsciousness where we don't have to think about doing it any more). Whether our client is trying to change a problematic behavior or find a more fulfilling job, affirmations - properly used! - will engage both the left and right brain as well and supply the power of synchronicity to create the desired state. An affirmation must:
    -   Be short (1 sentence is ideal)
    -   Be written in the present tense ("I am" vs. "I will")
    -   Be repeated several times each day

    One easy way to use affirmations is to write them on 3x5 cards or sticky-notes and put them on your bathroom and car mirror, desk, refrigerator, phone and anywhere else you will be regularly during the day. It can be as simple as "I am now moving toward my Ideal Job" to "I am now releasing anything that isn't exactly what I want."

4. **Support Group or Master Mind Team.** Let's face it: most of us won't make change if we're left on our own. We need to build some accountability into our change process! The Master Mind concept draws on the wisdom of Napoleon Hill and Jesus that when two or more people gather together with a common purpose (including a coach and client!), something greater emerges than the sum of the parts. A weekly meeting in person, over breakfast or lunch or via phone on a bridge line at which people celebrate each other's successes, articulate desired goals and support each other through challenges can make a big difference in each member's abilities to achieve their goals. You may want to sponsor such a group and charge each member a nominal fee to be part of a support or networking group that you facilitate to help them stay on

track! Alternatively, the client may wish to choose an "accountability partner" with whom they check in daily (and vice versa) to reinforce commitments to the goals.

5. **Meditation on a Power Question.** Many times, we can't reason our way out of our present state. Albert Einstein once said (paraphrasing) that we can't solve a problem in the same state of mind that created it. And often during the process of exploring a new career direction or making a personal change, taking action for the sake of "doing something" isn't appropriate. Meditating on a power question such as "What do I really want?" or "What do I want my life to mean?" - and staying in the question through the course of a week or two without having to come to a specific answer - can lead to some powerful insights. Even inquiring into the need for an answer can be helpful.

6. **Journaling.** One final practice that can be useful as clients are exploring Level 2 issues is free-form journaling. One of the best resources on this topic is Julia Cameron's *The Artist's Way*. Written for creative people who feel blocked, her concept of "morning pages" - writing 3 pages of rambling thoughts each morning and periodically reading back through them - will help increase our client's clarity about repeating patterns in their lives.

Key Coaching Concepts

1. Level 2 coaching works at the level of motivation, beliefs, assumptions, and interpretation to facilitate change.

2. Level 2 coaching does not do problem solving, focus on action steps, or inquire into the client's identity.

3. Chris Argryis' ladder of inference explains how observable data is distorted through a series of assumption-making and conclusion-drawing, ultimately becoming our unconscious beliefs about the world.

4. Traps in Level 2 coaching include using therapeutic techniques such as inventorying the past, focusing on the client's feelings instead of beliefs and being overly directive of the process.

5. Besides asking powerful questions, other Level 2 coaching techniques include visualization, role modeling, affirmations, support group, meditation on a power question and journaling.

The Role of Intuition and Deep Listening in Coaching

"Plotinus tells us that there are three ways by which we gather knowledge: through science, through opinion, and through intuition or illumination. These channels represent spiritual capacities since each is an avenue leading to self-knowingness, and self-knowingness is the very nature and essence of Spirit. Science is Spirit inducing Its own laws. Intuition is Spirit knowing Itself. Opinion is our estimate of Reality."

—Ernest Holmes
The Science of Mind

One of a coach's core competencies is listening to his/her intuition: "Accesses own intuition and trusts one's inner knowing - 'goes with the gut'" (ICF Competency 4b). However, the level of acceptability of a coach relying on his/her intuition, and even the commonly held definition of intuition, vary widely in different contexts.

Intuition: Practical Insight or Mystery?

Webster's Dictionary defines intuition as: "the capacity of knowing without the use of rational processes; keen insight." Of course, in the modern corporate world, knowing has traditionally only been valued if it were done with the use of rational processes. If we couldn't explain and document our knowing, it was discarded.

Thankfully, that is changing. Even as early as the 1980's, books such as *The Intuitive Manager* were being circulated among executives.

Laura Day's *Practical Intuition* has taken the mystery out of intuition - it is not the province of women or especially talented people only, but of people who take the time to recognize how intuition manifests for them. It is not a matter of either using intellect or intuition, but rather of combining both in a strategic way as the coaching interaction calls for it. Adding an awareness of your intuition to your coaching toolkit will enhance your effectiveness and, many times, will lead to the breakthroughs your clients are seeking.

How Intuition Manifests

Intuition is a very individual thing. While many (including psychologist Carl Jung) may suggest that our intuition is one way of tapping into the "collective consciousness" of mankind throughout the ages, each of us experiences it differently. Here are a few of the means through which it emerges - do you know which ones characterize your unique intuition?

- We may have passing thoughts or images in waking hours - often seemingly unrelated to what is being said by the client
- Dreams may represent a message the intuition is trying to give us about an individual issue
- We may feel a physical sensation, such as tingling, tension, heat or cold in a part of the body, etc.
- We may just "feel it in our gut" that something is "not quite right" or is "out of sync" with what's being said - or conversely, that it is in sync and authentic
- Aha's; or, sudden realizations may occur often at seemingly the wrong time

Intuition or Your Own Agenda?

Confusing the issue somewhat is the fact that it isn't always clear whether or not you are acting on intuition or from a personal objective. There are no hard and fast rules to know the difference, but it is a matter of gaining experience with your own intuition and having the courage to follow it. Some indicators that an impression is *not* intuition are:

- If the proposed idea or solution would harm anyone else, or be done at their expense
- If the insight is the "logical" answer

- If it is a rationalization
- If you're not client-focused
- If you've thought it out too much
- If it's a personal projection or a personal prejudice

On the other hand, intuition often:
- Doesn't make logical sense
- May contemplate something that you would not have thought of naturally
- Urges you to take some little step (e.g., call Joe or drive home a different way than usual), without your knowing where that step will lead
- Has an element of trust, a leap of faith
- Comes to you, you don't go to it

Knowing When to Share Intuitive Insights

Once you have a flash of intuition, as a coach you must then decide what to do with it. Do you share it? If so, how? When should you not? The answer may depend on the nature of the hunch. If, for example, you suddenly got an image of one person abusing another as a client was talking, that would be much more sensitive to raise than simply an insight into the client's emotional or motivational underpinnings of the issue being discussed.

We also need to be aware of the client's mental and emotional state. If he/she is relatively fragile, we may be less likely to share significant insights than if they are strong. But on the other hand, it may be your intuitive sense that helps the client move to a position of strength. Again it is an individual decision which depends on the overall situation.

If you do decide to share, it is best to "check out" our sense with the client to see if you are on track. You might say, "I'm getting a sense that... Does that resonate with you?" The client will know immediately whether or not that issue has relevance to what the he/she is discussing.

Deep Listening

In Chapter 22, we introduced the Reflective Model of Elaboration as a variation on Active Listening, one of our core competencies. We will now introduce a more advanced form of listening called Deep Listening. In this methodology, the coach tests assumptions, heeds intuitive hunches and draws distinctions between fact and interpretation of fact.

Figure 37 on page 244 compares Active Listening (Level 1) with Deep Listening (Level 2). After reviewing that chart, consider the following exercise:

> EXAMPLE: Which of the statements in the scenario that follows are facts? Which are interpretations of facts? How would you approach the situation differently if you were listening from Level 1 vs. Level 2?
>
> Question/Situation: Susie went to Coach John because she wanted to change jobs. Her company's profit margins had deteriorated from positive to negative in the past 6 months, and she was afraid that they would be laying people off soon. She said to John, "I just know that I'll be the first to go, since I was just hired 6 months ago when everything was going fine." As she did so, her voice got very soft, almost teary. She then launched into a long story about her best friend Jill and how Jill's company treated her when they started having financial problems. "I know that if it can happen to Jill - and she's an overachiever if I ever saw one - that it could happen to me too. I'd better get my resume updated and start sending some of them out."
>
> Answers/Facts: Deterioration of profit margins, that she was hired six months ago, and that she wants to change jobs. Interpretations: afraid she'd be laid off soon; that how Jill's company treated her was equivalent; Jill may not have actually been treated poorly; and the fact that she's an overachiever may also be an interpretation. Level 2 listening would ask: what's important about the friend being an overachiever. Is that true? How does she know what process will be used in deciding who will be laid off?

Level 2 Techniques to Augment Questioning

Much of coaching involves asking powerful questions to help increase the client's awareness, clarity, and well-being. But other

Contrasting Level 1 vs. Level 2 Listening	
Level 1(Active)	Level 2 (Deep)
Takes facts at face value	Listens beneath/beyond the facts to discern espoused theory vs. theory in use
Focuses on problem-solving right away, generating options for solutions	Focuses on testing assumptions beneath facts, bringing unconscious beliefs to awareness - and only then generating options for solutions
Active listening: "Summarizes, paraphrases, reiterates, mirrors back what client has said to ensure clarity and understanding" (ICF Competencies)	Goes beyond active listening to "deep" listening: "Distinguishes between the words, the tone of voice, and the body language"; "Helps clients to see the different, interrelated factors that affect them and their behaviors (e.g., thoughts, emotions, body, background)" (ICF Competencies)
Stays with client's perspective on the situation	Seeks openings which will shift client's perspective, perhaps to the other person/people involved in client's situation, to someone with different beliefs or thinking patterns, or a meta-perspective
Asks client to choose among several options	Asks client to see themes and underlying patterns among a set of options or behaviors

techniques, stemming from Level 2 listening, can also be have impact, including:

Bottom-lining

So-called "bottom-lining" is defined by the ICF as "understand[ing] the essence of the client's communication and help[ing] the client get there rather than engaging in long descriptive stories." This skill calls for not only the ability to listen deeply for this "essence" level of communication, but also for the confidence to interrupt the client's story to short-cut the process. The skillful coach will preview this possibility with the client during their initial session(s) so that the client will not view this technique as rude or disrespectful. Bottom-lining can allow the coaching to be done more quickly. It keeps the client from rambling about things that take up time but do not move the coaching forward.

Providing Feedback

Feedback often has a negative connotation, as in "May I give you some feedback?" (as you grit your teeth and wait!). When we facilitate the coaching practice sessions for our coaches in training at Career Coach Institute, we are careful to balance positive comments with suggestions for improvement. That allows the coaches to hold the idea of feedback in a more neutral way than they may have otherwise. Feedback may consist of observations, intuitive insights and other statements you make to the client regarding what he/she shared. Of course, you can only give meaningful feedback if you are listening carefully, making connections among the client's statements and doing some interpreting of what the client says.

The inherent risk in giving feedback is that it's easy to impose your own meaning on the client's statements in a way that is not in alignment with his/her meaning. You must be sure to get his/her response and to ensure that he/she doesn't say "yes that's true" just to please the coach.

Exploring Stretch Goals or Challenges

There may be times when your deep listening reveals an apparent barrier in the client's perception. She may not believe she can make any more than x number of phone calls in a week, or she may have become accustomed to working at a level of performance that is beneath her capability. This often happens when a client is not in an their Authentic Vocation™ and feels unable to bring her "whole self" to the work.

When you sense this may be limiting the client's perception of options and possibilities or even sabotaging her ability to advance in her career, you can explore with the client the possibility of a stretch goal which challenges her to a new level of performance, risk-taking or commitment. Stretch goals should challenge the client beyond her current comfort level but not be so aggressive as to set her up for failure. Just like the goals in the client's coaching plan, the stretch goal should be "just out of reach, but not out of sight." If the client's goal was to begin an exercise program, an appropriate goal would be to go to the gym three times a week and spend 20 minutes on the treadmill; an inappropriate goal would be to run a marathon in 45 days.

Discerning Subtleties of Client Communication

Another alternative to questioning focuses on discernment. "Discerning" is simply making distinctions between such things as:

- Words vs. tone of voice
- Stated vs. real priorities
- Stated vs. actual values
- Facts vs. interpretations
- Words vs. meanings
- Thoughts vs. feelings vs. actions
- Foreground vs. background
- Trivial vs. significant issues
- Situational vs. recurring behaviors
- Immediate vs. long-term goals/needs/issues

We might do this by providing feedback, sharing observations, or asking questions such as "Is it x or y?" or "Are you saying...?"

"Between the Lines" Issues

In our experience with career coaching clients, there are a few "classic" issues that you are likely to encounter as you listen deeply to the client's needs. Following are a few examples and some strategies for addressing them.

> **Guilt/not deserving/self-criticism** - The client feels like he should have done something to avoid being laid off or that he doesn't deserve more than a certain (under market) salary - or even that he doesn't deserve to do work he loves! Even if these beliefs do not serve us, we often hold hard and fast to them because

they are comfortable - and often, they have been with us much of our lives!

To address this challenging issue, it is critical first to ask if the client is willing to explore and face it (competency 3f: "Asks permission to coach client in sensitive, new areas)." If so, asking the client what he is giving up or losing out on by holding these beliefs (maybe even having him write this out), as well as what alternative beliefs might serve him better, he will then often become open to changing this beliefs. That process is most often done through:

- repetition of a short affirmation (e.g., "I deserve to be fulfilled in my work"), said with emotion;

- visualization how doing fulfilling work would look, feel, and be;

- using "the witness" by which we imagine we are observing ourselves from the outside, noticing when we engage in behavior that acts like we don't deserve x, and slowly but surely catching ourselves until we can integrate the new beliefs and, in turn, behaviors; and/or

- writing out a dialog between the Internal Critic and the grounded or Authentic Self. Writing the statements down makes them seem sometimes silly, inappropriate, or downright incorrect, which allows the client to begin to choose the inner dialog in which he/she wishes to engage.

Perfectionism/workaholism. Whenever a client exhibits extraordinarily high standards for himself, including long work hours, little or no vacation, work on weekends and holidays and/or difficulties with finding time for self or family, the coach should inquire as to whether the client is engaging in workaholism. Much recent research has been done to distinguish workaholics from people who work with passion (and may also work long hours). Key differentiating factors are that those working with passion may work overtime or weekends but also have a happy family life, are aware of appropriate boundaries between work and home/personal life and are actually very happy with their lives. Workaholics live for the recognition for their overworking, often engaging in overwork to escape an unhappy family life or difficult personal issues. For more on this topic, see *Working Ourselves to Death* by Diane Fassel and similar books. The workaholic may need therapy (either instead or in conjunction with coaching) to address the mental and emotional issues that underlie this addictive behavior, so a referral should be considered.

If, on the other hand, perfectionistic tendencies have led the client to work harder than they need to simply to meet their own high standards, coaching techniques can be very helpful.

- Ask the client to define success
- Query "How do you know when you have done or accomplished enough?"
- Probe the client's openness to having different standards for different projects
- Inquire into the client's desired balance between work and personal life

Fear. Fear is, of course, a normal reaction to any new experience as well as to any change or transition that takes us into uncharted territory (i.e., outside our comfort zone). What most of us tend to do is resist fear or try to ignore it. It's as though we see it as a "monster in the closet," and hope if we just ignore it long enough, it will die or disappear. What happens instead is that it occupies a lot of our mental energy and distracts us from our daily activities - not to mention that it holds us back from doing what we need to do in order to grow!

The secret to dealing with fear is to face it. As Susan Jeffers' book title states, *Feel the Fear and Do*

It Anyway.   In fact, we encourage you to take your clients even further than that: embrace the fear! Asking a question such as "What if this fear were a friend - what would it want you to know?" Or "What is the message in the fear?" Our bodies and minds are wise and we normally won't feel fear unless there is some good reason for it. Rather than let it stop us, we can face it, dialog with it and "get" the message it wants us to hear. After having considered the best case/worst case scenarios, we can help then move forward into the unfamiliar action step or transition that the fear is there to warn us about.

Career as identity.   Contrary to the popular statement, we are *not* what we do. Men and women moving up the rungs of corporate responsibility frequently feel as though they have lost their identities when they lose their jobs. Some probing coaching questions can reveal the fallacy in this way of thinking:

- Who were you before you were a [vice president]?
- What characteristics do you have that do not depend on work for expression?
- Who is the you that is asking these questions?

Have the client talk to some of his/her friends about how they view the client. It can be very revealing, and may even raise some career possibilities the client has not considered.

Key Coaching Concepts

1. Intuition can be defined as "the capacity of knowing without the use of rational processes; keen insight."
2. Intuition can manifest in many ways, each of which is unique to the individual. However, intuition will never suggest that one person harm another.
3. Deep Listening is an advanced listening skill beyond Active Listening or the Reflective Model.
4. Some techniques to augment Deep Listening include bottom-lining, providing feedback, setting stretch goals, and discernment.
5. Some common "between the lines" issues among career coaching clients include guilt/not deserving, perfectionism, fear, and career as identity.

25 LEVEL 3 COACHING

"For self is a sea boundless and measureless.
Say not, 'I have found the truth,' but rather, 'I have found a
   truth.'
Say not, 'I have found the path of the soul." Say rather, 'I
   have met the soul walking upon my path.'
For the soul walks upon all paths.
The soul walks not upon a line, neither does it grow like a
   reed.
The soul unfolds itself, like a lotus of countless petals."

—Kahlil Gibran
The Prophet

Level 3 is the highest level of the Ladder of Inference. Here, we explore how to clarify and transform one's very identity, the self as it expresses in the world. As the quote above illustrates, often what we have believed to be "the truth" about ourselves turns out to be just "a truth," one of may possible ways of viewing who we are. When a shift happens at Level 3, the client's beliefs and behaviors then tend to change automatically as a result. A parallel can be made with a computer:

> Level 1 is like the output a software program produces (e.g., a font in a document).
> Level 2 is like the software program itself (e.g. the default settings for a document that are automatically applied to every document created).

Level 3 is like the operating system, such as Windows, which is "hard wired" to impose certain features on documents created in any program. If a change is made at this level, it automatically impacts the software program and the output from the program. For example, the Windows operating system requires that margins be less than 7 inches, no amount of trying to adjust margins in Word, Excel, Power Point or other Windows-based programs will result in margins wider than 7 inches. This would also govern any documents generated by the programs. However, if we were to change the command structure within Windows to allow any size margins the user wanted, the other programs would automatically adjust, resulting in a change in how the documents printed.

What Level 3 Coaching Does:
- Inquires into identity
- Questions beliefs the person holds about him/herself
- Seeks personal transformation
- Asks about why something is important (especially a personal trait)

What Level 3 Coaching Doesn't Do:
- Try to improve performance
- Focus on observable data
- Lead to specific action steps
- Prioritize goals and actions to be taken - except regarding core beliefs about self

Premises of Level 3 Coaching:
- The objective is to change the person's very identity, who he sees himself to be.
- Personal transformation is the focus.
- Level 3 coaching does not problem-solve; to the extent it deals with beliefs, they are beliefs about the person him/herself, not the situation.

Level 3 Coaching Techniques

Figure 38 contains an addition to the Ladder of Inference from Chapter 23 that shows where Level 3 enters. Remember, we begin at the bottom and work up. Building on our beliefs (6th rung), we form our self-concept. That is the basis for our actions.

Figure 38: Ladder of Inference - Level 3

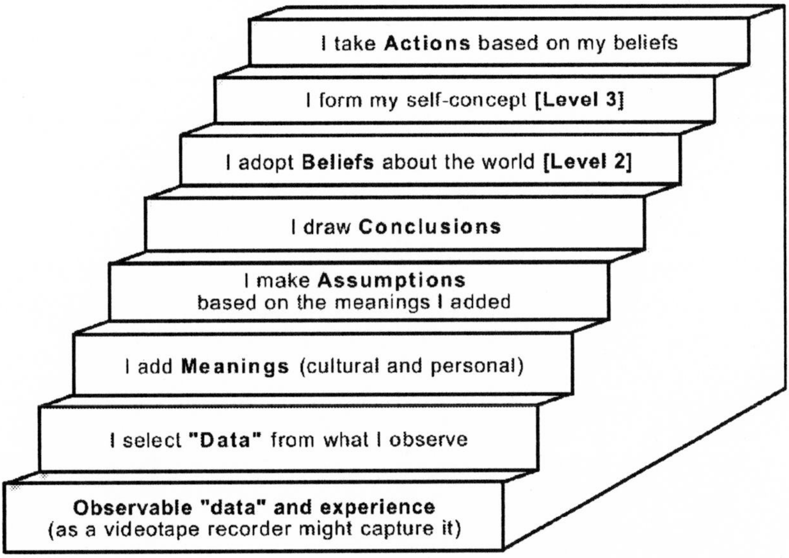

Often, as we are coaching clients, we (or they) will realize that they have internalized an aspect of themselves - from an observable life experience - that is not accurate (and probably never was!).

It can be confusing to differentiate between Level 2 and Level 3 issues. Some of the important features of Level 3 issues are:

- They go beyond beliefs about how the world works to beliefs about oneself
- They often bring up emotion
- They may be deep-seated, therefore the client may hang onto them and defend his/her position!
- They can often be stated by beginning with "I am a person who..." or "I am the kind of person who..."
- They may have been true at one time (e.g. in childhood) but are now inaccurate, irrelevant, or need to be changed to match current reality

- They may create pain
- The client may see the characteristic or principle as the "only way" to be; coaching and/or assessments can reveal others
- Because of the depth of Level 3 issues, the transformation may take some time to internalize - but when the QuantumShift!™ happens, it is obvious!
- It could be a blind spot that the coach can see more clearly than the client.

See how you do coaching a Level 3 issue in the following example:

Example/Situation: Dave shares that his challenge is having too many projects going. He says he always seems to be that way. Asked how long it's been an issue, he says "forever." He believes what's needed is better prioritization. However, upon further inquiry, it seems that the issue has more to do with his inability to say "no." What might the Level 3 aspect of this issue be? Start with "I am a person who..."

Answers: I am a person who doesn't turn people down; I'm a person who needs to please everyone; I am a person who wants to be liked; I say yes because I don't want to miss out on any opportunities; I am a person who is good at starting things but cannot follow through, etc.

     To continue coaching Dave, we would first bring these issues to conscious awareness; then determine whether or not he wants to change. If so, we ask what beliefs he wishes to hold instead: what would a person who felt they had the right amount of work for them embrace? We then work to shift the client's beliefs (see section on Transforming Beliefs below).

Traps in Level 3 Coaching; What It Is Not

Issues of style or personality type can be confused with Level 3 issues. For example, someone whose type according to the Myers-Briggs Type Indicator® assessment is ISTJ (introverted, sensing, thinking, judging) may state that he struggles with an extreme need for structure and organization. With the MBTI®, simply opening his perspective to the strengths and characteristics of that type and of others with similar preferences may allow him to soften his approach in some situations. However, this may or may not be a true Level 3 issue, depending on whether he believes his style is the only way he can be, or whether he can choose. The degrée of attachment to the behavior or how stuck a person is in that behavior will help determine whether it is a Level 3 issue or not.

Dealing with Level 3 issues is not therapy. Most therapy will explore the depths of the past - including childhood and even birth experiences - to find the root of the issue. Coaching generally doesn't go into the past. Instead coaching finds leverage for change in the present. We might ask, "How is the issue causing pain or holding you back from your desired life?" "What would the benefit or payoff be to be different?"

Coaches who become concerned when the client displays emotion or raises long-standing issues stemming from childhood are often afraid that they will uncover more than they can handle. We will discuss handling strong emotions in the next chapter. But as with Level 2, we need to keep our focus on staying neutral by inviting the client to explore her reactions, and asking her how she wants to move forward. This will keep us in the coaching role and empower the client to leverage the experience to her benefit.

Level 3 Coaching Questions

- Who would you have to become in order to x?
- What kind of person would act that way?
- What could have made you do/say that?
- What if [pleasing people] wasn't necessary/wasn't important?
- What would happen if you [said no]?
- What is your ultimate goal?
- How long has this been an issue for you? [If they say "all my life" or "forever", chances are it's a Level 3 issue] When did this start?
- Is that the only way to view yourself, or are there others?
- What's beneath those beliefs/that behavior?
- What would you need to believe about yourself in order to be [a loving person]?
- How would your life change if you became more [loving]?
- If you believed y about yourself, how would that change your behavior in this situation?

- What's beneath x [e.g. the over-commitment? Or the lack of confidence?]
- What is it that you're really committed/attached to here? Is that what you want?

Transforming Level 3 Beliefs

Level 3 questions are powerful in how they reveal identity issues to the client. Then comes the follow-up task of integrating the desired transformation. Once the client raises an issue of identity, it can be helpful to list the beliefs that support that identity. Often, one core belief may have many other beliefs connected to it.

Directly opposite that, the client can list the beliefs that would characterize a person who had the desired trait. For example, if someone felt they always had to please people, like Dave in the example above. Figure 39 illustrates the beliefs Dave could move toward.

Figure 39: Old Versus New Beliefs

Current Belief	Opposite/Future Belief
If I say yes, people will like me.	If I say no, people will honor my integrity and boundaries.
I must please everyone in my life, at all costs.	I can't please everyone in my life; I will act in congruity with what's right for me.
I'm not enough, doing things defines who I am.	My being-ness defines who I am; I am enough.
If I do enough different things, I'll fool people into thinking I'm successful and I don't have to worry about failing.	I can trust myself to excel at what I choose.

To integrate these beliefs will require consistent repetition through affirmations, visualization and similar processes we described at the end of chapter 23. Often, simply becoming aware of the broad-based impacts of the belief causes an immediate QuantumShift!™ Other times it takes days or weeks to completely embrace the new beliefs as part of one's identity.

Key Coaching Concepts:

1. Level 3 coaching works at the level of identity to facilitate transformation. It adds another rung to the ladder of inference: our self-concept.

2. Level 3 coaching does not problem-solve, focus on action steps, or inquire into the client's assumptions about the situation itself. Level 3 does inquire about the client's beliefs about himself as it relates to his current challenge.

3. Traps in Level 3 coaching include mistakenly characterizing type or personality issues as Level 3 issues (though sometimes they are!) and fearing to get into the realm of therapy with Level 3 coaching.

4. Besides asking powerful questions, Level 3 coaching should articulate the desired beliefs or state of mind the client wants to move toward. It also includes repetition to integrate those beliefs into the client's identity.

26

ADVANCED
COACHING SKILLS

"When you do not understand what a person is saying, do not grasp for every word. Give up your efforts. Become silent inside and listen with your deepest self...To know what is happening, push less, open out and be aware. See without staring. Listen quietly rather than listening hard. Use intuition and reflection rather than trying to figure things out. The more you can let go of trying, and the more open and receptive you become, the more easily you will know what is happening."

—John Heider,
Tao of Leadership

Progressing in expertise as a coach is not usually a linear process. It is not necessarily true, therefore, that someone who has been coaching 10 years is better at it than someone who has been coaching for 5 years. But if the coach has continued to learn and grow, using the self-awareness building process of "listening quietly rather than listening hard" as described above, she will continually become better at what she does.

This chapter explores 7 key coaching skills that add nuances to the use of the basic QuantumShift™ Coaching model we have described thus far. These are:

- Shifting perspective
- Identifying and eliminating self-defeating behaviors
- Handling strong emotions

- Powerful questioning
- Clear communication
- Celebrating successes, and
- Maintaining client focus

Shifting Perspective

The dictionary defines perspective as "...(b) a mental view of the relationship of aspects of a subject to each other and to a whole; (c) an idea of the relative importance of things." Both definitions are relevant in the coaching context. In Level 2 coaching, we examine the relationship of subject to object by testing to see if the client can separate themselves (the subject) from the people and situations in their lives (the object), and even from their beliefs and assumptions. And in all levels of coaching, we explore the relative importance of priorities: which of the options will lead to the best result? Which of those assumptions is most important in making this decision? Which will you choose? Which is most accurate?

Figure 40 provides some examples of opposing or complementary perspectives.

Coaching Questions to Shift Perspective

In helping a client shift his perspective, we first ask questions to identify their current perspective. Then, we test to see if he can also articulate other people's views or other filters through which he might look at the situation. Here are some sample questions to ask for this purpose:

- If you were x [the other person in the situation], what would they want/feel/need/say?
- If they say they're stuck:
  - "What's important about getting unstuck?"
  - "If you were advising yourself, what would you suggest to get unstuck?"
  - "How is it perfect for you to feel stuck right now?"
  - "If you weren't stuck, what might a step be..."
- If you were the coach, what question would you ask right now?
- What powerful question would your Wise Self ask right now?
- If that weren't true, what else could it be?

Figure 40: Sample Perspectives

Short-term .... Long-term
Immediate .... Distant
Limitation .... Possibility
Weakness .... Strength
Big picture .... Current issue
Behavior .... Motivation
Motivation .... Identity
Who you are .... Who you could be
People .... Things
Individual .... Family
Monocultural .... Multicultural/diverse
Black and white .... Shades of gray
Right and wrong .... Situational ethics
National .... Global
Selfish .... Selfless
Visual .... Auditory
Analytical .... Intuitive
Constant problems .... Lessons to be learned
Me .... Them
Challenge .... Opportunity
Old .... Young
Male .... Female
Conservative .... Progressive
Positive .... Negative
Small .... Large
Pessimistic .... Optimistic
Limited .... Unlimited

* Notice too that that our levels of coaching are themselves perspectives!

- What if x wasn't so important to you?
- How does that serve your life purpose?
- How else could you view this situation?
- What would you do if you knew you couldn't fail?
- Is there a broader perspective here?
- You've talked about yourself; what about them [the others involved]?
- I hear your analytical self speaking; what does your intuition say?
- What if you gave up your "script" around this?
- If you didn't have to blame x, what else might be possible?
- What's beneath the [stress, fear, guilt, etc.]? If it weren't that, what else could it be?

Other Perspective-Shifting Techniques

In addition to these powerful perspective-shifting questions, at least two other techniques can also help the client see a situation from another vantage point.

1. **Reframing.** When a client makes a statement reflecting a particular perspective, reframing through the use of a perspective-shifting question can create an immediate shift, as in:

    Client: "I just don't know how I'll make next month's mortgage payment."
    Coach: What could you do to stop living month-to-month?

    Client: "I'm just too stubborn to work for someone else."
    Coach: How could your stubbornness be used as an asset? [e.g. as an entrepreneur]

    Client: "It just seems like I can either make good money or do work I enjoy."
    Coach: How could you have both?

2. **Feedback.** By simply stating what you observe, the client may see the absurdity or "stuckness" of what they're saying. To take feedback one step further, use it to communicate a broader perspective that inspires the client to make a shift. The first example in the previous section illustrates how this can be done. A broader perspective is just one kind of "new" perspective, but it is critical that as you listen to your clients you mentally step back to see whether there might be a larger aspect to what they're saying. This kind of "dancing in the moment" demonstrates yet another of our coaching competencies. We must learn to be both present and flexible to help facilitate transformation in our clients.

Identifying and Eliminating Self-Defeating Behaviors

Nearly all of us engage in activities each day that either waste our time or drain our energy. The problem is, we're often unaware of them, but we tolerate them day in and day out and wonder why we aren't making faster progress toward our goals!

If a client either raises this issue or you suspect that it may provide an opportunity for her to reduce her stress level, perhaps the best way to identify these activities is to have the client keep a log of all of her activities for at least a week on a time log. Initially, she should just list the time of day and what she is doing. It should go from awakening in the morning until she goes to bed at night. Then, at day's end, she can come back and evaluate her activities to determine what was time or energy well spent, and what was not.

It is often amazingly clear from this exercise what is getting in the way of the client's fulfilling their career, job change, or other professional (or personal!) goals. Sometimes, the people we spend time with can be what wastes our time and/or drains our energy, so we want our clients to be on the lookout for that, as well as behaviors and activities!

Eliminating one behavior by itself is not enough, though, since it leaves an empty space or vacuum that must be replaced with another that is in alignment with one's purpose, goals and intention. This is because physics tells us "the universe abhors a vacuum." So the next step is to encourage your client to identify what actions or behaviors, however small or seemingly insignificant, would contribute to her being more focused, more on purpose, and with more time and energy available to fulfill her goals. She can then track how many days during a month she engages in that behavior, and keep another time log after working with the new behavior for a while to see if there are fewer time-wasting and energy-draining activities.

Even the stories the client tells during the coaching session may be time wasters. When this happens, see if you can cut to the essence of it by "bottom-lining":

- "What are you saying here?"
- "Can you summarize your point in telling this story?"
- "I just want to check in and see if this is how you want to spend your coaching time today, or if we could get to the point and do some further exploration."

Handling Strong Client Emotions

Periodically during our coaching experience, strong emotions such as fear, anger, frustration, tears, sadness and pain will arise in the client.

Depending on how comfortable we are personally with expressing emotion, this situation may be something we approach with ease or trepidation. Factoring in our client's comfort level makes the situation more complex yet!

What's important to realize about strong emotions is that they are communicating important information to the client. An effective coach will have developed the ability to be present with the client even during these times, knowing that working through the emotions will help them transform.

What Not to Do When Strong Emotions Arise
- Ignore them
- Ask the client why they feel that way [We don't need to know the cause of the feeling, but simply help the client embrace it.]
- Tell the client they shouldn't feel that way
- Tell them they should see a therapist (unless it keeps happening, of course, and they can't meaningfully participate in coaching)
- Encourage the client to bury, ignore, submerge or hide their feelings (from you or themselves)
- Confuse the client's emotions with your own issues, or get caught up in them

Strategies for Coaching When Strong Emotions Arise

Instead, try one or more of the following techniques:
- Mirror the client's intensity, pace, breathing and language - and then notice how it makes you feel, and what it tells you about the client's energy level and emotional state
- Focus more on simply "being there" with the client, rather than "doing" something or moving them to an "action plan"
- Since the client's typical desire is to avoid the emotions - and what lies beneath them - part of your role is to help them embrace (and even welcome!?) the emotions and include them in the experience of their life. You can even to encourage them to go deeper into the emotion and explore it with questions like:

- *"I sense that some powerful emotions are coming up. Can you describe them?"*
- *"What are you not willing to explore?"*
- *"Where do you feel this in your body? What does it feel like?"*
- *"Let's stay with that for a moment. Can you turn the volume [on the emotion or experience] up a notch? What do you notice?" [Then, when they are ready, turn the volume down and ask them what they're taking away]*
- *"What message is this emotion [or experience] telling you?"*
- *"What is the gift in this emotion?"*
- *"What would happen if [you did what you fear most]?"*
- *"What would you miss out on if you ignored this message?"*

- Notice whether the emotions seem to be about the conflict between a client's stated goal or desire (e.g. to lose weight - their espoused theory) and their actual behavior (overeating - their theory in use). Exploring that and asking the client whether that conflict is part of the issue can help the client voice what they're feeling.
- Use a metaphor to help the client see the emotions from a higher perspective:
- Ask the client to imagine they're floating above their situation and to share what they see
- Ask them to imagine that the situation is a lake into which they dive and swim around, exploring all aspects of the landscape/situation
- "Imagine that you could rewrite your life from here on, free of the deep issue beneath these emotions. What would be different?"
- If this were an animal, what would it be?
- Use humor (judiciously) - help the client laugh at their own situation
- Ask the client if they would like to go and get a glass of water (while you wait on the line) and come back to the call

Powerful Questioning

Asking questions in coaching is only powerful when we bring a sense of artistry to it, rather than a mechanical approach. This difference is more felt than described, more perceived than observed. The same element is obvious among students learning to play an instrument: some simply press the keys in a mechanical fashion as dictated by the musical score, where others make the instrument absolutely sing as they bring expression, soul, and feeling to the music.

We know a powerful question when we hear one - and sometimes when we ask one! But what is it about a question that makes it powerful?

- **Judgmental vs. non-judgmental:** One key to powerful questions is whether or not they contain judgment. It's the difference between "Why can't you do x as well as Sally?" and "How do you see the situation?" (Leading questions tend to do contain judgments.)

- **Short vs. long:** The more concise a question is, the less the possibility that it will contain judgment, include your own meaning-making/agenda, and/or confuse the client. If you tend to think aloud, you may frame the question as you talk, ending up with one long question or two or three questions in one. Instead, pause to take a breath, determine what you want to ask, and ask it simply and concisely. You'll be surprised how much it improves your coaching!

- **Open- vs. closed-ended:** Even in Level 1 coaching, we have learned to focus on asking open-ended questions to generate as many options as possible to resolve the client's issue. Closed-ended questions (those that can be answered "yes" or "no") tend to be weak, whereas open-ended questions have power in them.

   EXAMPLE: "Did you notice how he talked down to you?" (closed) versus "What did you notice?" (open)

- **Blaming/victim vs. empowerment :** Questions that bemoan the client's fate tend to look into the past and do not forward the session. Remember that as a coach your job is not to analyze the client's behavior! Instead, if you can ask a question that empowers the client to look at the present and the future. Examples are shown in Figure 41.

- Ask questions that include the client's language and/or communication style: Using your knowledge of the client's communication style (in neurolinguistic programming terms, visual, auditory, kinesthetic, or auditory-digital - see Figure 42 for details), you can reframe your question to fit their style.

Figure 41: Two Types of Questions

Blaming/Victim	Empowerment
Why do you think you did that?	What lesson can you take forward for next time this happens?
What did your parents teach you about this?	What do you want your philosophy or governing principle to be here?
Why can't I seem to find jobs I like?	What would your ideal job be like?
Why am I so afraid to take a risk?	How can you embrace the message in your fear as a catalyst for forward action?

Figure 42: Understanding Communication Styles Using NLP – Neuro Linguistic Programming Processing Order (Representation System)

	VISUAL	AUDITORY	KINESTHETIC	AUDITORY (DIGITAL)
Common Characteristics	They memorize by seeing pictures. They often have trouble remembering verbal instructions because their mind tends to wander.	They typically are easily distracted by noise. They can repeat things back to you easialy, learn by listening, like music, and like to talk on the phone.	They often talk slowly. They respond to physical rewards, and touching. They memorize by doing or walking through something.	This person spends a fair amount of time talking to themselves. They memorize by steps, procedures, and sequences.
Describing to them	They are interested by how the program looks	Tone of voice and the words used are important	They will be interested in a program that 'feels right' /"gut-feelings".	They will want to know if your program makes sense
Commonly used words	See Look Appear View Show Imagine Crystalize	Hear Listen Sound Tune in/out Click Ring a bell	Feel Touch Touch base Get hold of Comfortable Catch on Play, Together	Sense Experience Understand Think Process Decide I Know

	VISUAL	AUDITORY	KINESTHETIC	AUDITORY (DIGITAL)
Speech Pattern	Quickly grouped words	Lots of interruptions and 'uh', 'um', 'ah', etc	Deliberate phrasing	Long complicated sentences
Processing Patterns	Quickly with minimum of detail	Will let you know unconsciously when they understand by changing the subject	Extensive detail	Will not give indication of understanding unless you ask
Their Gifts	• Big Picture • Organized • Great planners • Get things done quickly • Great sellers • Visionaries	• Big Picture • Brilliant ideas • Little/no details • Inventors • Born leaders • Quality work • Good story tellers • Love telephone	• Love details • Creative • Work well with others • Patient • Loyal or devoted • Sensitive to people and environment • Supportive	• Problem solvers • Talent for 'figuring' it out • Work fast • Likes behind-the-scenes • Project planner

(c) Copyright 2002 All rights reserved Linda Storey
http://www.EveryDaySoulWorks.com

EXAMPLE: "How does that sound to you?"   is auditory;
        You could reframe it as:
"How does that look to you?" ·   Visual
"How does that feel to you?"   Kinesthetic
"What does that mean to you?"   Auditory-digital

- **Bypass rephrasing and go directly to the question you want to ask next:** Though as a beginning coach you may have tended to do a lot of rephrasing or reflecting of what the client was saying (using the Reflective Model), now you can be more directive. When tempted to say "So what you're saying is..." or "So what I'm hearing you say your options are is...," simply ask the question that would follow that statement for a more powerful question.
- **Use the optimum timing:** The right question asked at the wrong time becomes inappropriate, rather than powerful. How do you know when to ask a question? It's a combination

of listening to your intuition, deeply listening to what the client is saying, and determining why you are asking the question. Are you seeking to enhance the client's awareness, or do you need to know the answer for yoursself? Remember, "It's all about them" - your agenda does not enter into the coaching process. Experience is also part of this, and the more we are "in the flow" with the client, the less we will need to consciously be aware of timing because it will naturally be right. Trying to plan questions will throw the timing off.

- **Ask permission to coach in a sensitive area:** They may state this verbally ("I don't want to talk about x") or they may simply become resistant, change the subject, or otherwise nonverbally tell you that they're uncomfortable. Certainly, whenever we explore Level 2 or 3 issues there will be a level of discomfort - but we need to ask the client's permission to walk through the door of behavior to motive, beliefs, interpretation, and identity. This might take one of the following forms:
  - **"Do I have your permission to explore that area?"**
  - **"Would you like to go deeper into that issue now?"**
  - **"How would you feel about seeing what else is there regarding that issue?"**
  - **"I notice there may be some resistance; are you willing to explore it?"**

The Flow of Powerful Questions

Combining all of the elements above, we will now explore how to formulate powerful questions. How do we know that our questions are enhancing the self-awareness, purpose, effectiveness and overall life quality of our client? (If these sound familiar, they're our four desired career coaching outcomes.) And how do we continue to use questions, along with other coaching techniques such as feedback, observations, challenges, and role modeling, to further that awareness? The diagram in Figure 43 illustrates the use of un-powerful (weak) questions, which elicit "scripts" (the same old answer) instead of QuantumShifts!™

Figure 43: Unpowerful Questioning

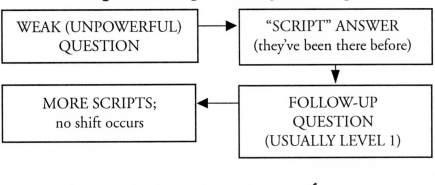

Contrast the process of powerful questioning. The client often pauses to "process" or reflect following the question. When encouraged to share more, an insight follows, and the process is repeated. At one of these levels, the client realizes a pattern and/or shifts their beliefs or perception. Voila—the QuantumShifts!™

Figure 44: Powerful Questioning

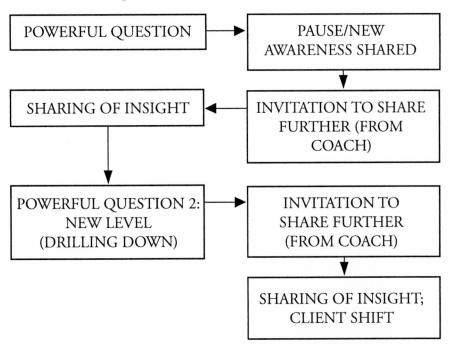

Clear Communication

Our coaching competencies make reference to several characteristics of clear and direct communication: direct feedback (which we have discussed), reframing and introducing other perspectives (also discussed previously), clear objectives, appropriate and respectful language, and appropriate use of metaphor and analogy. We will address the last two of these aspects here.

Using Appropriate Language

In our increasingly diverse culture, we must choose language that is both politically correct and culturally correct. This becomes more challenging as many of us work across international borders with clients in other countries.

"Politically correct" means avoiding slang, stereotypes, colloquialisms and offensive terms including racial slurs, derogatory or prejudicial language, or language that implies or states disapproval of lifestyle or sexual preferences. "Culturally correct" refers to terms that are clear and understandable based on the person's culture - e.g., "trunk" in American English vs. "boot" in British English. This latter term has more to do with being understood, both in language and in customs, than offending someone, which politically incorrect language can do.

In addition, we need to avoid the following:
- Grandiosities (always, never, all, every)
- Referring to the generic "they" or "people," thereby making untested assumptions about reality
- Noticing the client (or coach!) referring to "you" or "they" when they mean themselves ("I"), as in "When x happens, you feel like giving up"
- Making broad "how it is" statements ("That's just how engineers are," or "It's the economy, there just aren't any jobs out there.")
- Being inauthentic or hypocritical in any way (e.g. telling or encouraging the client to do something which you do not yourself do)

Use of Metaphor and Analogy

Metaphor - a visual or other image that can be likened to the client's issue or experience - can be a powerful way to access a more holistic perspective on the issue than the more obvious question. For example, asking "Do you feel like you're drifting at sea?" will be more powerful for some clients than "Are you confused?" (especially if they're kinesthetic or highly visual in communication style!). Analogy uses language creatively to draw parallels with the client's experience. An example might be "If the players in this situation were animals, what would they be?" or "Is there any parallel between what you're experiencing and a tidal wave? Describe it for me."

Coaching techniques using metaphor, analogy, and other images can also be used in a more directive way, as in "Imagine you can rise above the situation in a helicopter and see the entire landscape. What do you see? What else? What colors? What speed are things moving? What are the most important or visible elements?" Or, "Let's be a couple of miners, going deep into the earth to explore these beliefs further together. What do you notice as the elevator descends into the mine shaft? Where is the light coming from? Are there any creatures or other images that come to mind? What feelings do you feel? Let's go a bit deeper now, beginning to move toward the gold mine. The gold mine is where the answer to your dilemma lies. Now what do you feel? Where in your body?..."

Roadblocks to Clear Communication

Most of us desire to communicate clearly and be understood. So what gets in our way?

- **Complex questions:** If you process your thoughts aloud and form your question(s) as you go, rather than taking a moment to pause, formulate the question you want to ask, and then say it, you may confuse the client.
- **Lack of confidence:** When you lack confidence, you may hesitate, be unwilling to "tell it like it is," etc., so your communication will be unclear. You may also fail to instill confidence in the client due to your own lack of self-confidence.

- **Lack of familiarity with the client's industry, job, or situation (including terminology):** If you don't know a lot about the client's situation, you may feel the need to become more of an expert. Only learn as much as you need to know to coach her! Consider asking a generic coaching question and learn from her as she talks. Or ask her to provide you with a job description or other summary of her background to complete the "picture" you have of her.
- **Rushing or trying to slow the client's pace:** Indicators might be interrupting, long pauses by the coach, etc. - masterful coaches will only take a different pace than the client's when there is a specific reason for it, e.g., client thinks slowly and analytically and coach wants to "shake her up" by using a faster pace to generate new perspectives
- **Using a different communication style:** Your client may stumble over a visual question she processes auditorily; refer to chart in Figure 42 for tips on reframing question.
- **Other miscellaneous roadblocks:**
  - **Getting emotionally caught up in the client's issue**
  - **Mumbling; dropping your voice as you talk**
  - **Inadequate time establishing rapport**
  - **Failure to clear distractions from your mind before session**
  - **Failure to follow through on promised tasks**

Measuring the Clarity of Your Communication

Perhaps one of the best ways to increase your awareness of how effective (and clear) your communication has been is to record (with the client's permission, of course) your coaching sessions. As you listen to the tape (or listen to your statements and questions during the session itself), you might ask yourself questions such as those in Figure 45 to evaluate your communication.

Celebrating Successes

A business book entitled *1001 Ways to Reward Employees* by Bob Nelson and Kenneth Blanchard suggests that there are literally hundreds of ways to reward employees—and each person likes different rewards.

Figure 45: Questions To Evaluate Clarity Of Communication	Yes	No
1. Did the client understand what I said/asked? [How do you know?]		
2. Did the client answer easily or pause before answering?		
3. If the client paused after my question, were they processing (e.g. Introvert) or were they confused? [Again, how do you know?]		
4. Did I use the client's processing style in formulating my question (e.g., visual, auditory, kinesthetic, auditory-digital; thinking vs. feeling; sensing vs. intuitive)?		
5. Did my question further the client's understanding of their issue, or confuse them further?		
6. Did I mirror back what the client had said? Summarize/bottom-line? Or go deeper and probe to Level 2 or 3 aspects of the issue?		
7. Did the client's perspective on the issue shift as a result of my question or feedback?		
8. Did I use as few words as possible to communicate the idea or ask the question?		
9. Did I avoid asking more than one question at once or combining two issues into one question?		
10. Is the client more aware of their beliefs, systems of meaning-making, and/or self-concept because of my coaching and/or choice of language?		
11. Did I avoid getting caught up in the client's "story" or "script" and focus on the facts in my language?		
12. Did I avoid using language that conveyed my own prejudices or biases, but instead use gender- and race-neutral language?		
13. Did my questions and/or feedback help the client distinguish facts from interpretation?		
14. Was I direct, saying what I meant, and avoiding "beating around the bush"?		
15. Did I take time to prepare for the call, both mentally and by reviewing any notes from last time or coaching call prep forms prior to the appointment?		

Just getting our minds and arms around the idea that there could be that many ways to reward success is a shift. Knowing each each of us has our own ways that we like to be rewarded, what about our clients? How many ways are there to reward and celebrate their success?

We want to be sure that they are not taking the action they are to change just to satisfy us, or to get acknowledgement from us as their coach. While that is pleasant, it can create a codependency that stops their progress when the coaching ends. Some of the ways you may want to use to celebrate your client's successes include:
- Acknowledgement, appreciation
- Send free e-cards to clients
- Ask them how they could reward themselves
- Send inspirational message
- Novelty items with your company name on it
- Send balloons
- Send flowers
- What others can you think of?

Maintaining Client Focus

Our final coaching skill in this chapter is maintaining client focus. While goals seem quite palpable and important when set, over a period of weeks they can fade in order of priority - as can the client's commitment. Part of our role as coaches is to help the client stay true to what he stated was important to him as we began the coaching - and to his changing priorities as the coaching continues.

A challenge for us as coaches is balancing accountability with support; keeping the client true to their goals but also supporting them as they progress. The dictionary definition of accountability is to be "responsible and answerable; being held to the task and required to follow through on what you have promised." The common use of accountability, like feedback, has taken on a negative connotation - that of pointing out where the person (here, the client) has failed to keep their word. In fact, accountability is a neutral concept. It simply means "to give an account;" to tell what worked and what didn't and to learn from the results.

Holding clients accountable is more than babysitting, "checking up on" them, or even having them accountable to you—they're being held accountable to themselves to do what they've promised. In order to hold a client accountable, they need to articulate three things as part of their stated action step(s):

1. Action to be taken
2. Timeline
3. Means to measure progress (or value of the action, if it's a reflective action; note it is not necessarily completion, but progress in the right direction)

These elements should be integrated into their Coaching Plan.

When the Client Doesn't Do What They Promise...

When the client doesn't follow through, the coach is put in the difficult position of needing to mention what has happened and explore it. Yet our coaching competencies require that we confront them "positively." How do we do this? Here are some ideas:

- "I noticed you didn't complete x, [the action you intended at the close of our last session]. What are your observations about that?" Or, "What can you learn from this?" Or, "Has something prevented you from doing it?"
- "Based on your not doing what you set out to do, how do you want to re-define accountability in our relationship?" Or, "How can I help you be accountable to yourself around this issue?"
- "What's beneath your not following through here?"
- "Has this been a pattern? Does it pertain to a particular type of issues or to all issues?"
- "Imagine that you continue to not follow through on this action/behavior/issue. What will your life be like one year from now? Five years from now? Are you willing to reap those consequences?"

Ending the Coaching Relationship

When a client's need for our services ends, or they don't wish to renew their initial 90- or 120-day commitment, there is an art to the ending process. It's not so much "good-bye" as it is "farewell" or "adieu," since there is at least some likelihood that the client will be back to work with us again in a future career change or other work-related scenario. It's more like a "comma" instead of a "period."

So to end the relationship (for now) on the best of terms, here are a few tips:

1. Review with the client their initial goals, as stated in the Coaching Plan; were they achieved? Were new goals discovered that took their place?

2. Ask the client what surprised them, what disappointed them (if anything) and where they will go from here.

3. Ask the client to complete an evaluation on their coaching experience and return it to you within 24 hours if possible.

4. If the client has indicated any kind of dissatisfaction or disappointment, do what you can to make it right, including giving away additional sessions if need be, or otherwise correcting it. (Dissatisfied customers tell 10 people, satisfied customers usually only tell 1!)

5. Invite the client to keep in touch with you as they become acclimated in their new position or situation and to feel free to contact you if they want or need further coaching.

Key Coaching Concepts:

1. Shifting perspective means to see things in a different way.

2. To eliminate time and energy wasters, clients can keep a time log of their actual time spent during the day and evaluate what they can eliminate for more purposeful activity.

3. When a client expresses strong emotions, the best approach is to mirror their emotion, focusing on "being there," probing deeper into the emotion, or using humor.

4. Some keys to making questions more powerful include removing judgment, shortening them, changing closed-ended to open-ended, asking empowering questions, honoring the client's communication style, bypassing rephrasing, using optimal timing, and asking permission to coach in sensitive areas.

5. It is critical that we use appropriate language, meaning politically and culturally correct.

6. Metaphor and analogy can better illustrate a point in some cases than stating the situation directly.

7. Maintaining client focus requires a delicate balance between holding the client accountable and being supportive of them.

8. To be accountable, a client must state the desired action to be taken, a timeline, and a means to measure progress.

9. When the time comes to end a coaching relationship, it should be with a "comma" rather than a "period," since the client may return to you for their next transition!

Coach Self-Care for a Client-Centered Approach

"The best way is to understand yourself, and then you will understand everything. So when you try hard to make your own way, you will help others, and you will be helped by others. Before you make your own way you cannot help anyone, and no one can help you...So we say true understanding will come out of emptiness."

—Shunryu Suzuki
Zen Mind, Beginner's Mind

We have said throughout our discussion of career coaching that the process is "all about the client." And it is! But as with any helping profession, we must also ensure that we take good care of ourselves, "recharging our battery" regularly, so that we can give from a sense of overflow and not become drained. So in this, our final chapter, we will explore both the dynamics of being client-centered and some self-care strategies that will help keep us fresh and prepared to give our clients what they need.

Becoming Client-Centered

Our coaching competencies require that we develop a "coaching presence," one aspect of which is a focus on the client. Among the things that are involved in being client-centered are:

- Focusing our attention on the client exclusively during the session
- Showing genuine concern for the client and their welfare

- Being fully conscious
- Creating spontaneous relationship with the client
- Employing an open, flexible, confident style
- Using active and deep listening
- Adopting a neutral viewpoint, honoring and not judging
- Asking questions, being curious
- Being supportive
- Letting client set the agenda
- Allowing the client take responsibility for depth they want to go to
- Being sensitive to the client's limits, not pushing them past those limits without their permission
- Relating observations as appropriate (and listening for content to observe)
- "Dancing in the moment"

One of the traps that can keep us from being client-centered is starting to pursue (even if inadvertently) our own agenda. We know that we are doing this if we start asking leading questions, we miss nonverbal cues such as energy shifts, we start to rephrase the client's statements, do more talking than listening, or begin planning our questions in advance.

If our agenda is getting in the way, we first want to acknowledge what is happening (to ourselves first, and to the client only if appropriate). We might then ask for a moment to take a breath and refocus, ask an open-ended question that will get the client talking about their agenda, or if we are using a headset, get up and walk around to shift our energy invisibly. Then, we can ask a question that will help your client refocus on their agenda.

We discourage extensive note-taking during a coaching session, as it will distract the coach from both what is being said and not said. If you're concerned about missing important points, tape your sessions, or learn to trust that you will remember what is important. Or even better, ask the client to recap the important points and/or their "takeaways" after the call on the Post-session Worksheet, relieving you of the responsibility! (After all, the coaching is for them, right?)

The Ongoing Practice of Coaching

No other field outside of coaching - and particularly career coaching -

requires people to involve their entire lifestyle in their profession. Our life becomes a practice venue for choosing to live authentically, select work that expresses our passions and purpose, and continuing to engage in self-improvement so that we can be increasingly effective with our clients.

But there is a trap here: we may think we have to be perfect (??!!) to be a good coach...which of course is not true! Instead, we need to continually increase our openness to growth, addressing our issues as they arise, but knowing that perfection is an elusive state. The following quote from *A Path with Heart* by Jack Kornfield captures this idea:

> "In the beginning we may erroneously imagine spiritual growth [like learning coaching] to be a linear journey, traveling over a certain landscape to a faraway destination of enlightenment. But it is better described as a widening circle or spiral that opens our hearts and gradually infuses our consciousness to include all of life as a spiritual whole."

We encourage you to see your work in this way as you develop your practice or begin coaching within your organization. Masterful coaches never stop learning and growing - they know they need to do so to stay ahead of their clients!

Career Coach Self-Care

Caring for ourselves requires that we take a proactive approach toward our physical, mental, emotional, social, professional and spiritual health. Engaging in regular meditation, daily establishment of our intention for the day, quarterly or semi-annual personal retreats and/or re-evaluations of our roles, activities, and progress toward our goals plus setting our new goals for the next period will help us stay focused and fresh for our work. A few specific daily practices that may also be useful to this end include:

1. Focus on maintaining a positive outlook.
2. Be kind, courteous, and generous to everyone (i.e., follow the Golden Rule).
3. Eat lots of fresh vegetables and fruit each day, as part of a varied, balanced diet. Avoid excessive alcohol, tobacco, and drugs.
4. Surround yourself with positive, supportive people with

whom you feel mutual support and respect.

5. Exercise daily, as often as possible outdoors.

6. Love what you do for your livelihood, but don't mistake it for your identity.

7. Take time to cultivate meaningful friendships.

8. Stay in regular contact with God as you understand Him/Her/It.

9. Forgive yourself for past mistakes; refuse to feel guilty — you did the best you could.

10. Forgive others who have "wronged" you, and refuse to hold resentments, knowing they did the best they could at the time. Live fully in the here and now!

11. Keep growing and trying new things.

12. Let love rule all of your dealings.

13. Acknowledge others for their specialness. When you feel badly, give of yourself to someone else. Don't be afraid to ask for help and support when you need it.

14. Handle money joyfully and wisely.

15. Let your true self shine — express your ideas and your creativity in all you do.

16. Continually challenge yourself to see the new, to live a higher quality of life today than in the past, and to rise to ever increased awareness of yourself, God, and others.

17. Realize that the circumstances in your life are your "laboratory," and that they reflect your beliefs and thoughts. Be open to learning the lessons they present, and to accepting your part in creating what happens to you.

Summary of Coaching Skills

This also seems an appropriate juncture to review the coaching skills you have learned. The Career Coach's Toolbox in Part 5 offers a Coaching Skills Assessment to see how many of the 70 coaching skills you feel comfortable with at this point. Each of these skills can be used mechanically or artfully, by rote or strategically. Which will you choose? Remember our analogy of the musician, and how apparent it is when they have a natural gift and "flow" (as used in the book *Flow: The Psychology of Optimum Experience*, by Mihaly Csikszentmihalyi) in their performance, versus a musician that is simply executing the notes from the page in a mechanical way? By setting your goal to be a Masterful Coach, your clients will gain the added benefit of the "flow" in working with you, and their results will demonstrate it! And that opens the door for enhanced development for both you and your clients.

Characteristics of Masterful Coaches

Like any form of excellence, mastery is often judged subjectively. But we suggest that there are at least a few shared traits (a "Baker's Dozen") to which we can all aspire in our quest for mastery in this profession:

1. Masterful coaches never stop learning and growing, and engage in Continuous Self-Improvement™
2. Masterful coaches listen between the lines of what their clients say
3. Masterful coaches engage their intuition and/or Higher Self in their coaching
4. Masterful coaches see the small and the larger perspective
5. Masterful coaches hold a supportive, safe coaching space for their clients
6. Masterful coaches know how to "be" without the need to "do" anything
7. Masterful coaches use their coaching skills as an artist uses her paint brush and paints: an appropriate mix, applied artfully, to co-create a beautiful piece of art - the coaching interaction and its results
8. Masterful coaches know how to balance work and play
9. Masterful coaches are not afraid to "tell it like it is"
10. Masterful coaches focus on the client and his/her agenda and embody the principle, "It's all about them."
11. Masterful coaches know who their clients are, and who they are not - and are experts on their clients' needs
12. Masterful coaches are confident in delivering their service
13. Masterful coaches can be effective with a wide range of people

Key Coaching Concepts

1. Being client-centered is one aspect of developing a coaching presence, a core coaching competency.

2. A trap that can keep us from being client-centered is bringing our agenda into the coaching session.

3. Career coaching, in its truest form, is a practice rather than a set of skills to be learned. They can be used masterfully, or by rote: it is the coach's choice.

4. As we conclude this book, evaluating our coaching skills against the 70 coaching skills in the ICF competencies is a good measure of our current state of coaching expertise.

5. Masterful coaches share 13 traits, setting a standard to which we can each aspire and toward which we can work on a daily basis.

PART FIVE

THE CAREER COACH'S TOOLBOX

1. My Job Satisfaction Inventory
2. What Authentic Vocation Is
3. 8 Authentic Vocation Worksheets
4. Symbol Meditation
5. Ideal Job Template
6. What Career Coaches Do
7. Entrepreneurial Checklist
8. Are You Coachable?
9. Coaching Agreements
10. Intake Form
11. Coaching Plan
12. Pre-Session Worksheet
13. Post-Session Worksheet
14. Professional Balance Wheel
15. Ideal Day Exercise
16. Job Search Marketing Plan Template
17. Company Research Data Sheet
18. Wants/Needs Analysis
19. Coaching Skills Checklist
20. Professional Resources for Career Coaches

I. My Job Satisfaction Inventory

Please circle the appropriate response after each item. 1 = strongly disagree; 2 = no opinion; 3 = strongly agree.

1. I like my current job.	1	2	3
2. I am clear about my career direction.	1	2	3
3. It is easy for me to set goals for myself.	1	2	3
4. I usually attain the goals I set.	1	2	3
5. I have no fears about changing jobs.	1	2	3
6. I think of myself as a successful person.	1	2	3
7. I have high self-esteem.	1	2	3
8. Once I decide to make a change in my life, I usually move ahead and do so without making excuses or procrastinating.	1	2	3
9. I view change as a healthy occurrence.	1	2	3
10. The work environment in my current job meets all of my needs.	1	2	3
11. I know exactly which career field I want to enter (or in which I want to stay).	1	2	3
12. I understand what motivates me to work, and I make job choices based on those factors.	1	2	3
13. I understand the inner needs that I feel a job should fulfill.	1	2	3
14. My inner needs are fulfilled through my work.	1	2	3
15. I know the signs that tell me when it is time for me to change jobs or careers.	1	2	3
16. I enjoy nearly all of the tasks performed in my job.	1	2	3
17. My job allows me to satisfy my personal values and fulfill my personal goals as I do the work.	1	2	3

To determine your score, add the total of all numbers you have circled. The highest possible score is 51; lowest is 17. If your score is 40 or higher, you have a high level of satisfaction and may simply want to enhance that positive experience. If your score is 27-39, you have some work to do to achieve satisfaction. Those with scores less than 27 need to work carefully through the exercises in this book — your satisfaction level is extremely low.

2. What is Authentic Vocation™?

Have you been feeling restless or discontented in your job? Like something is missing, but you don't know what? The key may be a whole new approach to career development: Authentic Vocation.™

Authentic Vocation™ is an approach that is different that other skills-based approaches to identifying your calling or ideal work. Instead, it starts with your life purpose and builds a template for your ideal work from that critical base.

Simply, the elements of Authentic Vocation™ are these:

1. Life purpose: what is the purpose or mission of your life that *must* be expressed through your work?
2. Values: what values must be expressed in your work for optimal satisfaction?
3. Motivators: what motivates you to do your best?
4. Skills: what skills do you have that you want to continue using?
5. Experience: what experience can you leverage in your next position?
6. Desired Job/Career: what job titles and/or industries would suit your goals?
7. Environment: what location, culture, and other factors would be critical in your work environment?
8. Business Reality: Is your target financially viable? Can you make a living at it? If not, what needs to be adjusted so you can?

The diagram on the next page illustrates how the first 7 elements are the template, and must be filtered through the 8th element to have a true Authentic Vocation.™

If you are seeking greater fulfillment at a job that also meets your financial needs and allows you to "have a life," then Authentic Vocation™ coaching may be for you.

For more information, call us at 1-866-CCOACH-4 or email us at coach@careercoachinstitute.com.

AUTHENTIC VOCATION™

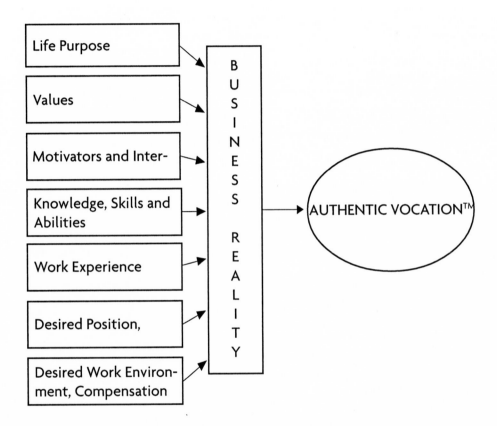

3. 8 Authentic Vocation™ Worksheets

Authentic Vocation™ Worksheet I: Life Purpose

The Authentic Vocation™ Process is designed to provide a focus in your work, from concept toimplementation. Please work through it thoughtfully, taking your time, and allowing your unique gifts and your true self to emerge as you do.

We begin by exploring the first element of your Authentic Vocation, Life Purpose. Find a quiet place and about an hour of undisturbed time, and respond to each of the following questions on a separate piece of paper (or on your computer).

Clue No. 1: What do you love to do when you have spare time?

Clue No. 2: What parts of your present job or life activities do you thoroughly enjoy? .

Clue No. 3: What do you naturally do well?

Clue No. 4: What have been your 10 greatest successes to date (in your eyes)?

Success	What Makes It A Success For You

Clue No. 5: Is there a cause or value or quality which you feel passionate about?

Clue No. 6: What are the 10 most important lessons you have learned in your life?

Lesson	What Makes It Significant/How You Use It

Clue No. 7: Think back over your life. Are there some issues or perceived problems that have occurred over and over again?

Clue No. 8: What do you daydream (or dream) about doing?

Clue No. 9: Imagine you are writing your epitaph. What things do you want to be remembered for? What things will your life be incomplete without?

Clue No. 10: What would you do if you knew you could not fail?

Now, narrow down your responses to glean the 10 most important aspects of your life purpose and write any themes you notice here:

Themes	(cont'd)

To compose your life's purpose statement, synthesizing your responses to the Clues, use the following format:

"My life's purpose is to_____ through _____."
      [ESSENCE]   [EXPRESSION]

The "essence" is relatively unchangeable over your lifetime, and might be something like "enhance peace in the world" or "make my world a beautiful place" or "help women find their own voice." The "expression" is the ways in which the essence is expressing (or can express) in your life right now, and it will change as life circumstances change. An example might be "working in a company that values authentic communication, dedicating myself to conscious parenting, and volunteering at the local library once a month."

Write your life's purpose statement here:

"My life's purpose is to _____ through

_____."

Authentic Vocation™ Worksheet 2: Values

You are now ready to explore the second element of your Authentic Vocation, Values. The second critical factor in job design is your values, as they relate to work. Fulfillment in work comes when the life and work values that are important to you are met through your work. At the same time, the company for which you work should share at least the most important of those values. Otherwise you will experience constant turmoil and conflict, as well as a feeling that you "can't be yourself" at work.

What are values? Values are simply things about work that, to you, are intrinsically valuable or desirable. They can be accessed most easily by asking yourself the question, "What do I want out of my work?" Or, "why do I work?" Begin by asking yourself these questions now, and write down your responses. If you get stuck, look at the previous value and ask what is important to you about that.

My Critical Work Values

I work because:

1.

2.

3.

4.

I want the following things out of my work:

1.

2.

3.

4.

5.

Some values commonly expressed are listed below. Rank each of the listed values as (1) not important, (2) moderately important, or (3) very important to you in your choice of career.

Values at Work

___ Enjoyment (having fun at what you do)
___ Helping other people (in a direct way)
___ Friendships (developing close relationships with co-workers)

___ Helping society (contributing to the betterment of the world)

___ Freedom (flexible schedule, independence)

___ Recognition (being recognized for your work in a tangible way)

___ Creativity (having opportunity to express your ideas and yourself in your work; innovation)

___ Location (being able to live where you choose)

___ Competition (matching your abilities with others')

___ Power and authority (being in managerial or leadership position; being responsible for supervising others; having decision-making authority)

___ Achievement (accomplishing desired objective; mastery)

___ Compensation (receiving equivalent in value or effect for services rendered)

___ Variety (a mix of tasks to perform and people dealt with during each day)

___ Security (feeling of stability, no worry; certainty)

___ Prestige (being seen as successful; obtaining recognition and status)

___ Aesthetics (beauty of work environment; contributing to beauty of the world)

___ Morality and ethics (working according to a code or set of rules; enhancing world ethics)

___ Intellectual stimulation (working in an environment that encourages and stimulates thinking)

___ Public contact (working with customers or clients, as opposed to working alone or working with objects only)

___ Pace (busy versus relaxed working atmosphere)

___ Risk (monetary or other risks — e.g., new product development or start-up enterprise)

Below, list your top 5 values:

1. _____
2. _____
3. _____
4. _____
5. _____

Now, think about your current job. How many of the values you have marked "3" for "very important" are being fulfilled through that job? Your answer gives you a very important insight as to why you may feel dissatisfied with that job.

Authentic Vocation™ Worksheet 3: Motivators and Interests

It is important to understand what motivates you to do something, so that you can include those considerations in your job design. Many of us believe that making more money or getting better benefits will keep us motivated. However, psychologists have found that increasing amounts of money, benefits, and status are only temporarily satisfying. What motivates most of us in the long run are challenging, interesting work; the opportunity to be creative; a chance to make a contribution; achievement; and recognition for our achievements. What is it that motivates you? The following exercise will help you answer this important question.

My Motivators

Think of at least 4 instances in which you felt highly motivated to do the activity. They may be in a job, school, a hobby, or another type of situation. List those on a separate sheet of paper or on your computer.

Now, consider what each of these situations had in common. Were you in a similar setting? With similar types of people? Doing a particular kind of task you genuinely enjoy? Did you feel a certain way (challenged, proud, etc.)? List those common threads next. These common threads that you have now identified are at least some of the things that will motivate you to do your best in your job. Can you think of others? Add them to your list.

Finally, list the top 5 motivators that are most important in your work for you to feel excited about doing the work and/or dedicated to doing your best.

Interests

Often (but not always), doing what interests us keeps us motivated. Please rank the following 10 functional areas found within an organization from 1 (most interested) to 10 (least interested). If desired, you can ask your coach to administer the Strong Interest Inventory and/or the Career Transition Report it generates to confirm your choices.

_____Administration   _____Information Systems

_____Customer Service   _____Manufacturing & Production

_____Finance & Accounting   _____Marketing

_____General Management   _____Sales

_____Human Resources   _____Research & Development

Authentic Vocation Worksheet 4: Knowledge, Skills and Abilities

You are now ready to explore the fourth element of your Authentic Vocation, Knowledge/ Skills/ Abilities. During your career thus far, you have developed some skills through schooling, further honed your natural aptitudes, and learned others on-the-job. The tool that follows helps you to assess how your skills fit into the most commonly sought skill areas, simply by indicating whether you have used that skill in a "hands-on" way, managed or supervised that function, trained in that skill, or obtained education in that skill.

FUNCTIONAL SKILL SETS

Jobs consist of a combination of functional skill sets plus management. You have probably used, with varying degrees, some of the skills in each set. The Functional Skills are:

- Administration
- Corporate Communications
- Finance
- Human Resources
- Information Systems/ Technology
- Legal
- Operations
- Research and Development
- Sales and Marketing
- Management

Functional Skillsets

Review **all** the Skill Sets and check the highest level of responsibility your experience warrants. Remember to read each section because your expertise overlaps from one Skill Set to another. The skills related to each of these functional skill areas are explained in detail in the next few pages. But first, we look at management generically, since those skills are used in conjunction with other functional areas by those in management roles.

M =Management T = Training H = Hands On E = Education

Management

Following are general skills used in management. Please check the areas in which you have specific experience, training or education.

M	T	H	E		M	T	H	E	
—	—	—	—	Budgeting	—	—	—	—	Developing Policies
—	—	—	—	Business Planning	—	—	—	—	Diversification
—	—	—	—	Business Reengineering	—	—	—	—	Divestitures
—	—	—	—	Change Management	—	—	—	—	Employee Evaluations
—	—	—	—	Consolidations	—	—	—	—	Financing-Public/Private
—	—	—	—	Corporate Finance	—	—	—	—	Government Relations
—	—	—	—	Cost Control	—	—	—	—	Growth Strategies
—	—	—	—	Cross-Functional Teams	—	—	—	—	Hiring/Firing
—	—	—	—	Decision Making	—	—	—	—	International Mgmt

M T H E

___ ___ ___ ___ Investor Relations
___ ___ ___ ___ IPO Strategy/
             Positioning
___ ___ ___ ___ Joint Ventures
___ ___ ___ ___ Labor Relations
___ ___ ___ ___ Manager Development
___ ___ ___ ___ Mergers &
             Acquisitions
___ ___ ___ ___ Methods & Measures
___ ___ ___ ___ Multi-Site
             Management
___ ___ ___ ___ Negotiations

M T H E

___ ___ ___ ___ Officer/Board Member
___ ___ ___ ___ Organiz'l. Development
___ ___ ___ ___ P&L
___ ___ ___ ___ Project Management
___ ___ ___ ___ Resource Management
___ ___ ___ ___ Restructuring
___ ___ ___ ___ Staff Development
___ ___ ___ ___ Business Start-up
___ ___ ___ ___ Strategic Partnerships
___ ___ ___ ___ Strategic Planning
___ ___ ___ ___ Supervision
___ ___ ___ ___ Turn Arounds

Operations – Manufacturing – Distribution Skill Set

The day-to-day operations that enable the company to produce its daily goals in making a product, getting the product to the customer, or performing a service.

M T H E

___ ___ ___ ___ Assembly
___ ___ ___ ___ Automation
             Engineering
___ ___ ___ ___ Bidding
___ ___ ___ ___ Call Center Operations
___ ___ ___ ___ Configuration
___ ___ ___ ___ Construction
___ ___ ___ ___ Continuous Process
             Improvements
___ ___ ___ ___ Contract Management
___ ___ ___ ___ Control Systems
___ ___ ___ ___ Distribution/
             Transportation
___ ___ ___ ___ Document Control
             Management
___ ___ ___ ___ Environmental Issues
___ ___ ___ ___ Equipment Design
___ ___ ___ ___ Equipment
             Maintenance &
             Repair
___ ___ ___ ___ Equipment
             Management
___ ___ ___ ___ Facility Management/
             Leases
___ ___ ___ ___ Fleet Management

M T H E

___ ___ ___ ___ Installation
___ ___ ___ ___ Inventory Control
___ ___ ___ ___ ISO 9000 series
___ ___ ___ ___ JIT / WIP / MRP
___ ___ ___ ___ Labor Control
___ ___ ___ ___ Lean Manufacturing
___ ___ ___ ___ Logistics
___ ___ ___ ___ Maintenance
___ ___ ___ ___ Manpower Planning/
             Budgeting
___ ___ ___ ___ Manufacturing
             Engineering
___ ___ ___ ___ Materials Handling/
             Management
___ ___ ___ ___ Methods & Standards
___ ___ ___ ___ Multi-Shift
             Management
___ ___ ___ ___ New Product
             Development
___ ___ ___ ___ Operations Research
___ ___ ___ ___ Operations Supervision
___ ___ ___ ___ Order Processing
___ ___ ___ ___ Outsourcing
___ ___ ___ ___ Plant Design & Layout
___ ___ ___ ___ Policies & Procedures

— — — — Process Control
       Supervision
— — — — Process Engineering
— — — — Production Planning
— — — — Project Coordination
— — — — Project Management
— — — — Prototype Operations
— — — — Purchasing/
       Procurement
— — — — Quality Assurance/
       Control
— — — — Safety Engineering
— — — — Service Support
— — — — Scheduling
— — — — Shipping & Receiving

— — — — Startup Operations
— — — — Supply Chain
       Management
— — — — Theory of Constraints
       Mfg
— — — — TQM
— — — — Traffic Management
— — — — Troubleshooting
— — — — Vendor Coordination
— — — — Warehousing
— — — — _____
— — — — _____
— — — — _____
— — — — _____

Research & Development Skill Set

Applies the processes, operations, and techniques of science and technology to create and improve products, processes, and services that may benefit an enterprise, an institution, or a society.

M T H E

— — — — Applied Research
— — — — Basic Research
— — — — Chemical Engineering
— — — — Contract
       Administration
— — — — Design and
       Specifications
— — — — Diagnostics
— — — — Electrical Engineering
— — — — Engineering Support
— — — — Environmental, Health,
       & Safety
— — — — Feasibility Studies
— — — — Field Studies
— — — — Lab Management
— — — — Lab/Facility Design &
       Construction
— — — — Manufacturing/
       Engineering Liaison
— — — — Mechanical
       Engineering
— — — — Modeling

M T H E

— — — — New Equipment
       Design
— — — — Patent Holder
— — — — Process Engineering
— — — — Product Applications
— — — — Product Development
— — — — Product Engineering
— — — — Product Re-engineering
— — — — Product Testing
— — — — Program Development
— — — — Project Management
— — — — Prototype Development
— — — — Quality Control
— — — — R&D Management
— — — — Regulatory Compliance
— — — — Research Publications
— — — — Security
— — — — Service Development
— — — — Simulation
       Development
— — — — Software Tools
— — — — Statistical Analysis

M	T	H	E	
—	—	—	—	Synthesizing
—	—	—	—	Technical Writing
—	—	—	—	Technology Evaluation
—	—	—	—	_____

M	T	H	E	
—	—	—	—	_____
—	—	—	—	_____
—	—	—	—	_____
—	—	—	—	_____

Sales & Marketing Skill Set

Marketing determines strategies/opportunities to sell profitably and directs the flow of goods from producer to domestic or international consumers or users. The sales force must achieve the targeted objectives.

M	T	H	E	
—	—	—	—	Account Management
—	—	—	—	Advertising
—	—	—	—	Brand Management
—	—	—	—	Budgeting/Expense Control
—	—	—	—	Business Development
—	—	—	—	Channel Marketing
—	—	—	—	Collateral Development
—	—	—	—	Compensation Plans
—	—	—	—	Competitive Analysis
—	—	—	—	Contract Negotiations
—	—	—	—	Convention Planning
—	—	—	—	Corporate Identity
—	—	—	—	Customer Relations/ Service
—	—	—	—	Direct Sales
—	—	—	—	Distribution Channels
—	—	—	—	Distributor Relations
—	—	—	—	Ecommerce/B2B
—	—	—	—	Field Liaison
—	—	—	—	Field Sales (Outside Sales)
—	—	—	—	Forecasting
—	—	—	—	Goal Setting
—	—	—	—	Image Development
—	—	—	—	Import / Export
—	—	—	—	Incentive Programs
—	—	—	—	Inside Sales
—	—	—	—	International Business Development
—	—	—	—	International Expansion
—	—	—	—	Logo Development
—	—	—	—	Market Research & Analysis

M	T	H	E	
—	—	—	—	Market Rollout
—	—	—	—	Marketing Communications
—	—	—	—	Marketing Plans
—	—	—	—	Marketing Promotions
—	—	—	—	Media Buying/ Evaluation
—	—	—	—	Media Relations
—	—	—	—	Merchandising
—	—	—	—	Multi-Media Presentations
—	—	—	—	New Account Sales
—	—	—	—	New Product Development
—	—	—	—	Online Marketing & Advertising
—	—	—	—	Packaging
—	—	—	—	Pricing
—	—	—	—	Product Demonstrations
—	—	—	—	Product Introduction/ Launch
—	—	—	—	Product Line Development
—	—	—	—	Product Management
—	—	—	—	Product Publishing/Sales
—	—	—	—	Product Sourcing
—	—	—	—	Product Specifications
—	—	—	—	Proposal Writing
—	—	—	—	Radio Media
—	—	—	—	Sales Administration
—	—	—	—	Sales Analysis
—	—	—	—	Sales Forecasting
—	—	—	—	Sales Kits

M	T	H	E		M	T	H	E	
—	—	—	—	Sales Management	—	—	—	—	Survey Design
—	—	—	—	Sales Presentations	—	—	—	—	Technical Sales Support
—	—	—	—	Sales Promotions	—	—	—	—	Telemarketing
—	—	—	—	Sales Recruiting	—	—	—	—	Television Media
—	—	—	—	Sales Support	—	—	—	—	Territory Development
—	—	—	—	Sales Training	—	—	—	—	Tradeshows
—	—	—	—	Showrooms	—	—	—	—	Trend Analysis
—	—	—	—	Strategic Alliances/ Partnerships	—	—	—	—	Video Productions
—	—	—	—	Strategic Planning	—	—	—	—	_____
—	—	—	—	Supply Chain Analysis	—	—	—	—	_____
—	—	—	—	Supply Chain Management	—	—	—	—	_____

Corporate Communications Skill Set

Plans, executes, and coordinates relationships of the company and its representatives with the company's various publics in order to achieve acceptance of the company, its objectives, and its conduct; and acquires knowledge of the business environment required for review and attainment of the company's objectives.

M	T	H	E		M	T	H	E	
—	—	—	—	Business to Business Communication	—	—	—	—	Internet Communications
—	—	—	—	Community Affairs/ Relations	—	—	—	—	Investor Collateral
—	—	—	—	Corporate Image	—	—	—	—	Media Presentations
—	—	—	—	Corporate Philanthropy	—	—	—	—	Press Releases
—	—	—	—	Corporate Publications	—	—	—	—	Proposal Writing
—	—	—	—	Corporate Relations	—	—	—	—	Public Relations
—	—	—	—	Educational Programs	—	—	—	—	Public Speaking
—	—	—	—	Employee Communications	—	—	—	—	Risk Management Communication
—	—	—	—	Employee Newsletters	—	—	—	—	Shareholder Relations
—	—	—	—	Event Planning	—	—	—	—	Speech Writing
—	—	—	—	Fund Raising	—	—	—	—	Trade Relations
—	—	—	—	Government Affairs/ Relations	—	—	—	—	Web Site Development-html
—	—	—	—	Industry/Association Relations	—	—	—	—	_____
					—	—	—	—	_____
					—	—	—	—	_____

Human Resources Skill Set

Broadly stated, HR refers to selection, staffing, development, and utilization of an organization's human resources. Organizations design programs to develop their human resources to their fullest capacities and to maintain ongoing worker commitment.

M T H E

__ __ __ __ Affirmative Action
__ __ __ __ Arbitration/Mediation
__ __ __ __ Benefits Vendor
            Management
__ __ __ __ Career Counseling
__ __ __ __ Career Development
__ __ __ __ Classified
            Advertisements
__ __ __ __ Company Orientation
__ __ __ __ Compensation &
            Benefits
__ __ __ __ Computer Based
            Training
__ __ __ __ Corporate Culture &
            Change
__ __ __ __ Cost Benefit Analysis
__ __ __ __ Course Development
__ __ __ __ Diversity
__ __ __ __ Downsizing
__ __ __ __ EEOC Compliance
__ __ __ __ Employee Coaching
__ __ __ __ Employee
            Communications
__ __ __ __ Employee Discipline
__ __ __ __ Employee Relations
__ __ __ __ Employee Selection
__ __ __ __ Executive Recruiting
__ __ __ __ Grievances
__ __ __ __ HR Generalist
__ __ __ __ HRIS
__ __ __ __ Human Resources
            Management
__ __ __ __ Industrial Relations
__ __ __ __ Interactive Training
            (Internet)

M T H E

__ __ __ __ International
            Employees
__ __ __ __ Job Analysis
__ __ __ __ Job Competencies
__ __ __ __ Labor Negotiations
__ __ __ __ Network Operations
__ __ __ __ Organizational
            Development
__ __ __ __ Outplacement
__ __ __ __ Performance
            Measurement
__ __ __ __ Policies & Procedures
__ __ __ __ Psychological
            Assessment
__ __ __ __ Records Management
__ __ __ __ Recruiting
__ __ __ __ Relocation
__ __ __ __ Salary Administration
__ __ __ __ Succession Planning
__ __ __ __ Team Building
__ __ __ __ Training
__ __ __ __ Training
            Administration
__ __ __ __ Union Coordination
__ __ __ __ Wage / Rate Analysis
__ __ __ __ Workers'
            Compensation
__ __ __ __ Workforce Forecasting/
            Planning
__ __ __ __ Workforce Security
__ __ __ __ _____
__ __ __ __ _____
__ __ __ __ _____
__ __ __ __ _____

Finance Skill Set

Plans, directs, controls, and measures the results of a company's monetary operations. Secures adequate operating funds at minimum cost, invests surplus funds to best advantage, and maintains a strong financial reputation for the company. Maintains records and prepares reports to meet corporate legal and tax requirements and measures the results of the company operations.

M T H E

__ __ __ __ Accounting
                  Management
__ __ __ __ Accounts Payable
__ __ __ __ Accounts Receivable
__ __ __ __ Acquisitions & Mergers
__ __ __ __ Actuarial / Rating
                  Analysis
__ __ __ __ Angel Funding
__ __ __ __ Auditing
__ __ __ __ Banking Relations
__ __ __ __ Budget Control
__ __ __ __ Budgeting
__ __ __ __ Capital Budgeting
__ __ __ __ Capital Investment
__ __ __ __ Cash Management
__ __ __ __ Cost Accounting
__ __ __ __ Cost Control
__ __ __ __ Credit / Collections
__ __ __ __ Debt Negotiations
__ __ __ __ Economic Studies
__ __ __ __ Equity/Debt
                  Management
__ __ __ __ Feasibility Studies
__ __ __ __ Financial Analysis
__ __ __ __ Financial Planning
__ __ __ __ Financial Reporting
__ __ __ __ Financial Software
                  Packages
__ __ __ __ Financing
__ __ __ __ Forecasting
__ __ __ __ Foreign Exchange
__ __ __ __ General Ledger
__ __ __ __ Insurance
__ __ __ __ Internal Controls

M T H E

__ __ __ __ Investor Relations
__ __ __ __ IPOs
__ __ __ __ Lending
__ __ __ __ Lines of Credit
__ __ __ __ Management Reporting
__ __ __ __ New Business
                  Development
__ __ __ __ Operations Research/
                  Analysis
__ __ __ __ Payroll
__ __ __ __ Pension & Fund
                  Management
__ __ __ __ Pricing / Forecast
                  Modeling
__ __ __ __ Private Placements
__ __ __ __ Profit Planning
__ __ __ __ Risk Management
__ __ __ __ Road Shows
__ __ __ __ SEC Reporting
__ __ __ __ Special Reports
__ __ __ __ Stockholder Relations
__ __ __ __ Systems Installation/
                  Training
__ __ __ __ Taxes
__ __ __ __ Treasury
__ __ __ __ VC/Investor
                  Presentations
__ __ __ __ Venture Capital
                  Relations
__ __ __ __ _____
__ __ __ __ _____
__ __ __ __ _____
__ __ __ __ _____

Administration Skill Set

Deals with support services, primarily focused on the facility and related topics.

M T H E

M	T	H	E	
__	__	__	__	Concierge
__	__	__	__	Construction
__	__	__	__	Contract Negotiation
__	__	__	__	Office Staff Training/ Supervision
__	__	__	__	Credit Transactions
__	__	__	__	Customer Service
__	__	__	__	Equipment Purchasing
__	__	__	__	Facility Managemen
__	__	__	__	Forms and Methods
__	__	__	__	HVAC
__	__	__	__	Leases
__	__	__	__	Library
__	__	__	__	Logistics
__	__	__	__	Telecommunications

M T H E

M	T	H	E	
__	__	__	__	Office Management
__	__	__	__	Office Relocations
__	__	__	__	Mailroom
__	__	__	__	Office Equipment
__	__	__	__	Parking
__	__	__	__	Policies & Procedures
__	__	__	__	Project Management
__	__	__	__	Real Estate
__	__	__	__	Reception
__	__	__	__	Records Management
__	__	__	__	Security
__	__	__	__	Space Planning
__	__	__	__	Utilities
__	__	__	__	_____
__	__	__	__	_____

Legal Skill Set

Performs functions required by law or by-laws of the corporation. Appraises and advises the company of all phases of its operations and relations from a legal viewpoint. Counsels on, prepares documents required by, and represents the company in connection with governmental controls, requirements, and statutory obligations.

M T H E

M	T	H	E	
__	__	__	__	Anti-Piracy Investigation
__	__	__	__	Antitrust
__	__	__	__	Board of Director Affairs
__	__	__	__	Case Management
__	__	__	__	City, County, State Issues
__	__	__	__	Contract Administration/ Mgmt
__	__	__	__	Copyrights & Trademarks
__	__	__	__	Corporate Secretary
__	__	__	__	Documentation
__	__	__	__	EEO, OSHA, EPA,

M T H E

M	T	H	E	
				FDA, etc.
__	__	__	__	Employment Law
__	__	__	__	Federal Issues
__	__	__	__	Financial Regulations
__	__	__	__	Government Contracts
__	__	__	__	Government/Legislative Affairs
__	__	__	__	Incorporation
__	__	__	__	Intellectual Property
__	__	__	__	International Agreements
__	__	__	__	Labor Issues
__	__	__	__	Leases & Records
__	__	__	__	Legislative Affairs
__	__	__	__	Licensing

___ ___ ___ ___ Litigation
___ ___ ___ ___ Lobbying
___ ___ ___ ___ Mergers &
    Acquisitions
___ ___ ___ ___ Patents
___ ___ ___ ___ Political Relations
___ ___ ___ ___ Purchase Agreements
___ ___ ___ ___ Real Estate Law
___ ___ ___ ___ Regulatory
    Compliance

___ ___ ___ ___ Safety Regulations
___ ___ ___ ___ Securities Registration
___ ___ ___ ___ Shareholder Proxies
___ ___ ___ ___ Stock Administration
___ ___ ___ ___ Taxes
___ ___ ___ ___ Transactions
___ ___ ___ ___ _____
___ ___ ___ ___ _____
___ ___ ___ ___ _____
___ ___ ___ ___ _____

Information Systems - Information Technology - Internet Skill Set

Works with the hardware, software, networks, data, and personnel supporting business objectives.

M T H E

___ ___ ___ ___ Analog Design
___ ___ ___ ___ Algorithm Development
___ ___ ___ ___ Applications Database Admin.
___ ___ ___ ___ Applications Development
___ ___ ___ ___ ASP Applications Systems Provider
___ ___ ___ ___ Broadband Networks
___ ___ ___ ___ Business Systems Planning
___ ___ ___ ___ Cabling
___ ___ ___ ___ Capacity Planning
___ ___ ___ ___ Chip Design
___ ___ ___ ___ CRM-Client Relationship Mgmt
___ ___ ___ ___ Computer Aided Design
___ ___ ___ ___ Computer Architecture
___ ___ ___ ___ Computer Configuration
___ ___ ___ ___ Computer Interface
___ ___ ___ ___ Computer Operations
___ ___ ___ ___ Computer Selection
___ ___ ___ ___ Computer Systems Conversion

M T H E

___ ___ ___ ___ Data Center Operations
___ ___ ___ ___ Data Mining
___ ___ ___ ___ Data Processing Management
___ ___ ___ ___ Data Security
___ ___ ___ ___ Database Administration
___ ___ ___ ___ Database Development
___ ___ ___ ___ Desktop Publishing
___ ___ ___ ___ Desktop Video Publishing
___ ___ ___ ___ Diagnostics
___ ___ ___ ___ Digital Design
___ ___ ___ ___ Digital Signal Processing
___ ___ ___ ___ Distributed Processing
___ ___ ___ ___ Ecommerce/B2B
___ ___ ___ ___ Electronic Data Interface (EDI)
___ ___ ___ ___ Enterprise Asset Management (EAP)
___ ___ ___ ___ Enterprise Level Applications
___ ___ ___ ___ Enterprise Resource Planning (ERP)
___ ___ ___ ___ Equipment Selection
___ ___ ___ ___ Field Support Engineering

— — — — Game Design
— — — — Graphics
— — — — Hardware
       Management
— — — — HTML/XML
— — — — Information
       Management
— — — — Information
       Technology Admin.
— — — — Integration Software
— — — — Intranet Development
— — — — Languages – Java,
       C++, etc.
— — — — Linear Programming
— — — — Linux Operating
       System
— — — — Methodology
       Engineering
— — — — Microprocessors
— — — — Modeling
— — — — Multiplexors
— — — — Network Engineering
— — — — Network Operations
       Management
— — — — Object Oriented
       Development
— — — — Office Automation
— — — — Performance
       Monitoring
— — — — Peripheral Equipment
— — — — Portal Design/
       Development
— — — — Process Development
— — — — Programming / Coding
— — — — Project Management
— — — — Release Management
— — — — Software
       Customization
— — — — Software Development

— — — — Software Engineering
— — — — Spreadsheets
— — — — Supplier Integration
— — — — Systems Analysis
— — — — Systems Applications
— — — — Systems Development
— — — — Systems Design
— — — — Systems Testing
— — — — Systems/Software
       Installation
— — — — Systems/Software
       Training
— — — — Technical Evangelism
— — — — Technical Support/
       Help Desk
— — — — Technical Writing
— — — — Telecommunications
— — — — Test Engineering
— — — — Tracking Systems
— — — — UNIX
— — — — Usability Engineering
— — — — User Education/
       Documentation
— — — — User Interface
— — — — Vendor Relations
— — — — Vendor Sourcing
— — — — Voice & Data
       Communications
— — — — Web Development/
       Graphic Design
— — — — Website Content
       Writer
— — — — Website Editor
— — — — Wireless Systems
— — — — Word Processing
— — — — _____
— — — — _____
— — — — _____
— — — — _____

Graphic Design/Desktop Publishing Skill Set

M T H E   M T H E

___ ___ ___ ___ QuarkXPress   ___ ___ ___ ___ Typing

___ ___ ___ ___ Illustrator   ___ ___ ___ ___ Formatting typing

___ ___ ___ ___ FreeHand   ___ ___ ___ ___ Web press

___ ___ ___ ___ Dreamweaver   ___ ___ ___ ___ Sheet press

___ ___ ___ ___ HTML coding   ___ ___ ___ ___ Creating die cuts

___ ___ ___ ___ Troubleshooting,   ___ ___ ___ ___ Naming conventions
problem solving   for file mgmt.

___ ___ ___ ___ FTP'ing on Internet   ___ ___ ___ ___ Package design

___ ___ ___ ___ Emailing files,   ___ ___ ___ ___ Printing terminology,
attachments   process

___ ___ ___ ___ Uploading files to   ___ ___ ___ ___ Communication skills
Internet   ___ ___ ___ ___ Team player/manager

___ ___ ___ ___ Preparing presentations   ___ ___ ___ ___ Able to meet deadlines

___ ___ ___ ___ Creating client mock-   ___ ___ ___ ___ Client relations skills
ups   ___ ___ ___ ___ Professionalism

___ ___ ___ ___ Color correction   ___ ___ ___ ___ Networking and social

___ ___ ___ ___ Color theory   skills

___ ___ ___ ___ Photoshop

___ ___ ___ ___ InDesign

___ ___ ___ ___ Adobe Acrobat

___ ___ ___ ___ Flash

___ ___ ___ ___ Action Scripting   ## Creative/Artistic/Musical Skill Set

___ ___ ___ ___ Converting from Mac
to PC and vice versa   ___ ___ ___ ___ Manual dexterity

___ ___ ___ ___ Organizing work flow   ___ ___ ___ ___ Fine motor control

___ ___ ___ ___ Project management   ___ ___ ___ ___ Eye-hand coordination

___ ___ ___ ___ Mounting artwork   ___ ___ ___ ___ Visual composition

___ ___ ___ ___ Pre-press, production   (balance, form,
work   color)

___ ___ ___ ___ Photo scanning   ___ ___ ___ ___ Drawing

___ ___ ___ ___ Understanding print   ___ ___ ___ ___ Computer design
bids   ___ ___ ___ ___ Musical composition

___ ___ ___ ___ Process color   ___ ___ ___ ___ Sense of rhythm

___ ___ ___ ___ Spot color   ___ ___ ___ ___ Musical ear

___ ___ ___ ___ Creative copy writing   ___ ___ ___ ___ Orientation to detail

___ ___ ___ ___ Typography   ___ ___ ___ ___ Imagination, creativity

     ___ ___ ___ ___ Ability to improvise

     ___ ___ ___ ___ Intuition, silencing
inner critic

Authentic Vocation™ Worksheet 5: Work and Other Experience

You are now ready to explore the fifth element of your Authentic Vocation, Work and Other Experience. One of the best ways to catalog your work experience is to do it in two parts. First, briefly describe the positions you have held and industries in which you held them in the table below:

Position	Industry

Now, for each position listed above, write at least 3 Work Experience Stories below or on your computer (for future reference). (You should have at least 8-10 stories in all.) If you wish, you can use the key words in the prior worksheet (AV Worksheet 4) to trigger ideas for stories. The 3 elements of a WES are:

C – Challenge or Circumstance when you began the project or task
A – Action you took to create a result or solve a problem
R – Result which followed, quantified whenever possible

Here's an example:

[Challenge:] When I was promoted to Sales and Marketing Director for Region 5, we were the lowest performing region of the 30 regional territories. My challenge was to bring the sales and overall performance numbers up as quickly as possible. [Action:] To do so, I met with the 20-person sales staff, jointly established some aggressive goals for the next 6-12 months, and developed a promotional strategy to increase customer awareness of our products which included incentives for new purchases within a stated length of time. [Result:] Within 90 days, sales were up by 15%, and by year-end we were second in the nation with $1.2 million in sales

For each position listed above, write at least one (ideally up to three) stories. Using the computer is best for this since you will also use the stories for your resume and for interview preparation.

Authentic Vocation™ Worksheet 6: Job/Career Targets

You are now ready to explore the sixth element of your Authentic Vocation, Job Descriptions and Career Paths. Now it is time to do some homework. (Did you think you were done with that?) With your responses to life purpose clue 1 (your spare time activities), 2 (aspects of your current job you enjoy), and 3 (your natural abilities), as well as the 4 subsequent factors, in hand, you can do some research. Your local library has a wide selection of resources to assist you in designing your new career. Begin by spending some time browsing through the *O*Net* web site at http://online.onetcenter.org/. This will give you all of the job classifications in various major career fields.

The purpose of this research is to expand your horizons. As you browse through this resource, note the Standard Occupational Classification (SOC) numbers and descriptions of the job classifications that *sound like fun to you*, that you would enjoy doing and feel you could do well (even if you might need additional training or education to do so). Please don't choose a code *only* because it "fits my training" or "is in the line of work I'm comfortable in." Be open to new ideas. Ignore (for now) all of the conditions such as money, location, education, experience, licenses, etc. *Don't rule something out because you don't think you can make enough money doing it.*

First, list the results of your research — that is, jot down the SOC codes and titles for up to 20 career fields and jobs that interest you.

Now, narrow your choices down to your top 10 favorites. To do this, keep in mind *first*, the choices which sound like the most fun, and *second*, those that are consistent with your leisure activities, favorite job tasks, and enjoyable natural skills. In this part of the exercise, you may take into account such things as education, location, and other "practical" considerations to some extent — but don't limit yourself too much. Mark each of your favorites — those that sound fun as well as within the realm of practicality — with a star.

You should now have a list of 10 career areas and/or job descriptions that sound like fun to you, and are at least within the realm of possibility for you to do. Now, let's return to your list of values from Worksheet 2. Can you narrow your list of job types further by comparing your important values with each of your 15 choices? If you can see at the outset that your important values cannot be fulfilled in one of your chosen careers or jobs, it should be eliminated from your list, since it will not result in the satisfaction you are seeking. (Note, however, that you may not be able to determine whether your values will be met until you have a particular company in mind.) Cross off any of your 10 favorites which are inconsistent with your important values and/or Life Purpose.

Be careful not to eliminate areas before you are fully informed. If some of the items on your list are areas you have not considered before, you may want to do some networking with others in the field, or do some additional research on that career area before deciding whether you can fulfill your value(s) in that job.

If you want to continue this research in more detail, other resources include directories such as *Dun and Bradstreet, Standard and Poors, Thomas Registry, Moody's,* and local and state directories, as well as individual industry reference books. The U.S. Department of Labor's *Occupational Outlook Handbook* is also helpful in generating ideas to expand your horizons.

Authentic Vocation™ Worksheet 7: Work Environment

You are now ready to explore the seventh element of your Authentic Vocation, Desired Work Environment. Your work environment can either enhance or detract from your enjoyment. The items listed below will help you evaluate each aspect of your work environment so that you can design it just the way you want it.

1. **Geographical Location.** Where would you like to work? In the state and city where you live — or somewhere else altogether? Perhaps this is a perfect time to explore that option realistically. Would you like to work in an office or outdoors? In an urban or rural setting?

2. **Pace.** A second aspect of your work environment is the pace of the business or office. Do you enjoy an environment that is bustling and busy, or do you prefer a peaceful, slower pace? How many hours do you want to work each week?

3. **Support.** The degree of support in the work environment is also important. One way to avoid burnout is to surround ourselves with a supportive environment — one in which we have a sense of significance, autonomy, challenge and support, and in which there are relatively few unmodifiable work stresses. In addition, mentoring programs, new employee orientation and similar programs create support. Indicate whether you prefer to have: __ little support; __ moderate support; __ a lot of support.

4. **Compensation.** How much money do you want to earn in your ideal job? Will you have certain fringe benefits? What are they? List those on a blank sheet of paper or computer screen, or use Authentic Vocation Worksheet 10, Wants/Needs Analysis, to distinguish your wants versus your needs in this regard.

5. Size. It is also important to evaluate whether you work best alone, with one or two co-owners, or in a large company setting. To help you evaluate your optimal work setting, consider the following profiles of the solo worker, the partner, and the team personality.

Solo Worker Profile

- Is independent
- Prefers working alone; likes privacy
- Is highly creative and contemplative
- Has a few carefully chosen friends
- Resists authority
- Is motivated by opportunity to create and to get credit for creation
- Likes to take risks
- Biggest fear: Loss of control

Partner Profile

- Enjoys (and needs) give and take feedback when making decisions and in conversation
- Is most creative in context of a close relationship
- Has a few long-term friends
- Needs equal amounts of time alone and with others
- Is an excellent listener
- Feels power comes from shared resources
- Shares risk-taking with partner
- Biggest fear: Rejection by partner

Team Personality Profile

- Enjoys esprit de corps of large organization, including process of gaining consensus
- Wants to be alone about 20% of the time
- Is motivated by competition
- Forms many friendships easily
- Comfortable with authority figures
- Is most creative in context of praise from team members and from leader
- Enjoys belonging to clubs
- Shares risks with team members and leader
- Biggest fear: Loneliness

You may find you have aspects of two of these profiles, or maybe even all three —but you probably have more qualities from one than any of the others. Which one most closely describes you: solo worker, partner, or team personality?

If you are a team personality type, also consider how large a company you wish to work for. Though the team dynamic is present in the 10-person company and a 1000-person company, your day to day experience in those two companies will be quite different.

The size of the ideal company for me is: _____.

6. **Primary Function.** Next, consider whether you prefer to work primarily with people, with data, or with things. Think about your hobbies and past jobs — what activities have given you the most joy: those involving interaction with people, working with data or information, or working on things with your hands?

7. **Corporate Culture: Vision, Values and Mission.** Culture, or "how we do things around here," is another important factor in work environment. Do you prefer a company that is conservative or radical, socially conscious or not, employee-oriented or bottom-line/results-oriented? Do you prefer that the company have a clear vision and mission, or that it "go with the flow"? Describe your ideal employer's culture.

To summarize: What would your ideal day at work be like? Where would you be doing it? What other aspects of environment are important to you? Write out your thoughts for future reference.

Authentic Vocation™ Worksheet 8: Business Reality

Now that you have explored your life's purpose and the other 6 factors of your ideal job, you should have a fairly accurate picture of the next job/career you wish to pursue. In the space below, describe your ideal job as accurately and completely as you can, stating it as though you already have the job. (For example, "I am working in a high tech company of approximately 35 people, in San Jose, California, doing computer assisted design. I make a salary of $_____ and have the following benefits: _____. I feel wonderfully satisfied in my work, since I work primarily with computers (my passion) and have two days off each week to pursue my hobby of hiking.")

Summarize the results of each of your previous worksheets on a separate screen or piece of paper using a format like this:

My life purpose (AV Worksheet 1):_____

My key values (worksheet 2):_____

My motivators (worksheet 3):_____

My motivated skills (worksheet 4):_____

My work and other experience (worksheet 5):_____

My job/industry targets (worksheet 6):_____

Desired work environment (worksheet 7):_____

Alternitavely, you can use the Ideal Job Template on page 310)

Then, incorporate these elements into a narrative summary on a separate screen or piece of paper describing the ideal job as though you already had it.

Business Reality

Your next step will be to "filter" your vision for your ideal job through the lens of "business reality." In other words, is it financially viable to pursue your job in the form you have stated it above? Does it meet a need in the business world or workplace? Or do you need to make some changes for that to occur? Using one or more of the salary sites on the Internet listed below, determine what the average salary range is for the type of work you have described:

www.careers.wsj.com   www.wageweb.com
www.jobsmart.org   www.salary.com
www.abbott-langer.com   http://stats.bls/gov/oes/oes_data.htm

My Minimum: $_____ per year

My Maximum: $_____ per year

Average for this Occupation: $_____ per year

Second, you may want to check the Occupational Outlook Handbook at http://stats.bls.gov/ocohome.htm and/or the Career Guide to Industries at http://stats.bls.gov/cghome.htm to determine whether the occupation you have chosen is projected to be growing, stable or declining over the coming years. If the specific occupation you have chosen does not appear financially viable, what related positions are available? (use the OOH to keyword search, consult O*Net at http://online.onetcenter.org, and ask people in your network – as well as your career coach – for ideas).

Finally, do you know how long to expect in which to complete your job search? The typical search takes three to six months, or one month for every $10,000 of salary. What plans have you made to support yourself financially during your search?

4. Symbol Meditation

Instructions: This guided meditation may be used to help an individual clarify his/her life purpose. It is a more "right brain" process than the 10 clues in Authentic Vocation Worksheet 1 and draws on the client's inner wisdom, as visualized by a wise being with whom they dialog. It can be read to the person by the coach or a friend, or tape recorded.

Sit in a chair with a straight back, or on the floor with your spine erect. If you are on a chair, your legs should be uncrossed, feet flat on the floor. Your arms should be lying loosely in your lap in a receptive position.

Relax your body completely. Begin with your feet, and move up through your legs, thighs, stomach, chest, arms, hands, shoulders, neck, head and face. Take a few minutes to do this.

Now close your eyes and take a deep, slow breath. Count to 4 as you inhale, hold just for a moment, and then release to the count of 2. Now again, slowly, breathe in, hold, and release.

When you are relaxed and breathing slowly, imagine a beautiful meadow. Everything is green and bright, the sun is shining, and there are beautiful flowers everywhere. You hear the sound of a brook babbling joyfully nearby. You have never felt so peaceful.

As you are sitting in this meadow, enjoying the tranquility and beauty of it, you notice a wise being coming toward you. You recognize it as your Wise Self, even if you have not seen it before. The being comes over to you and sits down near you. You realize that it is making itself available to you to provide whatever information you need for your growth and development.

You then ask this being to give you a symbol of your life's purpose, a symbol that represents your purpose in all of its aspects. Your Wise Self gives you this symbol now. Notice what it is. Do not judge of question it; simply accept it. Decide to remember this symbol. Hold it in your hands and examine it. Does it have a color? A shape? Is it large or small? Does it remind you of an object in the physical world? How does it make you feel?

Thank your Wise Self for this symbol. Now take the symbol and place it inside the center of your chest. This is your energy center of love, the highest love there is. Allow your symbol to energize you, to radiate light throughout every cell of your body. Feel it penetrate your being, allowing you to embody its essence. Allow yourself to experience what it is like to take the essence of this symbol, your essential life's purpose, into every aspect of your life. Your work, your relationships, your body, your possessions – all reflect your life's purpose as if in a prism.

You look across the meadow and see that your Wise Self is beckoning you to a bridge. The bridge is surrounded by other beings, all very joyful and happy. There is a mood of celebration. You walk slowly toward the bridge, feeling the presence of your symbol within you. You realize that the beings are celebrating you and your newfound awareness of your life's purpose.

Your Wise Self explains that the purpose of the bridge is to provide a connection between your life's purpose and the physical world in which you live. If you are now ready to begin to fulfill your life's purpose, as embodied in the symbol, walk across the bridge. Your Wise Self meets you at the center of the bridge and accompanies you to the other side, where the other beings are celebrating and supporting you. You and the other beings rejoice together that you have discovered your purpose, and that you are now allowing it to manifest in physical form. Everything that is necessary for the unfoldment of your life's purpose will now come to you, easily, in perfect time, exactly when you need it.

You pause now to savor the moment. You congratulate yourself on this experience of awakening, and on your dedication to your growth. You know that whenever you wish to remind yourself of your purpose and of the support you have for the fulfillment of that purpose, or when you have questions about how to proceed on your path, you can simply return in your mind's eye to this bridge, this special place of celebration.

Then, when you are ready, you become aware of your physical body once more. You return to the present moment, and gently open your eyes.

5. Ideal Job Template

1. **My life purpose statement.** My life's purpose is to
    _____through
    _____

2. **My work values.** My top 5 work values are:
    a.
    b.
    c.
    d.
    e.

3. **My motivators.** The factors and situations that motivate me are:
    _____.

4. **My skills.** My key skills that I enjoy using and want to use in my next job are:
    _____.

5. **My work experience.** The things that I have enjoyed about my past jobs that I wish to recreate in my next job are:
    _____.

6. **My ideal career area.** My chosen career area is: _____.
    My ideal job titles are: _____.

7. **My work environment.** My ideal work environment is described as:
    Geographic area:

    _____

    Pace:

    _____

    Degree of support around me:

    _____

    Compensation range: $_____to $_____
    Company size:

    _____

    Solo/Partner/Team Setting:

    _____

    People/Data/Things as Primary Focus:

    _____   _____

    Company Culture:

    _____

6. Entrepreneurial Quiz
Do You Have the Entrepreneurial Personality?

Question	Yes	No
Is it important to you to accomplish something meaningful with your life?	____	____
Do you typically set both short- and long-term goals for yourself?	____	____
Do you usually achieve your goals?	____	____
Do you enjoy working on your own?	____	____
Do you like to perform a variety of tasks in your job?	____	____
Are you self-disciplined?	____	____
Do you like to be in control of your working environment?	____	____
Do you take full responsibility for your successes *and* failures?	____	____
Can you place the needs of your business above your family when necessary?	____	____
Are you in excellent physical, mental and emotional health?	____	____
Do you have the drive and energy to achieve your goals?	____	____
Do you have work experience in the type of business you wish to start?	____	____
Have you ever been so engrossed in your work that time passed unnoticed?	____	____
Do you consider "failures" as opportunities to learn and grow?	____	____
Can you hold to your ideas and goals even when others disagree with you?	____	____
Are you willing to take moderate risks to achieve your goals?	____	____
Can you afford to lose the money you invest in your business?	____	____
When the need arises, are you willing to do a job that may not interest you?	____	____
Are you willing to work hard to acquire new skills?	____	____
Do you usually stick with a project until it is completed?	____	____

Give yourself 1 point for each "yes" answer. You should have a score of at least 15 if you are to be successful as a business owner. It is not necessary to answer all of these questions yes to be successful, but if you answer no to some of them, you will want to evaluate what that means to you and how significantly it may impact your ability to run your own business. Can you hire people to fill that need/trait or help you develop it?

7. Are You Coachable?

Please circle the number next to each of the following statements on the 1-4 scale as follows: 1 = not at all true, 2 = somewhat true, 3 = true, 4 = very true. You will then review the results of this quiz with your coach so that you can, together, determine whether coaching is the right option for you at this time so that you can gain maximum benefit.

NT	ST	T	VT	
1	2	3	4	I am prepared to be on time for all coaching appointments as scheduled, and to give at least 24 hours' notice if I cannot.
1	2	3	4	I am willing to take an active role in the coaching process and to follow through on action steps as agreed with my coach.
1	2	3	4	I am at a point in my life when I will try out new ideas and ways of doing things, as agreed with my coach.
1	2	3	4	I am willing to allow my coach to facilitate my process of discovery, and to freely share the insights I experience.
1	2	3	4	I am ready to willingly enter into a partnership with my coach to create a life that is even better than I have imagined alone.
1	2	3	4	I am willing to be open, honest and authentic with my coach.
1	2	3	4	I am willing to recognize my own "stuff" (limiting issues and beliefs) and to take responsibility for changing when it is in my best interest.
1	2	3	4	If at any time I feel the coaching relationship is not working for me, I will share this with my coach and work toward a mutually acceptable solution.
1	2	3	4	I have sufficient funds to invest in the coaching, and see coaching as an investment in my personal and/or professional future.
1	2	3	4	I do not have any depression, anxiety or other mental illness or other issue that would interfere with my ability to be coached.
_____				Add total score of all numbers circled

Scoring key: 10-16 – Coaching may not benefit you now; 17-25 – You may be coachable, but will need to adhere to all agreements carefully; 26-32 – You are coachable; 33-40 - You are very coachable and should be a delightful client!

8. What Do Career Coaches Do?

Career coaching is an interactive pocess of exploring work-related issues – leading to effective action – in which the coach acts as both a *catalyst* and *facilitator* of individual and, in turn, organizational development and transformation. Career coaches connect people with their passion, purpose, values and other critical aspects of their ideal work. They help their clients learn to manage their own careers – whether they work for themselves or for an organization. This empowers the client as he/she faces the typical 5-10 career changes in his/her life, so that he/she can continue to grow personally and professionally through his/her work. Career coaches also facilitate the client's process of developing and implementing a job search or business start-up plan to activate the client's Authentic Vocation.™

Career Coaches:

- Connect people with a deeper level of motivation than "just a job;" clients **discover their passion and purpose** to guide their decisions, empowering them to choose work they love, make a good living and still have a balanced life
- Distinguish themselves from career counselors and consultants by **building career management skills,** which enables the client to navigate future transitions
- Probe for **deeper levels of motivation** that, when addressed, cause permanent QuantumShifts!™ rather than providing just a "quick fix"
- Create effective **coaching interactions** by listening, providing feedback, asking powerful questions, observing and modeling
- **Remove blocks to career progress,** such as self-limiting beliefs, incomplete awareness of marketable skills, lack of purpose and more
- Improve clients' **ability to market and sell themselves** in the job market regardless of economic conditions
- Increase individual **potential for career growth** and **future earning power**
- Assist clients in becoming **"career self-reliant,"** taking control and ownership of their own career development
- **Enhance their clients' job satisfaction** through the discovery of their Authentic Vocation™

What Do Internal Career Coaches Do (Inside Their Organizations)?

- Increase the client's awareness of career paths and **enhance fit** to achieve "right person/right job"
- Improve the capability of both individual and organization to **manage constant change and transition**
- Provide and model **communication styles** that enhance internal problem-solving skills, appreciate differences, and lead to long-term progress, rather than creating dependency on the coach
- Promote a **win-win balance of work/life priorities**, using the desired states of both individual and organization as benchmarks
- Guide organizational systems to **evolve their culture** by increasingly valuing their employees, implementing career development as a priority, and retaining human capital
- **Blend training, organizational development, career/ employee development and coaching** at every level in an organization

To get results and to learn more about how to enhance your personal and/or organizational capability, please call for more information. Your initial telephone consultation is free.

Career Coach Institute
1-866-CCOACH-4
www.careercoachinstitute.com
email: coach@careercoachinstitute.com

9. Coaching Agreements

COACHING AGREEMENT "A"

This agreement, between _____ (referred to as "Coach") and _____ (referred to as "Client") will begin on _____, 200_, and will continue for a minimum of three (3) months. At the conclusion of three months, this agreement will convert to a month-to-month renewable contract.

Fees. The fee for the initial intake meeting is $_____ and for the initial three months of coaching is $_____ per month [or, alternatively, $_____ for the XYZ Coaching Package, which shall include (insert description)]. Fees are payable (check one) ____ in advance, in exchange for a ___% discount off the full fee; ___at the beginning of each month at or before the first session of each month. An average of four sessions per month is used in calculating the monthly fee (if any). The monthly fee is not waived for periods when Coach or Client may be on vacation. Assessments to be administered during the coaching interaction shall be billed in addition to the monthly coaching fees unless otherwise agreed in advance.

Dates and Times. Coaching sessions shall take place each _____ (day of the week) beginning on _____, at _____ a.m./p.m. Unless otherwise agreed, coaching shall be done by telephone, and each session shall be approximately 30 minutes in length (except for the initial intake session, which shall run _____ minutes). Client shall call Coach at the agreed upon time; if the line is busy or goes to voicemail or Coach does not answer, Client shall call again in 5 minutes. If Coach again does not answer, the session shall be deemed to be postponed.

Cancellation. Client is required to give Coach at least 24 hours' notice of intended cancellation of a weekly session, or the session is forfeited. There is a $25.00 fee assessed for each missed appointment. This fee is in addition to the monthly fee. If a session is missed due to Coach unavailability as described in the previous paragraph, the session shall not be forfeited, but shall be rescheduled at the Client's and Coach's mutual convenience.

Client's Responsibilities. Client agrees to:
1. Arrive at each session on time
2. Bring an issue or agenda to the session
3. Turn off any cellular phone, call waiting, pager and other distractions during the session
4. Let the Coach know if at any time the coaching is not working as desired and use his/her best efforts to resolve any issues that may arise with the Coach.

Coach's Responsibilities. Coach agrees to:
1. Hold all of the information disclosed in the coaching sessions in confidence
2. Facilitate Client's progress toward his/her goals

3. Use his/her best efforts within the guidelines of the coaching relationship

Termination. This agreement may be terminated by either party upon at least thirty (30) days' written notice to the other.

Entire Agreement. This written agreement constitutes the entire agreement between the parties. It shall be governed by the laws of the state of _____. If any provision of this agreement shall be deemed invalid, the remaining provisions shall remain intact. If any dispute should arise from this agreement, it shall be resolved according to rules of the American Arbitration Association.

So agreed this _____ day of _____, 200__.

_____   _____
Client   Coach

COACHING AGREEMENT "B"

Date

Dear _____,

I am pleased to have the opportunity to work with you in the capacity of Coach, with the intention of facilitating your achievement of personal and professional goals and desired outcomes. These goals and outcomes will be of your own design. In the course of this process, I will not provide expert advice, but will facilitate your strategies for discovering and achieving what you choose. The purpose of our interaction is to keep you on purpose and aligned with your intentions and to support your success.

Coaching services will be provided at mutually agreeable times and places. Each coaching session will consist of one-half hour in-person or telephone session per week for a period of three months, renewable month to month thereafter. The fees for the coaching services shall be $_____ per month, due and payable at the beginning of each month. If you desire to pay your three months of services in advance, you will be entitled to a ____% discount off the full fee.

The services to be provided by the coach to you, the client, are designed jointly with you. Client acknowledges that coaching is not expert advice, therapy or counseling, but is a professional service designed to facilitate your forward progress on the issues of your choice.

All matters discussed in our sessions will be held in strictest confidence. The coach will be honest and straightforward, asking clarifying questions and making requests, among other techniques. As the client, you will also be honest and straightforward, will appear for your sessions on time, will give at least 24 hours notice if you must cancel a session, and will bring an agenda or issue to be discussed to each session.

If these terms are agreeable to you, please so indicate by signing in the appropriate space below. I look forward to working with you.

_____   _____
Client   Date   Coach   Date

COACHING AGREEMENT "C"

Coach Name

Address

Phone

Email

1. I agree to be on time for each phone or in person appointment. If the session is conducted over the phone, I agree to call Coach at the agreed time.
2. I agree to an initial series of 12 sessions within a 3-month time period.
3. I understand I can terminate the project at any time, and that if I decide to do so it will be in context of a scheduled session for that purpose. I understand that I can seek a second opinion from another consultant/coach at any time.
4. Sessions are approximately thirty minutes in length.
5. I agree to pay
    $_____each_____starting_____.
6. I agree to have the payment in Coach's office by the 1st of the month.
7. I agree to make session cancellations by calling at least 24 hours before the scheduled appointment. I understand that if I fail to do so I will be charged.
8. I agree to take an active role in the consulting process by being absolutely honest with Coach and myself. I especially agree to be absolutely honest about my feelings or issues I have about the coaching process or about Coach as my coach.
9. I understand that Coach is not a licensed psychotherapist and will not diagnose or treat mental or emotional disorders for a fee.
10. I understand that Coach uses coaching techniques such as assessments, interviews, feedback, [etc. – you fill in].
11. I agree to complete all agreed-upon assignments and requests for information.
12. I agree to fax or send assignments so that they arrive at Coach's office three days before a scheduled session.
13. I understand that I am absolutely responsible for my own business, life, and actions, and that I initiate the consulting/coaching process with this in mind.
14. I understand that Coach does not work with clients actively in the grip of a chemical addiction (drugs, alcohol and tobacco). I agree to report any use of such substances immediately to my coach. I understand that at least 14 days' substance-free must be attained before beginning the consulting/coaching process.

15. I understand that Coach actively markets his/her practice based on a formalized referral system. If I am satisfied with the results of this work, I will refer two other individuals for a risk-free, explorative consultation.

16. My most important consulting/coaching goals are:

_____

_____

_____

_____

_____

17. My coaching/consulting history:

Experience   Outcome   Reason Terminated

18. I agree to take 100% responsibility for my complete understanding and agreement of all the information above. I understand that my honoring these agreements I double the effectiveness of the coaching process.

Name _____

Date _____

10. Coaching Intake Form

Name: _____

Address: _____

City/State/ZIP: _____

Telephone: Day_____Evening_____Cell_____

Fax:_____

Email address:_____

Web site (if any):_____

Name of Employer (if any): _____

Employer's Address:_____

City/State/ZIP:_____

Your Position/Title:_____

How Long?_____

Duties:_____
_____
_____

Previous Position/Title:_____

How Long?_____

Duties:_____
_____
_____

Summary of Prior Work Experience:
_____
_____

Previous Assesments Completed:

Assessment	MBTI	DISC	PVQ	ECI	Proscan
Date					
Result (if known)					

What degree(s) and certifications do you have?

Degree/Certification	College/University	Major	Year Obtained

In the past, have you worked with:

A coach?   Y/N   How long/what years?

A therapist? Y/N   How long/what years?

Major issues addressed:

What is the primary reason(s) you are entering into a coaching experience at this time?

Marital Status: Married   Divorced   Single

                   Widowed   Other

NOTE: Our coaching relationship is confidential. Unless you disclose issues which your coach is required to disclose to the authorities (e.g., intent to harm yourself or others), all of the content of our conversations will be held in confidence.

Is this confidentiality policy acceptable to you? Y/N

How would you rank your current level of satisfaction with each of the following areas of your life?

Life Area	**Very Satisfied**	**Satisfied**	**Dissatisfied**
Work	_____	_____	_____
Emotional health	_____	_____	_____
Physical health/well-being	_____	_____	_____
Mental health	_____	_____	_____
Finances	_____	_____	_____
Spirituality/religion	_____	_____	_____
Relationship with spouse/significant other	_____	_____	_____
Relationship with children	_____	_____	_____

Relationships with boss or coworkers	_____	_____	_____
Social network/friendships	_____	_____	_____
Self-confidence/self-esteem	_____	_____	_____

What was your greatest success in the past year?

In your lifetime?

What is your biggest challenge right now? Or asked another way, what factor(s) is/are holding you back from having everything you want?

Describe below your ideal life, assuming you could create your life exactly as you want it to be:

What are your most important goals for the next 6 months?

1

2

3

4

5

6

What are you like when you are at your best?

How would you like me to be as your coach? (e.g., demanding, gentle, challenging, etc.)

What else would you like your coach to know about you and your current life situation?

Thanks for completing this form!!!

II. Coaching Plan

COACHING PLAN WORKSHEET

Goal (with timeline)	Action Steps	Result

Remember, "Goals" are what you want to accomplish and should be specific, realistic, measurable (including a timeline) and depend on your own responsibility. They should answer these questions:

    a.   What do I want to change in my life in the next 3-6 months?

    b.   What do I want to improve?

    c.   What is in my way? Or what do I want to overcome?

"Action Steps" are the steps you take to achieve your goals. They should answer the questions:

    a.   What specific actions will I take to achieve my goal(s)?

    b.   What action steps are most urgent (i.e. must be done first) and which are less urgent?

    c.   If I need more resources, information or contacts to achieve my goal, where will I find it?

"Results" are the ultimate outcome of achieving your goals. For example, if your goal is to get your web site designed and uploaded to the web, the result would be providing a source of information through which to attract clients and in turn build your business. These should answer the question "What is the payoff for completing the Action Steps?"

12. Pre-Session Worksheet

Coaching Call Preparation Form
Email to [COACH] 24 hours BEFORE your call
EMAIL ADDRESS: _____

Name: _____ Date: _____

My greatest wins since our last call

The commitments that I made to myself on our last call were

What I was able to do around those commitments included

Challenges I am facing

Opportunities that I am facing

What I want to focus on with my coach today is…..

13. Post-Session Worksheet

After Coaching Call Reflection
Email to [Coach] within 12 hours AFTER your call
EMAIL ADDRESS: _____

Name: _____   Date: _____

Here are the ways I benefited as a result of our call

Commitments I'm making to myself for this week include

Systems, habits, practices or programs I am working on to support me include

Questions, ideas or issues that I'm still thinking about that we didn't discuss

What I'd like you, [COACH], to do more or less of to coach me optimally...

What you can do for me that I would love the most is

14. Professional Balance Wheel

Reprinted with permission from Advantage Coaching (www.advantagecoaching.com)

1. Within each of the following eight areas, circle the number that best represents **your level of satisfaction** in that area of your career ("7" = Completely satisfied; "1" = Completely dissatisfied):

2. Connect the numbers around the circle to form a wheel.

The rounder the wheel, the more balanced your life is. Imagine how your car would travel if all the wheels were in this shape!

15. Ideal Day Exercise

A powerful tool to help a client break through barriers is to ask them to describe their "Ideal Day." Even the instructions for the exercise are a stretch for many people. They must go beyond "I see myself as a sales representative for a consumer products company working with Fortune 500 customers." That's a start! But for it to penetrate to the subconscious level – which is critical to activate the powers of individual creativity – the client must use both intellect and emotions in the exercise. Here are the instructions:

"Imagine that you are writing a movie script which depicts a day in your ideal life. You must describe every detail of the scenery, your feelings, and your activities, as well as the people with whom you are interacting. Describe it in such vivid form that a producer (someone besides you!) could read your description and instruct others in building the props, casting the characters, bringing the right personality and style to the acting, and sequence the activities the actors are doing! Include your work, your home, your family life, your leisure activities, any special aspects in your environment, the pace, and each activity you do from dawn till bedtime. Imagine there are no restrictions in time, money, or any other aspect. Ready? Write that description in the space below, on a separate sheet, or on your computer. Take 10 to 20 minutes to do this."

16. AV Worksheet 9: Job Search Marketing Plan Template

Designed for   Date:

Action	Total	Week 1	Week 2	Week 3	Week 4	Week 5	Week 6	Ltr Sent	Calls	Actual Activity		
										Interviews	Offers	
UNPUBLISHED (60%)												
1. Networking	30	5	5	5	5	5	5					
Follow up calls plus new contacts	75	N/A	15	15	15	15	15					
2. Direct Targeted to Employers	60	10	10	10	10	10	10					
3. News events	30	5	5	5	5	5	5					
PUBLISHED (40%)												
4. Recruiters	60	10	10	10	10	10	10					
5. Ads	60	10	10	10	10	10	10					
6. Job Board Postings	60	10	10	10	10	10	10					
7. Job Fairs	6	1	1	1	1	1	1					
TOTALS	381	51	66	66	66	66	66					

17. Company Research Data Sheet

Company Overview:

History, Size, Growth:

Products and/or Services:

Clientele/Customer Base:

Key Management People:

Company Culture:

Possible Needs/Areas of Expansion:

Other Notes:

18. Authentic Vocation Worksheet 10 — Wants/Needs Analysis

Item	Amount Needed (or yes/no for core requirement)	Amount Wanted (or yes/no for whether desired)	Job Offer No. 1	Job Offer No. 2
Compensation				
Salary				
Bonuses/commission				
Stock options				
Relocation package				
401k plan, match				
Medical insurance				
Holidays/vacation				
Life insurance				
Disability insurance				
Sick/personal leave				
Travel expense reimbursement and/or company car or allowance				
Severance package				
Health club membership				
Computer allowance				
Tuition reimbursement				
Other benefits desired				
Authentic Vocation Fit				
Expresses my life purpose				
Job/company in alignment with my key values				
Activates my motivators				
Fits my desired job/industry target				
Uses my motivated skills				
Leverages my past experience				

Item	Amount Needed (or yes/no for core requirement)	Amount Wanted (or yes/no for whether desired)	Job Offer No. 1	Job Offer No. 2
Embodies desired work environment				
Conforms to business reality and meets my financial needs				
Career Development:				
Training provided/required for skills development				
Future career growth				
Cross-training encouraged				
Career development plans used in performance evaluation and planning				
Work/Life Balance				
% travel required				
Flexible work options				
Hours expected/required				
Family-friendly policies (e.g. time off for children's needs allowed/ encouraged)				
Commuting time/distance from home				
Company Analysis				
Risk factor (e.g. start-up vs. well-established company)				
Turnover levels				
Revenues expanding, static or declining				
Competitive pressures in industry				
Expected job stability				
Merger/acquisition potential				
Reputation (consult Better Business Bureau, customers of company, and other staff)				

19. Coaching Skills Checklist
Coaching Competencies Self-Assessment

_____ 1. Understands and exhibits the ICF Standards of Conduct

_____ 2. Understands and follows ICF Ethical Guidelines

_____ 3. Clearly communicates the distinction between coaching and other related professions

_____ 4. Refers client to other professionals as needed

_____ 5. Understands, effectively discusses with client the guidelines and parameters of the coaching relationship (logistics, fees, scheduling, inclusion of others)

_____ 6. Reaches agreement about what is appropriate in the relationship and what is not

_____ 7. Determines whether there is an effective match between coaching style and client needs

_____ 8. Shows concern for client's welfare and future

_____ 9. Demonstrates personal integrity

_____ 10. Establishes clear agreements, keeps promises

_____ 11. Demonstrates respect for client

_____ 12. Provides ongoing support for and champions new behaviors (including those involving risk taking and fear of failure)

_____ 13. Asks permission to coach in sensitive areas

_____ 14. Is present and flexible during the coaching process; dances in the moment

_____ 15. Accesses his/her own intuition, trusts his/her own inner knowing, "goes with the gut"

_____ 16. Is open to not knowing, takes risks

_____ 17. Sees many ways to work with the client, chooses in the moment what is most effective

_____ 18. Uses humor effectively

_____ 19. Confidently shifts perspectives, experiments with new possibilities for own action

_____ 20. Demonstrates confidence in working with strong emotions

_____ 21. Attends to client and client's agenda

_____ 22. Hears client's concerns, goals, values and beliefs re: what's possible

_____ 23. Distinguishes words, tone of voice and body language

_____ 24. Summarizes, paraphrases, reiterates, mirrors back

_____ 25. Encourages, accepts, explores and reinforces client's expressions

_____ 26. Integrates, builds on client ideas, suggestions

_____ 27. Bottom-lines

_____ 28. Allows client to vent or "clear" a situation

_____ 29. Asks questions reflecting active listening, understanding of client perspective

_____ 30. Asks questions that evoke discovery, insight, etc.

_____ 31. Asks open-ended questions

_____ 32. Asks questions that move client toward what they desire

_____ 33. Is clear, articulate and direct in giving feedback

_____ 34. Reframes, articulates to enhance client understanding

_____ 35. Clearly states coaching objectives

_____ 36. Uses appropriate language

_____ 37. Uses metaphor and analogy

_____ 38. Goes beyond what is said

_____ 39. Invokes inquiry

_____ 40. Identifies for client his/her underlying concerns

_____ 41. Helps client discover new thoughts, beliefs, perceptions, emotions, moods etc. to assist them achieve what is important to them

_____ 42. Communicates broader perspectives to client, inspires commitment to shift viewpoint and find new possibilities

_____ 43. Helps client see different, interrelated factors affecting them

_____ 44. Expresses insights in useful, meaningful ways

_____ 45. Identifies major strengths vs. areas for learning and growth

_____ 46. Asks client to distinguish between trivial and significant issues

_____ 47. Brainstorms and assists client to define actions to deepen new learning

_____ 48. Helps client focus on and explore concerns, opportunities central to coaching goals

_____ 49. Engages client to explore alternative ideas and solutions and evaluate options

_____ 50. Promotes active experimentation and self-discovery

_____ 51. Celebrates client successes

_____ 52. Challenges client's assumptions and perspectives to provoke new ideas, possibilities

_____ 53. Advocates points of view aligned with client goals and, without attachment, engages client to consider them

_____ 54. Helps client "do it now"

_____ 55. Encourages stretches and challenges as well as comfortable learning pace

_____ 56. Consolidates collected information, establishes coaching plan

_____ 57. Creates plan with results that are attainable, measurable, specific and with target dates

_____ 58. Makes plan adjustments as warranted

_____ 59. Helps client identify and access resources for learning

_____ 60. Identifies and targets early successes

_____ 61. Clearly requests actions to move client toward their goals

_____ 62. Demonstrates follow-through by asking client about actions committed to during prior session

_____ 63. Acknowledges client for actions taken, learnings since last session

_____ 64. Effectively prepares, organizes and reviews with client info obtained during sessions

_____ 65. Keeps client on track between sessions, holds attention on coaching plan

_____ 66. Focuses on coaching plan but remains open to adjusting it

_____ 67. Can move back and forth between big picture [and current situation]

_____ 68. Promotes client's self-discipline, holds client accountable (including specific plan and time frames)

_____ 69. Develops client's ability to make decisions, address key concerns, develop self

_____ 70. Positively confronts client when they do not take agreed-upon actions

20. Professional Resources for Career Coaches

Professional Associations:

Coaching:
International Coach Federation www.coachfederation.org
Coachville www.coachville.com
Professional Coaches and Mentors Association www.pcma-online.com

Career Development:
International Association of Career Management Professionals (IACMP) www.iacmp.org
International Board of Career Management Certification (IBCMC) www.ibcmc.com
International Career Development Conference www.careerccc.com
National Career Development Association www.ncda.org
State Career Development Associations (www.ncda.org lists some)

Books

Career Coaching and Career Development

Baber, Anne & Waymon, Lynne, *How to Fireproof Your Career* (Berkley 1995)
Beck, Martha, *Finding Your Own North Star* (Crown 2002)
Bench, Marcia, *The Career Workbook* (High Flight Press 1992)
Berman Fortgang, Laura, *Take Yourself to the Top* (Warner 1998)
Berman Fortgang, Laura, *Live Your Best Life* (Warner 2001)
Bolles, Richard & Figler, Howard, *The Career Counselor's Handbook* (Ten Speed Press 2000)
Buckingham, Marcus & Coffman, Curt, *Now Discover Your Strengths,* (Simon & Schuster 2001)
Buckingham, Marcus & Coffman, Curt, *First Break All the Rules,* (Simon & Schuster 1999)
Enelow, Wendy, *101 Ways to Recession-Proof Your Career* (McGraw-Hill 2002)
Gallwey, W. Timothy, *The Inner Game of Work* (Random House 2000)
Levoy, Gregg, *Callings* (Three Rivers Press 1997)
Lore, Nicholas, *The Pathfinder: How to Choose or Change Your Career for a Lifetime of Satisfaction and Success* (Fireside 1998)

Change and Transition

Bridges, William, Ph.D., *Transitions* (Perseus 1980)
Bridges, William, Ph.D. *Managing Transitions* (Perseus 1991)
Perkins-Reed, Marcia, *Thriving in Transition* (Simon & Schuster 1996)

Changing Workplace

Bridges, William, *Creating You & Co: Learn to Think Like the CEO of Your Own Career* (Perseus 1998)

Bridges, William, *Jobshift: How to Prosper in a Workplace Without Jobs* (Perseus 1995)

Goleman, Daniel, *Working with Emotional Intelligence* (Bantam 2000)

Handy, Charles, *The Hngry Spirit: Beyond Capitalism – A Quest for Purpose in the Modern World* (Broadway 1999)

Handy, Charles and Bennis, Warren, *The Age of Unreason* (Harvard Business School Press 1998)

Johnson, Spencer & Blanchard, Ken, *Who Moved My Cheese?* (Putnam 1998)

Naisbitt, Nana et al, *High Tech, High Touch* (Nicholas Brealey 201)

Rifkin, Jeremy, *The End of Work* (Tarcher 1996)

Coaching Techniques

Crane, Thomas, *The Heart of Coaching* (FTA Press 2002)

Hargrove, Robert, *Masterful Coaching* (Pfeiffer & Co. 1995)

Richardson, Cheryl *Take Time for Your Life* (Broadway 1999)

Whitworth, Laura, et al, *Co-Active Coaching* (Davies Black 1998)

Corporate Career Development

Bridges, William, *The Character of Otganizations: Using Personality Type in Organization Development* (Davies-Black 2000)

Hendricks, Gay & Ludeman, Kate, *The Corporate Mystic* (Bantam 1996)

Knowdell, Richard, *Building a Career Development Program* (Davies-Black 1996)

Niemela, Cynder & Lewis, Rachael, *Leading High Impact Teams,* (High Impact Publishing 2001)

Senge, Peter, et al *The Dance of Change: The Challenges to Sustaining Momentum in Learning Organizations* (Doubleday 1999)

Whyte, David, *The Heart Aroused* (Currency/Doubleday 1996)

Creativity and Motivation

Cameron, Julia, *The Artist's Way* (Tarcher/Putnam 1992)

Csikszentmihalyi, Mihaly, *Flow: The Psychology of Optimal Experience* (Harper Collins 1991)

Executive Coaching and Leadership Development

Bolman, Lee G. & Deal, Terrence, *Leading with Soul* (Wiley 2001)

Goldsmith, Marshall (Ed.), *Coaching for Leadership: How the World's Greatest Coaches Help Leaders Learn* (Jossey Bass 2000)

Goleman, Daniel et al, *Primal Leadership: Realizing the Power of Emotional Intelligence* (Harvard Business School Press 2002)

Job Search Techniques

Baber, Anne and Waymon, Lynne, *How to Fireproof Your Career* (Berkley 1995)

Bench, Marcia, *How to Find the Job You Want* (High Flight Press 1995

Wendleton, Kate, *Getting Interviews* (Five O'Clock Club 2000)

Wendleton, Kate, *Interviewing and Salary Negotiation* (Five O'Clock Club 1999)

Wendleton, Kate, *Building a Great Resume* (Five O'Clock Club 1999)

Wendleton, Kate, *Targeting the Job You Want* (Five O'Clock Club 2000)

Ladder of Inference

Argyris, C., Increasing Leadership Effectiveness. (Wiley 1976)

Argyris, C., On Organizational Learning. (Blackwell 1993)

Argyris, C. & Schon, D. (1974). Theory in Practice. (Jossey-Bass 1974)

Argyris, C., Reasoning, Learning and Action. Individual and Organizational. (Jossey-Bass 1982)

Argyris, C., Knowledge for Action. (Jossey-Bass 1993)

Argyris, C., Putnam, R. & Smith, D., Action Science. (Jossey Bass 1985)

Senge, Peter, *The Fifth Discipline Fieldbook* (Currency Doubleday 1994)

Life Purpose and Work

Adrienne, Carol & Redfield, James, *The Purpose of Your Life* (Eagle Brook 1999)

Leider, Richard, *The Power of Purpose* (Berrett-Koehler 1997)

Leider, Richard, *Whistle While You Work* (Berrett-Koehler 2001)

Perkins-Reed, Marcia, *When 9 to 5 Isn't Enough* (Hay House 1990)

MBTI Assessment

Tieger, Paul & Barron-Tieger, Barbara, *Do What You Are* (Little Brown 2001)

Krebs Hirsh, Sandra, *Introduction to Type and Coaching* (Consulting Psychologists Press 2000)

Krebs Hirsh, Sandra, *Introduction to Type and Career* (Consulting Psychologists Press 1993)

Recruiters

Gurney, Darrell, *Headhunters Revealed!* (Hunter Arts Publishing 2000)

Resumes

Crispin, Gerry & Mehler, Mark, *CareerXroads* (2002)
Criscito, Pat, *Designing the Perfect Resume* (Barrons 2000)
Criscito, Pat, *Resumes in Cyberspace* (Barrons 2001)
Enelow, Wendy, *Best Resumes for $100,000+ Jobs* (Impact 2002)
Farr, Michael & Kursmark, Louise, *America's Top Resumes for America's Top Jobs*
Yate, Martin, *Resumes that Knock 'Em Dead* (Adams Media 2001)

Sabbaticals

Dlugozima, Hope et al, *Six Months Off* (Holt 1996)
Rogak, Lisa Angowski, *Time Off From Work* (Wiley 1994)

Self-Employment

Edwards, Paul and Sarah, *Working From Home: Everything You Need to Know about Living and Working Under the Same Roof* (Tarcher 1999)
Gerber, Michael, *The E-Myth Revisited* (Harper Business 1995)
All Business - http://www.all-biz.com/
CCH Business Owners - http://www.toolkit.cch.com
Entrepreneur Magazine - http://www.entrepreneurmag.com
Information for Small Businesses - http://www.sec.gov/smbus1.htm
National Foundation for Women Business Owners - http://www.nfwbo.org

SBA: Small Business Administration Home Page- http://www.sba.gov/
Small Business Development Centers - http://sbinformation.about.com/smallbusiness/sbinformation/library/reference/blstate.htm
http://smallbizmanager.com/

Spirituality and Work

Barrett, Richard, *Liberating the Corporate Soul* (Butterworth-Heinemann 1998)
Belf, Teri-E, *Coaching with Spirit* (Jossey-Bass/Pfeiffer 2002)
Briskin, Alan, *The Stirring of Soul in the Workplace* (Berrett-Koehler 1998)
Casto, Michelle, *Get Smart! About Modern Career Development* (Get Smart! Publishing 2000)
Coombs, Ann, *The Living Workplace* (Warwick 2002)
Fox, Matthew, *The Reinvention of Work* (Harper Collins 1994)
Guillory, William, *The Living Organization: Spirituality in the Workplace* (Innovations International 2001)
Heider, John, *The Tao of Leadership* (Bantam 1988)
Jaworski, Joseph, *Synchronicity: The Inner Path of Leadership* (Berrett-Kohler 1996)
Jones, Tom, *A Career Devotional Journal* (Career Life Publishing 2002)
Klein, Eric & Izzo, John, *Awakening Corporate Soul: Four Paths to Unleash the Power of People at Work* (Fair Winds Press 1999)

Mitroff, Ian, *A Spiritual Audit of Corporate America* (Jossey-Bass Business 1999)

Peppers, Cheryl, *Bringing Your Soul to Work: An Everyday Practice* (Berrett-Koehler 2000)

Renesch, John, *Getting to the Better Future: How Business Can Lead the Way to New Possibilities* (NewBusinessBooks 2000)

Richmond, Lewis, *Work as a Spiritual Practice* (Broadway 1999)

Sisk, Dorothy & Torrance, E. Paul, *Spiritual Intelligence: Developing Higher Consciousness* (Creative Education Foundation 2001)

Williams, Nick, *The Work We Were Born to Do* (Element Books 1999)

Teleclasses

www.teleclassinternational.com (CCI's vendor of choice)

www.teleclass.com

www.teleclass4u.com

Appendix I – Frequently Asked Questions About Career Coaching

Q: I'm thinking about career coaching but don't want to go back to school. Don't career coaches have to have a Master's Degree in counseling?

Career *counselors* are usually required to have a Master's degree; coaches are not. Currently, there are no educational requirements in most states in the U.S. for coaches. (However, some states subject some coaches to state regulations; check with your state's employment or labor department to see what the requirements are where you live.) Career coaching is *not* the same as career counseling, as we will see below. If one were going to be a counselor, they should certainly get a degree in that field! But career coaching is a discrete skill, the primary prerequisite for which is specific coaching training and a knowledge of career development principles. Whether practicing in the U.S. or abroad, degrees in counseling or psychology are *not* required to be a highly effective coach.

Q: If I can talk to people about their job-related issues, then can't I call myself a career coach?

The short answer? No. While there are no specific requirements for career coaches (unlike career counselors, who usually need a Master's Degree and have to register with their state agency), career coaching does require specific training in coaching knowledge, skills and abilities (KSA's). A coaching interaction is much more than a mere conversation; it has a strategic component and a transformational impact that puts it at a much higher level than a mere conversation. And the client's professional future is at stake; are you willing to risk giving uninformed "advice" versus becoming (through training and experience) a trained professional – or referring the client to one?

Q: Since I've been doing career counseling or career consulting for years, can't I just use the "career coach" label since it seems to be the latest thing in career development?

Again, the answer is no. Coaching is much more than simply a repackaging of career counseling; rather, it is a discrete approach and skillset that must be learned. Career counselors often have a structured approach to their work with clients, and are frequently expected to give the client advice about which career path or job opportunity they should pursue. Career coaches, on the other hand, are charged with asking questions and using other coaching skills to elicit the client's own answers, drawing on their inner wisdom. If someone is giving advice, they are not coaching.

Q: I'm already a coach, so when people come to me about a job-related issues, can't I call myself a career coach?

Maybe, if you meet certain conditions. Remember, there are no legal requirements in most states in the U.S. for coaches to get specific training or register with a government agency to call themselves coaches. If you have received formal coach training and have an effective coaching model that you are using, your coaching skills may be transferable. However, to coach individuals in career issues also requires knowledge of career development theories and principles as well as the science/art of resume writing, helping a client capitalize on their strengths and minimize weaknesses in an interview, components of an effective job search campaign, and the like. Specific training in these areas is needed to supplement coaching skills for one to truly call themselves a career coach.

Q: Aren't other kinds of coaching, like business and executive coaching, more "advanced" and specialized than career coaching? Seems like career coaching is just a point to begin one's practice; career coaching by itself isn't a substantial enough specialty area on which to build a practice, is it?

To put it simply, career coaching isn't as easy as it looks! But it *is* a viable practice specialty. The best career coaches make six-figure incomes. Some of them choose to supplement their actual 1:1 coaching with writing books, ezines and articles, teaching, training, teleclasses, or speaking because they enjoy the variety of activities around the career development theme. But far from being a "basic beginning" for a coaching practice, it is a very viable ongoing business.

Q: I don't think career coaching would be right for me because I don't enjoy writing resumes, practicing interviewing, and helping the client with negotiations.

This is one of the best things about career coaching: you can do it in whatever way fits your personality and preferences! Some career coaches prefer to focus on the "direction-setting" or personal exploration part of the process, helping clients figure out "what they want to be when they grow up," as we like to put it. Others prefer the tangible, immediate-results work involved in designing a job search strategy, writing (or critiquing) resumes, role-playing interviews and negotiation sessions, and the like. And still other independent practitioners do all of this! Internal career coaches (employed by an organization) may have additional responsibilities. So career coaching is a field that can be tailored to the individual coach's preferences.

Q: I notice that your Authentic Vocation™ model explores several areas before it gets to skills and my work experience. Isn't it best to focus on what I'm good at in determining my next job?

> This is a premise of many career development theories. It can be effective with new graduates or new entrants to the workplace, or to those wishing to find a new job within the same industry and/or position they have held in the past. However, for the majority of people who will seek out career coaching (having exhausted their own resources and ideas about what would most fulfill them), a skills-based model will not achieve their desired result. Instead, the process must begin at a deeper level with their overall life purpose or mission, values, and the like in order to match what they do with what they love and what has meaning for the client. CCI's Authentic Vocation™ model does this.

Q: Isn't it tough to make money at career coaching, especially during tough economic times?

> On the contrary! Career coaching is the one specialty in the coaching field that is recession-proof and actually expands during economic downturns. Why? When the economy turns down, companies lay off workers, requiring outplacement services (and these firms have added coaching as one of their services to such companies) as well as career centers (which can be set up and/or staffed by career coaches). In addition, there are more individuals in job or career transition at these times, and those who are not are overworked and worried if they will be the next to be laid off. So while the independent practitioner may find that they need to offer fee incentives and/or affiliate with an outplacement firm or other organization to serve the clients who have needs during the economic lows (if we assume individual clients have less disposable income to invest in coaching), they will find a lot of work to be done!

Q: Why should I pay for career coaching when I can get helpful advice about my career from my family and friends?

> Remember the old saying, "you get what you pay for"? There are several reasons family and friends' advice may not be in your best interest regarding your career. First, they lack the objectivity and training that a coach has. And second, even if the change you're considering is good for you, it may impact them in a way that is uncomfortable, causing them to discourage or sabotage you. And finally, they may be unwilling to provide the unconditional support (even "cheerleading") that a coach will do as you pursue your dreams.

Q: Isn't career coaching usually be done in person?

One thing that is fascinating to most people when they first discover coaching (as a prospective coach or a client) is that most coaching is done by telephone. This is appealing to the coach because it allows them a flexible lifestyle. But it is also appealing to the client because of its convenience! In fact, if you receive training via teleclass (a kind of conference-call format used by Career Coach Institute and some other coach training programs where class members gather "virtually" over the phone for the weekly sessions), you are receiving the very best preparation to be a highly effective coach – over the phone! Coaches learn to hone their listening abilities to listen "between the lines" to the client's energy shifts, hesitations, excitement, style, and other cues that lead to deeply thought-provoking questions from the coach. Coaching in person is done by some (though a minority of) coaches, but between the logistics required to physically get together and the sometimes distracting visual cues that are added with in-person coaching, telephone coaching can be an even superior medium to use!

Appendix 2 – International Coach Federation Coaching Core Competencies

The following eleven core coaching competencies were developed to support greater understanding about the skills and approaches used within today's coaching profession as defined by the ICF. They will also support you in calibrating the level of alignment between the coach-specific training expected and the training you have experienced.

Finally, these competencies were used as the foundation for the ICF Credentialing process examination. The core competencies are grouped into four clusters according to those that fit together logically based on common ways of looking at the competencies in each group. The groupings and individual competencies are not weighted - they do not represent any kind of priority in that they are all core or critical for any competent coach to demonstrate.

A. SETTING THE FOUNDATION

1. MEETING ETHICAL GUIDELINES AND PROFESSIONAL STANDARDS
2. ESTABLISHING THE COACHING AGREEMENT

B. CO-CREATING THE RELATIONSHIP

3. ESTABLISHING TRUST AND INTIMACY WITH THE CLIENT
4. COACHING PRESENCE

C. COMMUNICATING EFFECTIVELY

5. ACTIVE LISTENING
6. POWERFUL QUESTIONING
7. DIRECT COMMUNICATION

D. FACILITATING LEARNING AND RESULTS

8. CREATING AWARENESS
9. DESIGNING ACTIONS
10. PLANNING AND GOAL SETTING
11. MANAGING PROGRESS AND ACCOUNTABILITY

NOTE: These competencies and the more expanded version outlining specific coaching skills for each competency are current as of 2002. For the expanded and updated version, see www.coachfederation.org/credentialing/en/core.htm

About the Author and Career Coach Institute

Marcia Bench is a Master Certified Career Coach™ and nationally respected expert in the job/career transition field. She has been coaching and consulting both individual and corporate clients since 1986.

A former attorney, Marcia has authored 9 previous books, including *When 9 to 5 Isn't Enough* (Hay House) and *Thriving in Transition* (Simon & Schuster) and has been a featured speaker/trainer at over 400 local, regional and national conferences, as well as a guest on numerous television and radio programs.

Marcia's coaching experience includes work with managers and executives from such firms as Qualcomm, Intel, Intuit, Kelloggs, FedEx, Westinghouse, Willamette Industries, Raytheon, US West, Shell, PetCo, and Kimberly Clark, among others, as well as dozens of business owners, professionals, and military officers entering the civilian workforce.

Marcia founded Career Coach Institute in 2001 and currently serves as its Director and CEO. The firm is the premier virtual career coach training program, and offers a six-month teleclass-based training program to both those who wish to become individual, independent career coaches and those who wish to do career coaching inside their organizations.

Prior to her tenure with CCI, she was a Senior Vice President in a dot-com career management firm for 4 years, and previously spent 10 years as President of New Work Directions, a business and consulting firm she founded. Ms. Bench developed her expertise in business start-up and management in part through her 4 years as a practicing attorney specializing in business and employment issues.

Marcia's education includes a Juris Doctorate from Northwestern School of Law of Lewis & Clark College and a Bachelor of Science in Psychology from Western Oregon University. In addition, she is a Certified Career Management Practitioner through the International Board of Career Management Certification, a Certified Business Coach, a Certified Teleader and Master Certified Career Coach.

For further information or to contact Ms. Bench:

Career Coach Institute
1799 Kiowa Ave. #107-526
Lake Havasu City, AZ 86403
coach@careercoachinstitute.com
www.careercoachinstitute.com

INDEX

Printed in the United States
961700001B